CLEARING THE FIELDS

OTHER BOOKS BY KEVIN M. CAHILL, M.D.

The Untapped Resource: Medicine and Diplomacy
Health and Development
Health on the Horn of Africa
Somalia: A Perspective
Irish Essays
The American Irish Revival
Threads for a Tapestry
Famine
The AIDS Epidemic
Tropical Medicine in Temperate Climates
Tropical Medicine: A Handbook for Practitioners
Clinical Tropical Medicine: Volume I
Clinical Tropical Medicine: Volume II
Teaching Tropical Medicine
Medical Advice for the Traveler
Health in New York State
Pets and Your Health
A Bridge to Peace
Imminent Peril: Public Health in a Declining Economy
Tropical Medicine: A Clinical Text
A Framework for Survival: Health, Human Rights, and
Humanitarian Assistance in Conflicts and Disasters

CLEARING
THE FIELDS

Solutions to the
Global Land Mines Crisis

EDITED BY

KEVIN M. CAHILL, M.D.

A Joint Publication of BasicBooks and the
Council on Foreign Relations

Designed by Ellen Levine

Library of Congress Cataloging-in-Publication Data
Cahill, Kevin M.
  Clearing the fields : solutions to the global land mines crisis / Kevin M. Cahill.
    p. cm.
  ISBN 0–465–01177–2
  1. Mines (Military explosives) (International law.)   2. Human rights.
I. Title.
JC597.C34 1995
327.1'74—dc20   94–22737
                                                                      CIP

The publisher has agreed to donate proceeds from this book to the Center for International Health and Cooperation.

95 96 97 98 ◆/RRD 9 8 7 6 5 4 3 2

For Cy and Gay Vance

who have, for so many years,
given generously of themselves
in healing the wounds of war

CONTENTS

ACKNOWLEDGMENTS

This book was made possible by the generous contributions of many individuals and organizations.

All of the participants accepted my invitation on short notice and came, many from long distances, and for no honorarium, because they shared my belief that the topic deserved attention and the timing was critical. I know my colleagues realize the depth of my respect and gratitude for their efforts, and I hope that my editing of their manuscripts into a cohesive book fulfills part of my debt to them.

The board and staff of both the Center for International Health and Cooperation and the Council on Foreign Relations graciously supported the entire effort, willingly offering their resources and skills to assure success. I particularly thank Leslie Gelb, president of the Council, and Dr. Kenneth Keller, director of science and executive vice president of the Council, for their always gracious and wise counsel. Dr. Enid C. B. Schoettle, former director of the Project on International Organizations and Law at the Council on Foreign Relations, and Dr. Jessica Tuchman Mathews, senior fellow at the Council, helped organize the symposium that led to this book. Drs. Schoettle and Mathews were ably supported by Jennifer Hobbes and Renée Cahill. These friends made a complex and difficult task a pleasure.

Michael J. O'Neill, the former editor-in-chief of the New York *Daily News* and president of the Association of Newspaper Editors, graciously attended the entire symposium as official rapporteur; he then, typically and selflessly, reviewed all of the manuscripts and offered his sage and warm counsel in the midst of his own busy writing schedule.

The rapid editing was made pleasant and possible by Dore Hollander, as well as Kermit Hummel and Jo Ann Miller of Basic Books. I would also like to thank George Craig of HarperCollins for his steady interest and generous assistance throughout this project.

Essential funding for the symposium was provided by a major grant from the Ford Foundation to the Council on Foreign Relations, and grants from the Tropical Disease Center of Lenox Hill Hospital, the Alexander Bernstein Foundation, and the Albert Kundstadter Family Foundation to the Center for International Health and Cooperation.

FOREWORD

Thousands of people are killed and maimed by land mines every month. In the hinterlands and countrysides of the world, the blinded and ravaged bodies of victims are an increasingly common sight.

More than 100 million mines have been deployed in over sixty countries. This proliferation has brought a triple crisis: individual lives are shattered; families, communities, and societies bear an increasing medical burden; and states cannot proceed to develop lands and infrastructure rendered unusable by the presence of mines.

The United Nations funds most of the world's mine clearance programs. The cost of clearance, including training, support, and logistics, is somewhere between $300 and $1,000 per mine. Most antipersonnel mines cost less than $25, and some cost less than $3. Mine clearance is labor-intensive, and slow because it is so dangerous.

Experience shows that the most cost-effective clearance teams are those using civilian mine clearers recruited locally and trained for the task in their own country. The United Nations objective, therefore, is to help the afflicted nations build a capacity to deal with this desperate situation. United Nations programs for mine clearance and victim assistance are in urgent need of greater international financial and political support.

Mines do not discriminate among military and civilian victims. As such, they are prohibited under customary international law. But as the recent upsurge in death and devastation caused by mines demonstrates, reliance on this approach is not sufficient. As world opinion is beginning to awaken to this growing danger, this symposium, sponsored by the Center for International Health and Cooperation and the Council on Foreign Relations, is an important step toward necessary action. The aim should be to build widespread support for an international agreement on a total ban on the production, stockpiling, transfer, and export of mines and their components. Only in this way can the community of nations begin to make sustained progress against the killing, maiming, and societal destruction caused by these terrible weapons.

BOUTROS BOUTROS-GHALI
Secretary-General, United Nations
April 1994

CLEARING THE FIELDS

Introduction

KEVIN M. CAHILL, M.D.

In the fertile grazing grounds of Somaliland mothers now tie toddlers to trees so that the young children cannot crawl, innocently but dangerously, out among the more than 1 million mines that have been haphazardly laid there over the last decade. Camels, and the youngsters and adolescents who tend them, are less fortunate, since to survive in the Somali savannah, animals must endlessly search for water and nourishment. The fields are littered with camel carcasses, and stone mounds mark the graves of herders. The towns are crowded with amputees. Mine injuries have become one of the major health hazards in that sad country, reaching epidemic proportions in the north.

Numerous international conferences, congressional and United Nations hearings, and extensive media coverage have heightened our awareness of the growing problems posed by land mines. These efforts have documented the horror of mine injuries and the vast—indeed, global—scope of the crisis. The educational process, however, has almost become an end in itself, with articles repeating articles, using the same data in an orgy of condemnations. But the emphasis has rarely, if ever, been on possible solutions. One has been expected to find solace merely in continuing to express outrage. However, the growing number of mine victims, if nothing else, demands that we move beyond rhetoric, beyond merely reconstructing limbs, to stop the spread of a devastating epidemic and devise a permanent cure.

Physicians know, perhaps better than others, that no amount of sophistry can mask the human suffering that war inevitably brings. I have seen the land mine crisis firsthand as a physician. In directing medical and public health programs in Nicaragua and Somalia, I have had to deal with the mutilated bodies; the crippled and blinded; the psychologically traumatized; and the devastating effects on families, communities, regions, and countries. But a physician's view is not merely medical; he does not cease to be an involved citizen merely because he wears a stethoscope or uses a scalpel. In fact, those experienced and skilled in international health can offer unique insights, and even solutions, not usually found in foreign policy debates, legal formulations, or military lore.

The special evil of antipersonnel land mines is that they do not discriminate between the civilian and the soldier, and they continue to maim and kill innocent victims long after the conflict in which they were deployed is over. But that is neither the beginning nor the end of the problem. Land mines are considered by military establishments to be indispensable defensive weapons in interstate warfare; they have also become offensive weapons of choice in internal conflicts, as can be seen in many Third World countries. Additionally, they are easy to make, profitable to sell, and relatively inexpensive to acquire.

Mines no longer have to be laid individually, but can be scattered over vast areas, dropped from airplanes or delivered by rockets. It is virtually impossible to map the location of mines delivered by such "sophisticated" systems. Both sides employ mines in war, but media interpretation and official condemnation are the prerogatives only of the victor. In the Persian Gulf War, for example, much attention was devoted to the minefields Iraq laid inside Kuwait. However, little notice was given to the millions of mines rocketed by the allied forces deep into Iraq, far from the battlefields—one mine for every Iraqi man, woman, and child.

The constant development and refinement of the instruments of war has been the most malignant result of the technological revolution of our times. Public protest has rightly been aroused, and international action taken, against the threat of biological, chemical, and nuclear weapons. Land mines do not just pose a threat; they blow up innocent people every hour of every day. It is time to consider whether they, too, should be deemed a particularly inhumane weapon that should be circumscribed by international law.

Dimensions of the Crisis

Land mines are one of the great scourges of history. They are turning vast areas of the earth into wastelands of death, economic ruin, and social disintegration. More than 100 million land mines are now scattered wantonly across the fields, roads, and other strategic areas of some sixty countries. Up to 30 million mines have been laid in Africa. In the Middle East, mines used during the Iran-Iraq and Persian Gulf wars have been added to those still lying in wait from World War II. Since 1989, an estimated 3 million mines have been sown, without markers or maps, among embattled civilians in the former Yugoslavia, and the total there is growing by some fifty thousand per week.

Part of the problem is the sheer number of mines, and of the manufacturers and exporters of them. More than 250 million land mines, including approximately 200 million antipersonnel land mines, have been produced over the past twenty-five years. Antipersonnel land mines continue to be made at an average rate of 5–10 million per year. Approximately fifty nations produce these weapons, and about thirty export them. With such widespread distribution, no one escapes; in the recent Somali conflict, 26 percent of U.S. casualties were due to inexpensive, low-technology, easy-to-use, conventional land mines—the same mines that are currently contaminating so much of the developing world.

Land mines are now used to terrorize and disrupt whole populations, not simply to block or control battlefield movements, as during World War II. The very concept of a "battlefield" that can be demarcated in space and time is, in fact, no longer valid. The entire countryside is now fair game in most conflicts, and the hapless inhabitants become part of every conflict. In World War I, only 5 percent of those killed or wounded were noncombatants; by World War II, the level was 50 percent, and the figure has approached 90 percent in recent conflicts. Defending the use of land mines by invoking obsolete battlefield definitions and military logic offers a seriously flawed argument in which unchallenged language distorts reality.

Long after armies leave, long after cease-fires and even peace treaties have been signed, still-hidden mines continue to do their terrible work on a devastating scale, especially in the twenty most ravaged countries, from Cambodia, Afghanistan, and Vietnam to Angola, Mozambique, and Somalia; from El Salvador and Nicaragua to Iraq and Kuwait. Because of the presence or fear of land mines, almost half the land area of Cambodia is unsafe for farming or any other human use. After eighteen years of civil war and 2 million land mines, no major road in Mozambique is usable. In Angola, the loss of arable land is so massive that the World Food Programme had to earmark $32 million of its 1994 food aid budget merely to offset nutritional deficiencies.

Refugees are afraid to return to their homes, creating a growing financial burden on international relief agencies. Land mines have cut the expected rate of repatriation in Cambodia from 10,000 to 1,000 per week. In Afghanistan the situation is even worse. Some 3.5 million refugees will not return because mountain roads and fields are infested with mines. The bill for refugees refusing to leave the camps in Pakistan was $50 million in 1993. In southern Sudan, mines have paralyzed agricultural production, leaving thousands trapped in a drought-stricken region. Everywhere, power plants, transportation centers, water supplies, and other essential services are primary mining targets so that the basic infrastructure of society collapses, and economic independence becomes a painful mirage.

In land mine–infested areas, medical and public health teams are overwhelmed; the problems of evacuation, triage, and surgical treatment are daunting, but the challenges of rehabilitation are staggering. While over 1,000 people are killed by mines every month, many more are injured and permanently disabled. In Cambodia, one in every 236 people is a land mine amputee; the rate is one in 470 in Angola, and one in 1,000 in northern Somalia. One of the most significant, and most neglected, features of land mines is that the cost of clearing a minefield is at least one hundred times that of laying it; in addition, clearance is a highly dangerous and painfully slow process. The number of deminers killed in Kuwait since the Persian Gulf War exceeds that of U.S. combatants killed during the conflict.

The Search for Solutions

The enormity of the global land mine crisis, and the increasing rage against the special crimes that mines commit against the innocent, in times of peace as well as conflict, are finally and belatedly generating public demands for action. But what action? What can be done? For answers, the Center for International Health and Cooperation and the Council on Foreign Relations invited UN Secretary-General Boutros Boutros-Ghali, former Secretary of State Cyrus Vance, and other leading authorities to present their ideas at a symposium in New York City on April 29, 1994.

The meeting was part of an innovative effort of the Center and the Council to promote a multidisciplinary approach to global problems that no longer fall neatly into the old pigeonholes of power politics and conventional diplomacy. The fundamental premise is that in most contemporary international crises, specialists in many apparently unrelated fields are as relevant as foreign affairs experts.

This thesis was borne out in 1992 at our first joint symposium, *A Framework for Survival: Health, Human Rights, and Humanitarian Assistance in Conflicts and Disasters.*[1] Participants at that meeting concluded that physicians, nurses, and disaster workers should not be left in the rear echelon of policymaking when they are operating on the front lines of epidemics, famines, and massive human rights violations, the putative bases most often used to justify costly interventions in foreign conflicts. Health workers frequently have more local experience and understanding than visiting scholars or foreign policy representatives. In the very act of relieving suffering, health and humanitarian workers develop relationships that are often intimately personal and trusting. By building on common objectives, they establish corridors of cooperation that can sometimes help resolve conflicts that otherwise elude conventional negotiation.

It was in a spirit of partnership, then, that leaders in a wide variety of fields—diplomacy, international law, military, medicine, ethics, humanitarian service, and technology—met to consider ways to deal with the land mine crisis. The participants all agreed on the urgent need for action, but were immediately confronted by a maze of practical dilemmas: conflicting military and humanitarian interests, the different perspectives of rich and poor states, and the special challenges of civil wars and ethnic conflicts raging outside the pale of moral restraint and international law.

One might view the land mine crisis in the same way as the ruler in *The King and I* saw the confusing challenges of change—as a "puzzlement" that no single approach and no single actor can solve. Certainly, no amount of ranting will help any longer, and a piecemeal approach is obviously inadequate for the growing disaster. Yet, the problem was created by man's ingenuity—perverse, to be sure—and ultimately will have to be solved by the combined, cooperative, and coordinated efforts of many people. The solutions will depend on technical and military experts with innovative technological ideas. They will depend on lawyers who are willing to grapple with the elusive and frustrating verbal nuances that must be overcome if new, enforceable conventions, regimes, and agreements are to be fashioned. They will depend on doctors and humanitarian workers who can create models that may solve some of the most pressing problems posed by land mine injuries. And they will depend on diplomats and politicians who are willing to move beyond the boundaries of Cold War power politics to forge new treaties and provide innovative leadership, rather than merely repeat the slogans of the past. Solutions are possible.

Clearing the Fields is the effort of men and women, in and out of government, representing different disciplines and ideologies, all searching for solutions to a universally recognized disaster. Rooted firmly in the hard reality of their experiences, the contributors to this volume document the crisis and then explore possible avenues of escape.

Calls for a Total Ban

In his foreword, UN Secretary-General Boutros-Ghali calls for total banishment of antipersonnel land mines: "The aim should be to build widespread support for an international agreement on a total ban on the production, stockpiling, transfer, and export of mines and their components. Only in this way can the community of nations begin to make sustained progress against the killing, maiming, and societal destruction caused by these terrible weapons."

Secretary of State Vance is also unequivocal. In a position paper coauthored by Ambassador Herbert S. Okun, Vance acknowledges that land mines have "some military use," but questions whether they are "worth the immense costs that society is forced to pay to repair the enormous damage and the horrendous suffering they cause." The clear answer, he argues, is no. Rejecting a variety of partial control measures, some of which the United States supports, Vance insists that "nothing short of a total ban on the production, transfer, and use of antipersonnel land mines will stop the killing and maiming of civilians. . . . Bombs can be aimed at military targets and bullets fired by soldiers against soldiers, but land mines are radically different, lying in wait—as they do—until triggered by the target."

The former secretary of state calls on President Clinton to take the lead in seeking a total worldwide ban despite the Pentagon's insistence that nations must continue to keep land mines in their arsenals. So far, however, the military view has prevailed, not only in the United States, but in other countries, big and small. Whatever humanitarian and moral imperatives there may be, professional soldiers and guerrilla leaders alike contend that land mines are an essential weapon of war. And this position emerged at the symposium as the principal obstacle facing the total ban movement.

Thomas E. McNamara, principal deputy assistant secretary of state, lays the Clinton administration's position on the line: Washington opposes the total ban on the grounds that it fails to recognize the legitimate battlefield utility of land mines. "It would make no sense to pursue a solution to the land mine problem," he explains, "that increases the risk to American uniformed men and women." While the administration supports a limited ban on the sale and transfer of land mines, it has yet to ratify the 1980 Conventional Weapons Convention and Landmines Protocol, and therefore cannot participate fully in the review conference to revise those flawed documents.

More troubling, however, is that the administration opposes a total ban on antipersonnel land mines even as a long-term, humanitarian goal. The United States was one of only three nations to abstain on the 1993 United Nations resolution establishing the review conference; the United States objected to an amendment asking the conference to discuss all aspects of the land mine problem, including a total ban. President Clinton asserted simply that the "U.S. armed forces continue to require land mines to accomplish certain military missions."

Retired Colonel Richard H. Johnson, a U.S. army expert on munitions and mines, cites the classic use of mines to control battlefields in all kinds of engagements from World War II to the Persian Gulf War. He notes their continuing defensive value in danger zones like the border between South and North Korea. He also argues that now, with the end of the Cold War, when standing armies are shrinking, mines are even more necessary to block enemy movements until counterforces can be deployed. And in the case of Third World conflicts, he says, mines are often the "weapons of choice . . . because of their availability, low cost, and relative ease of use."

The Moral Argument

If land mines are so important to military professionals and local warlords, then what are the grounds for outlawing them? Why is a land mine any more uncivilized than a bomber, which no one is proposing to banish? The moral argument, which Harvard University's J. Bryan Hehir develops in exquisite detail, is that land mines are "inherently indiscriminate . . . in terms of time and targets." The targets are no longer just enemy troops or armored forces, but civilians and, in many of the ethnic and tribal conflicts that are now so prevalent, whole populations. Moreover, because the damage mines do to humanity continues long after wars have ended, new generations fall victim to conflicts in which they were not even involved.

"The fundamental test of limitation in the ethic of war is the ability to preserve noncombatant immunity," Hehir argues. "It is the only principle in the framework of the Just War ethic that places an absolute barrier on the kind of force that can be used in a morally justified way. . . . The prohibition of direct attacks on civilians constitutes an absolute standard in the ethic of war."

He also emphasizes an obvious ethical dilemma in the U.S. argument that this country should be allowed to retain military use of land mines while smaller nations or rebel groups should be barred from employing cheaper versions of these weapons. It is unlikely, to say the least, that others will accept America's claim to world leadership if we insist on a double standard for which weapons can be used in conflicts for freedom.

International Law and Public Opinion

Of course, if land mines are to be banned or even controlled in some limited ways, then international law comes into play, and so far it has been pitifully inoperative. As Professor Richard Falk of Princeton University observes, the logic of military necessity continues to prevail, and although public opposition to land mines is increasing, "this pressure has not made sufficient inroads on the professional military ethos to create the basis for effective law." He develops the thesis that humanitarian law can succeed only if two conditions are fulfilled: combatants must have a "mutual interest" in accepting some restraints, as in the case of prisoners of war or the sanctity of hospitals; and the view must be widely shared that certain weapons, like biological and chemical agents, are shunned by the military profession itself. The trouble, as several participants note, is that while the military consider biological and chemical warfare only marginally useful, they still view land mines as essential.

Although the contemporary laws of war say that combatants must discriminate between civilian and military targets, that any harm inflicted must be necessary and proportionate to the military need, and that weapons must not cause cruel or gratuitous suffering, these standards do not hold fast in the context of war and, especially, in the low-technology conflicts ravaging so many of the world's trouble spots. In these circumstances, Falk notes, "legal language . . . is mainly a kind of moralistic charade" that is "not taken seriously in the context of weapons design, military planning, or belligerent practice." He adds, "The patterns of disregard are so pronounced and widespread as to invite the most cynical view of the role played by international humanitarian law."

Janne E. Nolan of the Brookings Institution makes a similar point. "There is reason to be cautious about crafting regulations that cannot be widely supported and credibly enforced," she contends. "Weak agreements, like weak laws, invite cynicism and fatalism." She notes that no international law or voluntary agreement proscribes the production, possession, or export of land mines, and the Landmines Protocol applies only "imperfectly" to the use of mines. To be credible, she observes, there must be "a verifiable arms control regime that covers production, stockpiling, and exports, as well," and the only way to move in this direction is to totally "stigmatize" land mine use.

Like Boutros-Ghali, Vance, and several others, Nolan comes down on the side of calling for a total ban rather than pressing only for interim agreements on piecemeal limitations. "If a total ban were embraced as a common goal for a large number of countries," she argues, "it would be easier to stigmatize land mines as an illegitimate instrument of warfare. . . . The control of land mines, in fact, may be feasible only if these weapons are delegitimized internationally, which is unlikely to occur if some uses remain acceptable under partial controls."

Sweden's Jan Eliasson, a mediator in the Nagorno-Karabakh conflict and former UN under-secretary-general for humanitarian affairs, similarly argues in favor of a total ban. "Regardless of the likelihood of this solution being chosen now," he contends, "it should still be recognized and remain the aim of international and national groups concerned with land mines." Brigadier General Patrick Blagden, the UN's demining expert, with long, firsthand experience in one of the world's most hazardous professions, cites the need for public advocacy to drive the anti–land mine movement forward despite military opposition and many other practical obstacles. He notes that nations will have to be dragged and pressured into action, the supply of mines must be attacked by moratoria and outright banning, and, above all, the public in the developed world needs to be informed that unless and until they generate some of the outrage toward land mines that they show to nuclear and chemical weapons, the number of people per year currently killed or injured, more that 15,000, will continue to rise.

Falk also concedes that "if the public campaign gathers more steam, and heads of important states join the campaign, then it becomes more plausible to override the views of military commanders and their advisors," but he is not optimistic about a near-term breakthrough.

Policy Roadblocks

The movement toward a ban involves not only the resistance of professional military establishments, but a series of other policy challenges:

- Sharp differences between the strategic view of land mines among major nations and their life-and-death value to poor countries, ethnic groups, and others involved in low-intensity conflicts where mines are the readily available weapons of choice.
- The ability of high-technology nations to produce sophisticated self-neutralizing or self-destructing mines to reduce carnage and ameliorate the demining problem, but the continuing preference of poor countries for much cheaper, if also more destructive, conventional mines.
- The fact that much mine warfare is carried out by irregular forces—from tribal warlords to guerrilla armies—that pay no attention either to rules of war or to the opinions of the international community.
- A deep and pervasive resentment in the developing world against a perceived double standard by which industrial nations demand that others give up or limit weapons that they insist on keeping themselves, as in the case of nuclear bombs.

It is clear that there are many ways to limit the impact of mines, but also, unfortunately, just as many ways to multiply their devastating effects. As Col. Johnson and others report, technology has led to mines that planes, artillery, and "vehicle-mounted mine dispensers" can scatter easily and indiscriminately over large areas so that the old image of minefields laid and mapped in geometric order is obsolete.

Modern mines also have almost no detectable metal content and are therefore extremely difficult and dangerous to locate and remove. Fuses can be triggered remotely, by the magnetic field of a tank, for example, so that direct contact is no longer necessary. By contrast, detection and demining technology has lagged. In Gen. Blagden's words, "although little or no money has been spent on research into clearing mines, many millions have been spent making mines more effective, more wounding per unit cost, and more difficult to clear."

Partial Measures

In the light of these dismal facts, the question is what, if any, kind of progress can be made, short of a total ban. A variety of approaches is possible. On the technological front, one could develop a land mine protocol that mandates using only self-destructing and self-neutralizing mines, to reduce the long-term impact on innocent civilians and societies. Vance, however, echoing the sentiments of others, argues that this idea is "well intentioned" but "faulty in concept and, in practice, would actually impede realization of a total ban." One of many arguments is that high-technology mines simply cost too much. Why should a poor nation spend $30 for one of these mines, asks W. Hays Parks, assistant to the U.S. judge advocate general for law of war matters, when it can buy an ordinary mine for as little as 50 cents?

To deal with the horrendous problems of detection and demining, Thomas R. Evans of Johns Hopkins University, a long-time Defense Department consultant, urges a two-pronged approach by the industrial countries: do more to develop "affordable improvements" in technology and, in the near term, share low-technology demining systems with Third World nations. General Blagden similarly argues for expanded research, technological development, and information exchanges to produce fieldable technologies by the year 2000 and to double global mine clearance capabilities by 2005.

Modern technology offers the best hope for solving the land mine crisis, providing that political will is present to force integration of existing military systems with civilian needs. Evans notes that the current military database on land mines, functioning optical reconnaisance and global positioning systems, enhanced mathematical correlation techniques, and multispectral sensor and neutron bombardment projects could, in the near future, permit far more extensive, more rapid, and safer detection and destruction of land mines.

But even if all the technological advances were to be implemented immediately, the carnage would continue. It is imperative, therefore, that health workers devise simple, effective, standardized programs that can work in the poor, underdeveloped areas of the world, where the great majority of land mine accidents occur, and where medical personnel and material are already scarce. Effective surgical and rehabilitation programs for mine victims must be based, to the greatest degree possible, on the most basic techniques that can be performed by semiskilled health workers. My colleague Abdulrahim Abby Farah and I, learning from our failures in Nicaragua, developed in Somalia a field approach in which local amputees were rapidly trained to fit simple prostheses in the midst of civil anarchy. This program can be replicated in other war zones, thereby offering an opportunity for amputee mine survivors to return to a productive role in the community. The program offers a practical, cost-efficient interim step to recovery after—or even during—conflicts in developing countries.

Physicians Chris Giannou and H. Jack Geiger emphasize the importance of teaching simple first aid to all combatants, and the need to instruct every doctor in principles of fundamental trauma surgery. Too often, well-intentioned but inept medical efforts complicate war wounds and result in more extensive amputations. These authors also emphasize the impact that land mines have on public health, in the tragic transfer of scarce resources from primary medical and preventive programs to costly and time-consuming surgical care of the injured. Nutrition, immunization, sanitation, and water purification projects cannot then be funded, and the negative impact of land mine injuries on preventable diseases expands exponentially.

The loss of productive human labor, the burden of large, disabled populations, and the diversion of resources from primary health services only hint at the enormous price that mines extort from societies they infest. The mass suffering, constant fear, corrosive anger, moral degradation, and collective despair that result from such an inordinate insult to the very essence of human dignity simply cannot be measured.

International Policy

In terms of international policy, the focus at the symposium fell mainly on proposals to put more teeth into the Landmines Protocol of the Conventional Weapons Convention, which the United States, among others, still has not ratified. The Clinton administration position, as reported by McNamara, is that the "crux of the problem" is not land mines per se, as Vance and others argue, but "civil unrest and warfare in the Third World." The Clinton policy, therefore, centers on a call for a worldwide moratorium on the export of land mines that "pose a grave risk to civilians." The United States has already imposed such moratoria, and the UN General Assembly endorsed the idea in 1993. The administration is also trying to develop a multilateral land mine control regime, but has made no decisions on specifics.

While urging an international ban, Janne Nolan suggests that given the political and technical complexities involved, some "interim steps" should be considered. One measure, she mentions, might be to establish restrictions or an outright prohibition against the production, possession, and transfer of mines that pose "the most severe risks to noncombatants." The difficulty is that these are the very mines that are most in demand, because they are so cheap and easily available. As Parks asks, "Why should, for example, a manufacturer nation make a relatively expensive high-technology mine when it still has inexpensive low-technology mines that sell?"

Like several other speakers, Nolan supports the idea of export controls, noting that a number of countries besides the United States have passed moratoriums and that the action had been passed by the European Parliament even before the 1993 General Assembly vote. She concedes that control violations would likely occur, but says limiting commercial sales still makes sense because some of the nations with the worst problems have to import mines from other countries. Having said this, however, Nolan contends the real goal of the international community should be to seek a comprehensive ban. The ban campaign itself, she argues, would help to create the same kind of taboo against land mines that won worldwide condemnation of biological and chemical warfare.

In one discussion at the symposium, Jessica Tuchman Mathews cited with approval the example of the 1993 UN Conference on the Environment, where unanimous and coordinated nongovernmental leadership forced powerful nations to conform to new international regulations that protect the land, air, and water we all share. She noted: "Governments, responsive to their militaries, might never get there alone. But there is a new force in the global village, a body of international public opinion that can be mobilized through dozens of channels and grow until governments are forced to respond. It was this largely unrecognized force that drove the global climate treaty through against all expectation. A land mine ban can become the cause of international networks of doctors and health care workers, of development economists and nongovernmental organizations, of veterans' groups (which know the personal agonies caused by mines), of those who care about refugees, of humanitarian agencies, of environmentalists worried about the supply of arable land, and of children's advocates who have seen children tied to trees by their mothers to keep them alive."

Despite ample reasons for pessimism, a common thread ties these chapters into a unified theme—an appreciation that even the most heinous and complex problem created by man must ultimately also be solved by man. *Clearing the Fields* offers many reasons for optimism;

good people came together to try to tame—and maybe eliminate—a monster that is threatening to destroy vast portions of our globe, as well as the lives of future generations of innocent victims. It presents technological, legal, medical, and diplomatic options that can help bind the terrible wounds inflicted by mines. Time and the combined efforts of many will, as with other epidemics, eventually allow healing to occur.

I

THE CURRENT SITUATION

1

An Overview of the
Global Land Mines Crisis

KENNETH ANDERSON

War is always terrible, but the use of antipersonnel land mines in many of the international and internal conflicts prevalent in the world today adds an extra dimension of terror and instability. These wars never really end, at least not for the civilians—the agriculturalists, pastoralists, and peasants—who must live in the midst of these "explosive remnants of war."[1] Every time they go off the known "safe" path or into their fields, these people risk losing life or limb to injuries caused by mines—left and forgotten from some long-ago battle, or left by some patrol making camp for the night, or deliberately placed by armies in order to drive civilians out of the area years before.

Land mines are aptly described as weapons that cannot distinguish between the boot of a soldier and the footfall of a child. And the most common types of mines in use today remain active and ready to kill for decades, silent sentinels lying in near permanent ambush. Their prey all too frequently turns out to be civilians gathering firewood or plowing a field.

The author acknowledges the assistance of Stephen D. Goose in the preparation of this chapter.

The land mines crisis has many dimensions; it is simultaneously a matter of human rights and humanitarian law, economic development, arms control and disarmament, health care, social services, and the environment. Similarly, solving the land mines crisis—clearing the fields—will require the combination of many strategies and ideas from many fields of endeavor. The purpose of this chapter is to give an overview of the crisis, introducing the facts necessary to understand the solutions that are proposed throughout this volume.

The Extent of the Land Mines Crisis

Although it is estimated that there are 15,000 victims of land mines worldwide per year, mostly civilians, too many people believe that the problem of land mines is fundamentally a problem of a few severely mined places—Afghanistan and Cambodia, principally. These two countries are indeed among the most mine-infested places on earth, but they are unfortunately by no means alone.

About 100 million land mines are scattered in about sixty countries around the globe.[2] Of these sixty countries, approximately twenty face a severe land mine problem, that is, large infestations of mines causing daily hardships.[3] Significantly, virtually all of the severely infested countries are in the developing world, and many are among the world's poorest nations.[4]

Africa, to add to its many problems, is the most heavily mined continent, with 18–30 million mines laid in eighteen countries.[5] Still, south Asia and east Asia have tens of millions of mines in many countries; the Middle East has mines dating from World War II in Libya, and ones laid in the Iran-Iraq and Persian Gulf wars. Nor is Europe free of mines; besides those that continue to take a toll in Poland and Russia from World War II, an estimated 3 million mines have been laid in the former Yugoslavia.[6]

This would be bad enough if it were a static situation, but in fact, mines continue to be laid, sometimes in locales previously cleared at great time and expense. In Cambodia, for example, the UN estimates that mines are being laid faster than they are being cleared. Some experts believe that the former Yugoslavia,[7] during intense periods of conflict, is being sown with mines at a rate of fifty thousand per week—faster than anyplace else in the world. Where wars suddenly break out or hostilities are renewed, mine use often follows. In Abkhazia, Georgia, for example, mines have suddenly emerged as a problem for any peace settlement in that separatist war; international mediators warned both sides in the conflict of this, but to no avail.[8] The horrendous bloodshed in Rwanda will be compounded by the victims of the mines strewn so liberally in that conflict.[9]

The world is losing ground against the spread of mines—perhaps (although reliable facts are hard to come by) at an accelerating rate. In any case, the problem of mines is compounded by the fact that they *accumulate.* Physical deterioration and mine clearance take relatively few mines out of action, while successive years of warfare—especially in long-running civil wars, such as those in Angola and Cambodia—pile layer upon layer of mines. Mines accumulate like sediment in the developing world, and eventually the accumulation becomes so great—as occurred in the early 1990s—that the rest of the world begins to notice. Dealing with that accumulation will be one of the key social, development, health, environmental, and human rights problems of the 1990s.

The Nature of Mines and Mine Warfare

A land mine is a specialized piece of ordnance designed to explode in response to pressure or proximity of a person, on a time-delayed basis. A mine is designed not to need an operator who chooses to detonate it; it is designed to require no initiation to set it off apart from a footstep or other movement by the target. The key facts about a land mine are that it operates automatically and on a time delay.

Over the past two decades the technology of mines has shifted, and so, too, has mine warfare. These shifts have a considerable amount to do with the reasons why so many mines are emplaced in the developing world.

The original military use of antipersonnel mines, going back to World War I, was to protect antitank mines, and that function remains at the heart of conventional military doctrine. Both antitank and antipersonnel mines were seen as weapons of the defense—to make it harder for an attacker to break through ground, to slow down an attacker, and to channel the attacker's forces to ground where they could most easily be destroyed.[10] This understanding of mines' defensive and tactical role tended to limit their use in World War II and the Korean War, at least by comparison to the wars of the 1980s. Laying minefields was also labor-intensive, which further tended to reduce the promiscuous use of mines before the introduction of mechanical emplacement devices.

Land mines have now evolved from a tactical, defensive, battlefield weapon to an offensive, sometimes even strategic, weapon operating in environments far larger than what classically would have been regarded as the "battlefield."[11] The track of advanced technology allows this to happen through the use of remotely delivered scatterables. The use of such mines to put barriers between the front line and supplies, for example, is a straightforwardly offensive use.

Unsophisticated mines can also be put to offensive uses. An all-too-typical use of mines in the internal wars of the developing world involves their deliberate sowing in civilian agriculture, for the purpose of disrupting agriculture and, very often, to create refugees. Used on a vast scale in places like Angola, across whole theaters of war, land mines take on certain aspects of strategic weapons in that they have their worst effects on civilians and poison the land practically forever. Although the analogy can easily be overstated, mines are in some respects like weapons of mass destruction, in slow motion.[12]

While technologically dissimilar mines thus achieve the same effect, the crisis in mines that began to emerge in the 1980s has relatively little to do with scatterables, whose deployment has been limited. Rather, the land mine crisis as it exists today is a function of the accumulation of unsophisticated mines, emplaced either without regard for their effects on civilians or for the very purpose of attacking civilians, and is largely a product of long-running internal wars—although that situation could change if sophisticated scatterable mines were used in other types of wars, in the ways anticipated by the standard military doctrines of nearly all conventional armies.

The Effects of Land Mines

One approach to examining the effects of land mines is to use the various disciplines from which the land mines crisis is being addressed.

Land mines have a disastrous effect on development, and particularly agricultural development, following an armed conflict. At precisely the time when there is the greatest need to restart agricultural production, to put people back to productive work, to ensure food supplies, and to bring refugees back to their lands, land mines impose a high barrier. The need to remove land mines, even when it can be done, raises the cost of development immensely.

The health and social services of developing countries suffer devastating effects of mines. Where medical care is available, the amputations typically required for mine wounds generally necessitate not just one but several operations. Large transfusions are usually needed, as well as antibiotics. And once the amputation is complete, the rehabilitation and fitting of prosthetics are expensive. Nor can very many developing world societies absorb a large number of amputees into economies that depend on physical labor. The ripple effects and indirect costs of mine wounds in economically marginal societies go on and on.

The effects of land mines as a pollutant in the environment are just now beginning to be understood. It is a long-lived pollution, one that requires physical cleansing of the earth to eliminate. And since land mines are often laid in places of human habitation, land mine pollution may in some cases have the effect of pushing people who cannot return to their own land out into otherwise unused land.

Mines thus set off a long chain of direct and indirect effects; their costs stretch over decades and reach far beyond the initial tragic victim of a mine who loses a limb; all of society pays, over and over again.

Who Supplies Mines?

Combatants use mines, particularly unsophisticated mines, because they are efficient and cheap. One reason why mines are a crisis today is because they are a true commodity in the international arms market—cheap to make and cheap to buy. Thus, combatants rarely need to think about the cost of mines in deciding whether to use them; to judge by the results, it appears they rarely do. While it is true that unsophisticated mines can be made locally by virtually any combatant, government, or guerrilla force, in fact the great majority of mines deployed today were manufactured and then transferred abroad, whether from Italy, China, the former Soviet Union, or elsewhere. Few of the combatants in today's wars make their own mines in any but minor circumstances—not in Angola, for example, or Mozambique—and if they did, they would likely incur greater overall costs than they do by obtaining them from outside sources.

The cheapness and universal availability of mines in the international markets is therefore a major factor in finding solutions to the land mines crisis. Manufacturers have likely produced an average of ten million mines per year in recent decades.[13] More than one hundred companies and government agencies in fifty-six countries have manufactured more than 340 types of mines in the past several decades.[14]

The total value of all mine production worldwide is likely $100–$200 million annually.[15] China, Italy, and the former Soviet Union were probably the largest producers and exporters of land mines in recent decades, if not necessarily in that order. Although official data would seem to place the United States far behind these countries in production and export—current U.S. law prohibits the export of mines completely—data from mine clearance groups suggests that not long ago the United States must have been in the front ranks.[16] Other large exporters and producers in the past twenty-five years include Belgium, Bulgaria, the former Czechoslovakia, France, Hungary, the United Kingdom, and the former Yugoslavia. Developing nations are also becoming active in the land mine export market; it is a product that suits their competitive advantage in labor and the commodity economics typical of mines. Countries of the developing world that have become players in mine exports include Egypt, Israel, Pakistan, Singapore, and South Africa (although South Africa has now imposed a unilateral moratorium on mine exports).[17]

There have been attempts recently to dampen the export market. This effort has been partly through unilateral bans, such as those in effect in the United States, Germany, France, and South Africa. It has also involved initiatives at the United Nations, especially in the General Assembly, to encourage a worldwide moratorium on mine exports. It is too early to tell, however, what effects these efforts will have, given that barriers to entry into the mines export market are minimal.

Mine Clearance

The costs of mine clearance, if undertaken in a serious way, would likely equal the full development budgets of some of the poorest mine-infested countries. The reason for this is that mine clearance still consists principally of a person with a stick, probing the ground a few centimeters at a time. It is slow and dangerous work, and progress is measured in square meters rather than kilometers. Available alternatives all have significant limitations, and methods appropriate to battlefield mine breaching are not suitable for the large-area clearance necessary for civilian mine clearance.

New technologies for civilian mine clearance are being discussed but are still in limited use or under research and development. Mine clearance experts generally agree that although new technologies may provide significant cost and time savings in some clearance situations, no technological "silver bullet" will cause the problem to go away.

Conclusion

The land mines crisis has reached a critical point. Other areas of social concern will feel ripple effects. Finding solutions to the land mines crisis requires, in the first place, a hard look at the facts of the current crisis and the reasons why it has come to be. With those facts in hand, it is possible to go forward to propose solutions that will, finally, clear the fields.

2

Why Mines? A Military Perspective

RICHARD H. JOHNSON

Armed conflict is the ultimate means to resolve disputes between nations and states when all other efforts fail. As man has become more sophisticated in peaceful pursuits, he similarly has refined the methods he uses to wage war. As tactics have evolved, so, too, have a wide range of weapons to enable military commanders to achieve success when combat becomes necessary. One weapon found on the modern battlefield is a family of devices known as mines or, more specifically, land mines.

Many key words are associated with the conduct of war. *Mobility, maneuver, firepower, mass, economy of force, surprise,* and a plethora of others are used to describe the principles of war and the tenets of military operations. From these comes a requirement to force an enemy into a disadvantageous position by controlling terrain and the situation on the battlefield while conserving combat power. Ideally, any weapon used in war should meet this requirement; it should inflict a maximum penalty on the enemy with no deleterious effect on the user. Mines can trace their lineage to devices developed to meet this objective.

A simple device developed to control mounted forces, the four-pointed caltrop, has probably been in existence in some form since the horse was first used in combat. Other historical examples also illustrate attempts to influence the outcome of battle by providing inanimate aids to combatants. The Hundred Years' War provides two good examples. During the Crécy Campaign, in 1346, English archers dug potholes in front of their positions to hinder enemy horsemen.[1] In 1415, before the battle of Agincourt, both sides used explosive mines and countermines to breach fortified positions. (The term *mines*, refering to a type of explosive charge in, or on, the ground comes from instances like these.) At Agincourt, each English archer carried six foot stakes to be driven into the ground with the point facing the enemy to repel cavalry.[2] In these and similar instances of devices developed to supplement direct and indirect fire weapons, the purpose was clear—control the battlefield at the lowest cost to the defender.

In the nineteenth century, mines were used in the American Civil War. Most complex were the naval mines both sides used against shipping. The Russians had used naval mines in the Crimean War; during the Civil War, both sides manufactured complicated explosive devices for use in offensive and defensive naval operations.[3] The land mines first used by the Confederates around Yorktown in 1862 were simply artillery projectiles buried base down. A soldier would cause this antipersonnel mine to explode when he stepped on the fuze. The Civil War also saw the explosive mining of fortified positions by tunneling; the most famous (or infamous) occurrences of this tactic were at Vicksburg in 1863 and at Petersburg in 1864.

World War I introduced the machine gun, the tank, the airplane, and other weapons to the battlefield. To counter the introduction of the tank by the British, the Germans fabricated explosive mines. These were improvised in the field from artillery projectiles and had limited application. By the end of the war, a limited inventory of antitank mines existed. Land mines finally became a prominent fixture on the battlefield during World War II. Because of the widespread use of armor, with its inherent mobility, mines were developed as a counterforce. The potential has today expanded to use mines in all conflicts across the spectrum of tactical operations. Mines provide a means to achieve economy of force, surprise, and security.

With the introduction of high explosives in the late 1800s, large-scale uses of explosive devices became common. They span the range of munitions projected, dropped, thrown, and placed from artillery and airplanes, as well as individual items like hand grenades and land mines. Inevitably, some proportion will fail to function as intended, or will "dud." While each item has an associated dud rate, historically about 5 percent of explosive ammunition has failed to function as intended. These items remain on the battlefield, along with uncleared land mines, as explosive debris posing a threat to the reoccupying civilian populace. As an article in *Smithsonian* states about the aftermath of Verdun, "The soldiers moved on. The war moved on. The bombs stayed."[4] Seventy-five years after the end of hostilities, large areas are so contaminated, they are unusable. Even partial statistics for France are awesome: Since 1946, 630 deminers have died; 18 million artillery shells, 10 million grenades, and 6 hundred thousand aerial bombs have been found and destroyed. In 1991, thirty-six farmers died and another fifty-one citizens were injured by unexploded ordnance.[5]

To understand the utility of mines and to explore their disutility, it is useful to first examine how explosive ordnance works.

A Brief Primer on Mines

HOW MINES WORK

All explosive ordnance contains about the same types of components; all have a firing train consisting of a fuze, detonator, booster, and main charge. The objective is to have the most sensitive explosive in a small quantity in the fuze, protected from inadvertent initiation. As the firing train progresses toward the main charge, the explosive increases in quantity and decreases in sensitivity. The manner of launch or employment distinguishes one type of ordnance from another and will define the shape, hardness, and, to some extent, configuration of the main charge.

The fuze dictates how and when the item functions. A general goal is to have the fuze safe so the munition can be handled in storage, transportation, and tactical movement; the fuze becomes armed only when the item is employed. A hand-emplaced mine will become fully armed when it is emplaced in or on the ground and all safeties are removed. A fuze may dud for a variety of reasons, but the cause will not be readily apparent. Most important is the real possibility the dud fuze may function and detonate the ordnance if it is disturbed or moved. All unexploded ordnance is a potential hazard.

The complexity of a fuze is as varied as the ordnance to which it is attached. It can be mechanical (such as a firing pin and a stab detonator), chemical (for example, acetone that decomposes a plastic disk), electrical (for instance, a battery-operated electrical circuit), or a combination of types. The specific details of how the fuze functions are most important to the designer, the soldier user, and the ordnance disposal technician. Most significant to all who encounter an explosive munition is the simple fact that removal or neutralization of the fuze is generally the way to render the ordnance inoperative. A second method to achieve neutralization is to interrupt the firing train so the explosive reaction cannot propagate to the main charge. Another means of rendering explosive ammunition safe is to remove the main charge, so even if the fuze and the rest of the firing train operate, the intended effect is not achieved.

To produce a desired effect on the intended target, the main charge is designed in a number of ways. The character of the target may require the addition of fragmentation or even molding or concentrating the explosive effects through use of a shaped charge or explosively formed penetrators to get the required result.

A not-so-subtle difference distinguishes mines from most other explosive ordnance. With mines, the target causes the fuze to function as the mine lies dormant and the target approaches or contacts it. There is normally a delay from employment (emplacement), which provides the user with a safe separation from the effects of the main charge if it fires prematurely. In some respects then, mines are more precise than other ordnance, since action of the target on the ordnance causes it to function, as opposed to the more conventional approach of having the item explode when it arrives at its destination. The main drawback with most mines is the lack of a feature to discriminate friend (or noncombatant) from foe. Therefore, with land mines, the potential exists to attack nonhostile targets in probably a greater proportion than with aimed ordnance, such as artillery projectiles, bombs, or even hand grenades. Additionally, most mines, like all unexploded ordnance, work in all weather and light conditions.

MEANS OF EMPLACEMENT

Land mines can be categorized by their method of emplacement. A means requiring little or no technology is hand emplacement, and the mines are identified as conventional mines. Mines sown this way may be either buried or placed on the surface of the ground and as a result may or may not be readily visible. Ideally, mines placed by hand will be arranged in a pattern to simplify marking and, after they have served their purpose, removal. A problem occurs, though, when mines are left in position for extended periods—they may change position because of erosion; the terrain surrounding them is also subject to change because of climate and environmental effects. Unfortunately, over time, the chance increases that environmental effects will make minefields hard to locate and remove.

Several mechanical aids have been developed over the last fifty years or so to hasten hand emplacement. There are vehicle-towed plows used to lay rows of mines and augers that emplace mines individually. Even with these supplemental aids, the logistics and manpower involved in constructing a large minefield are extensive. Hand and mechanical emplacement is quite simply a very time-consuming task and requires the diversion of manpower from other combat requirements.

A variant of the hand-emplaced mine is the "off-route" mine. Such devices are placed alongside a road or trail and project a warhead or fragments toward the target. Fuzing may be target-activated (such as passive infrared or tripwire) or command-detonated (for example, the U.S. M-18 Claymore). Targets may be either vehicles or dismounted soldiers.

To decrease the logistics and personnel tax conventional mines impose on military commanders, several countries have developed scatterable mines. These can be delivered by air, artillery, or ground launch. With both air- and artillery-delivered mines, the people dispensing them are remote from the emplacement site. By design, many scatterable mines have electronic fuzes powered by a reserve cell (battery) activated when the mine is dispensed. The fuze will function in several modes: when activated by the target, when a self-destruct time has elapsed, or when the energy of the cell degrades to a lower limit. In all three cases, the main charge will function and no hazardous residue will be left. This feature is called "self-destruct." If, for some reason, the fuze fails to fire, the cell will eventually reach a point where it will be incapable of firing the electric detonator, the main charge will not fire, and the mine is "self-neutralized" or "self-sterilized." The main charge in the mine still presents a hazard, but it is much reduced. Some individuals have recovered the electronic lens (fuze) from scatterable mines used in the Persian Gulf War. The fact the lens can be recovered without injury is testimony to the effectiveness of the self-neutralization feature of electronic fuzed mines.

While hand- or mechanically emplaced conventional mines are normally arranged in patterns, scatterable mines are not. Conventional minefields, particularly those expected to remain in place for long periods, are usually marked with signs and barbed wire to prevent friendly forces from entering them. Most scatterable minefields are marked only on maps, not on the ground at the time of dispensing. Scatterable mines can be dispensed at the time and place of need, and because of the electrical power source, most have a finite active life, measured in months. Because of the methods used to dispense them, scatterable mines are surface-laid, but as with conventional minefields, environmental effects may cause movement and concealment of individual mines.

DETECTABILITY

Originally, all mines had a significant metallic content. Even mines fabricated from wood, as were popular with the Soviets, or the ceramic-body mines developed by the Japanese in World War II, had metal components in the fuze. Some mines on the market today have only trace metal elements in the fuze or body. Some better-known types, for instance, come from the former Yugoslavia, Italy, and China. They are not just a recent invention; the United States developed and produced two low-metal-content mines around mid-century.[6] The reason for keeping the metal content low is to make detection difficult, since the most common detectors in use by military forces today rely on detecting the metal in the mine. The nondetectable mine was introduced as a counter to hand detection; however, hand detection is no longer a preferred method when breaching complex obstacles. The objective in breaching a minefield is to clear a path to support the momentum of offensive combat. When possible, the breach will be conducted by armored forces using explosives, plows, and other tools. Though the presence of antipersonnel mines greatly increases the complexity and difficulty of the breaching operation, detectability of individual mines becomes a moot issue. The only utility they provide is in low-intensity conflict when no mechanized breaching equipment is available; the advantage provided in this situation is offset by the increased hazard the user faces when the mines have served their purpose.

While mines are commonly called metallic or nonmetallic, there is no international agreement on what amount of metal is necessary to make the distinction. If the force that places a minefield expects to reoccupy the terrain where the mines have been employed, it appears rational to expect the mines will be removed at some point. Nondetectability seems to work against this goal and appears to have little or no tactical utility. It does, however, impose a penalty on the people clearing land areas of explosive hazards when a peace agreement has been concluded.

ACTIVATION OF THE FUZE

As mentioned earlier, the contact or proximity of the target is a distinguishing feature of mines. Early generations of mines required that the target come in direct contact with the fuze or with a trip wire to cause activation. Refinements in fuzing design no longer require direct contact. The magnetic field generated by an armored vehicle is sufficient to fire a fuze designed to fire on magnetic influence. This feature was present in sea mines almost from their inception and has lately been incorporated in some land mines. Acoustic signatures can be used to arm firing circuits. Infrared can be used to passively detect a target within the mine's range and fire the main charge. Antihandling devices can be incorporated to preclude easy removal or neutralization. In short, many advances in fuzing and firing systems place the sophistication of current conventional and scatterable mines on a plane far removed from their ancestors. But, bear in mind, some of their ancestors are still in use.

CLASSIFICATIONS OF MINES

The most common way to designate differences between land mines is by referring to them by type of target they are designed to attack. There are two types: "Antipersonnel (AP) mines are designed to kill or wound soldiers."[7] "Antitank (AT) mines are designed to immobilize or destroy tracked and wheeled vehicles and the vehicles' crews and passengers."[8]

One might think the weight, shape, or appearance of the mine could be used as a determinant of its use and function. Not so. Antitank mines can vary in weight from about four pounds to over thirty pounds; antipersonnel mines, from an ounce or so to several pounds. They both may be either cylindrical or rectangular solids. Fuzing may be visible or may be integral to the mine and thus not readily accessible. These factors combine to make external features an imprecise way to differentiate between types.

The same is true to some extent when trying to use the fuze or the main charge as identifiers. Some antitank mines will function if disturbed by personnel because they contain an antihandling device, effectively turning them into antipersonnel mines. If they use a magnetic influence fuze, simply changing the orientation of the mine in relation to its original resting position may be sufficient to cause the fuze to function.

Mines can also be categorized as manufactured or improvised. Manufactured items are easily recognizable as such by general appearance and sometimes the presence of markings. Improvised mines are usually fabricated in the field from explosives on hand or from dud-fired ordnance. In conflicts at lower levels of intensity or when the combatants do not have access to standard weapons sources, improvised mines are common. During the Vietnam War, Viet Cong and North Vietnamese forces made extensive use of dud-fired U.S. ordnance as improvised mines. This condition will prevail in the future, particularly in less-developed nations. Occasionally, insurgency forces will develop procedures to recover dud-fired ordnance and remanufacture it into mines and other explosive devices, as was done in Vietnam. With improvised mines, the line between an antipersonnel and antitank mine is almost nonexistent, since the items can range in size from a pound or so to several hundred pounds and targets are usually targets of opportunity.

Common in the realm of improvised mines is the command-detonated mine. Again, the main charge may be almost any size, and the effects it produces vary. Manufactured mines may be designed to be fired on command. Dud-fired ammunition may be also modified into command-detonated mines. Anyway, the item is a form of mine, and the target may be either people or materiel (and people).

So much for a brief description of mines. While one approach is to make a distinction by calling them either antipersonnel or antitank, a more detailed examination shows this characterization may not be sufficient. To fully consider all the implications of uses of land mines, it is more balanced to place them into the perspective of all similar types of hazardous explosive debris left on the battlefield when hostilities end.

Uses of Mines

The classic combat tasks mines accomplish are to protect friendly forces, attack the enemy, shape the battlefield, and deny freedom of movement to the enemy. A more general statement, applicable to all countries, is the published U.S. policy on the use of mines:

"Minefields are used to

- Produce a specific effect on enemy maneuver, thereby creating a vulnerability that can be exploited by friendly forces.
- Cause the enemy to piecemeal his forces.

- Interfere with enemy command and control.
- Inflict damage to enemy personnel and equipment.
- Protect friendly forces from enemy maneuver."[9]

As the range of military operations escalates from peacetime to large-scale combat operations, the weapons employed increase in number and complexity. As the tempo of operations picks up, the size and type of force committed will probably change also. The range of possibilities is almost endless, but some examples are illustrative of the role mines may play in defensive and offensive operations.

Following the Six Day War in 1967, both the Israelis and the Egyptians established large defensive minefields on their respective sides of the Suez Canal. The mines' primary purpose was to provide protection from maneuver by the other side and to deny the opponent the element of surprise. Their existence gave the defenders an appreciable economy of force measure and provided what amounted to "on-call" defensive firepower in case of attack. Other recent examples of classic defensive minefields have been in North Africa, Normandy, and Russia in World War II; at places along the Iron Curtain during the Cold War; in the Persian Gulf War; and in Korea today. Mines used for defense are most effective when employed as part of other obstacles and watched over by direct and indirect fires; mines become one element of an integrated combat plan. Defensive minefields can always be breached, but they do provide a measure of tactical advantage to the defender.

Defensive minefields emplaced on a large scale traditionally have been associated with attrition warfare and were designed to remain in place for a long time. They can provide a stay-behind obstacle to opposing forces with no real-time involvement of the defender. Large minefields deliberately emplaced as part of a complex obstacle may take several weeks or months to put in place; they may remain for months or even years (along the Suez Canal, for example, they remained in place from 1967 to 1973). Minefields on this scale will consist of conventional mines laid either by hand or mechanically.

In the Persian Gulf War, Iraqi forces emplaced extensive defensive minefields to protect their forces in Kuwait. To a lesser extent, coalition forces also used defensive minefields to protect their forces, particularly in the early stages of the buildup. Available in large numbers were ground-scatterable mines that could have been dispensed by coalition forces to defend their positions in the early stages. The first U.S. elements in Saudi Arabia were, of necessity, light and readily deployable.

Such a force has a limited anti-armor capability. Mines provide added capability with little cost in manpower and other resources. Since this operation, the United States has fielded more scatterable mine systems. It will soon deploy a wide-area mine that will destroy armor targets approaching within one hundred meters. As the U.S. military gets smaller, there is a decrease of forward deployed forces in foreign countries. Subsequently, threats such as Iraq must be met by sending troops from the continental United States—"power projection from home country"—a major change and difficult task. Mines will be a key antiarmor element for early deploying troops establishing a lodgment pending assembly of a fully capable force.

Mines have also become an integral part of offensive doctrine. It takes imagination to integrate them into fast-paced maneuver warfare, given the traditional association of mines with static situations. Particularly applicable to the offense are scatterable mines, which are dispensed rapidly and at extended ranges, and thus are ideally suited to maneuver warfare. Scatterable mines can block movement of opposing forces or fix them in place. They can protect flanks during penetrations and interdict logistical and reinforcing forces. However, the use of mines in offensive operations is limited. This is consistent with the reality that attacking forces in an offensive operation consume less of all kinds of ammunition than similar forces in a defensive posture.

Scatterable mines were used effectively in Operation Desert Storm. For instance, air-delivered Gator mines were used to interdict deep targets and restrict enemy movement. In one case, two Iraqi divisions on the right flank of the VII Corps attack into Iraq were fixed in place by strikes of Gator mines while coalition forces exploited their attack into Iraqi territory. As another example, a primary mission of artillery in ground combat is to fire counterbattery to suppress and destroy opposition forces. The doctrinal guidance to use artillery-delivered antipersonnel mines as the last rounds fired in counterbattery was common in the Gulf.

Insurgency/counterinsurgency operations and low-intensity conflict are ideal opportunities for mines. In defensive positions, whether they are strongpoints or field locations, such as night defensive positions, mines play an integral role with other defensive measures. Insurgent forces make extensive use of mines, mainly as an economy of force measure. These mines can range from improvised devices to manufactured items, as was the case in the Vietnam War. Mines will often be the weapons of choice in Third World conflicts because of their availability, low cost, and relative ease of use. The existence of locally available materials from unexploded ordnance exacerbates the situation.

It is possible to find antitank or antipersonnel mines used by themselves; doctrine supports this application. It is normal to use them in combination, however. In breaching an obstacle, an objective of the attacking force is to neutralize or remove as many components of the obstacle as possible at the outset. An objective of the defender, meanwhile, is to harden the obstacle against this to enhance its effectiveness. If antitank mines are used alone, the probability that dismounted troops can cross the minefield while removing the mines rises. If direct and indirect covering fires are suppressed or neutralized, then a minefield consisting solely of antitank mines can be breached rapidly by dismounted soldiers. Obviously, the breach is even easier to accomplish if the mines do not have antihandling devices. In combat involving light forces, the threat of armor must always be considered; therefore, pure antipersonnel minefields are rare also. Most doctrinal approaches to minefield composition call for a mix of antitank and antipersonnel mines, to preclude easy breaching by the opposition. It is not unusual to include antihandling or antilift devices on antitank mines to prevent easy removal and to retard breaching.

Doctrinal approaches to patterned emplacement vary regarding positioning of antitank and antipersonnel mines relative to each other. Some patterns have rows containing mines of one type, while other applications specify laying antipersonnel mines in a cluster around an antitank mine. Scatterable mines, of course, will not be laid in a pattern; the ratio of antitank mines to antipersonnel mines in scatterable mine systems is not subject to adjustment in the field because of the dispensing method.

In any case, minefields must be marked to preclude casualties to friendly troops. Conventional minefields, whether laid by hand or with mechanical assistance, can be marked with physical barriers and signs on the ground. Detailed maps should be prepared both to preclude fratricide and to enable removal when the purpose of the minefield has been served. Minefields composed of scatterable mines will usually be marked on maps and similar media to preclude inadvertent entry by friendly forces. Map notations will indicate the expected self-destruct times for the scatterable minefield. When scatterable mines are laid by ground-mounted systems, it is possible at the time of emplacement to mark the boundaries of the field.

A necessary consideration during placement of any mine must be the plan for removal when the device has served its purpose. Removal can be achieved through a reversal of the process used to emplace the mine, as with conventional hand-laid mines, or through self-sterilization or self-destruction in mines with electronic fuzes. Mine clearance depends on detectability. As mentioned earlier, there is no discernible tactical utility to nondetectable mines; the use of nondetectable mines today is at best a terrorist tactic.

If unconventional warfare is the province of the nondetectable mine, there are other distinctions found in this type of low-intensity conflict. Conventional, low-cost mines will be prevalent in insurgency/counterinsurgency operations. In addition, there will be a mix of manufactured and improvised mines made from unexploded ordnance. Minefields generally will be smaller than those found in engagements between large or mechanized forces. Potential exists for heavy use of booby traps.[10] Locations will be known to the user, but fields are generally not marked according to any convention, and location data are not always available after the end of hostilities. All of this makes the mines used in low-intensity conflicts hard to clear and one of the greatest threats posed to civilian populations both during a war and afterward.

Use of conventional (hand-emplaced) mines requires extensive logistical support and large operational forces. The Iraqi minefields in Kuwait were put in place over several months. The ones along the Suez Canal similarly took months to construct. Scatterable mines will appreciably decrease the logistical and operational burden and may herald an increase in mine use in offensive operations.

"The offensive is the decisive form of war—the commanders' ultimate means of imposing their will upon the enemy."[11] An axiom of armies worldwide is they will "fight as they train." Maneuver-oriented commanders have a natural bias against the use of tactics (such as mine warfare) traditionally associated with attrition warfare; use of scatterable mines and their associated offensive utility is a recent innovation. Training simulations for scatterable mines and unexploded ordnance are just now being introduced, and the effect on mine usage is hard to judge. It is inherently difficult and unglamorous to train troops in emplacement and removal of mines (including countermine operations). The large logistical requirement of conventional mines is a deterrent to training because it is time-consuming and requires static positioning of maneuver forces while troops construct minefields. All these factors conspire to limit training in mechanized forces, but do not affect unconventional or guerrilla forces, for whom the mine is often the most sophisticated weapon available.

The Military Effectiveness of Mines

All the preceding serves to explain the rationale for acquiring land mines. It may be possible to statistically analyze mines in relation to other weapons or weapon systems and arrive at some quantified judgment of their relative utility. Such a study, though, would undoubtedly contain an extreme number of caveats and assumptions, and thus be of questionable value. It may be as meaningful to examine some historical and personal examples, besides doctrinal guidance, and draw conclusions on the advantages and disadvantages mines offer to military operations.

HISTORICAL PERSPECTIVE

The successful instances mentioned earlier, taken from the Hundred Years' War, of mechanical aids or modifications to terrain support the utility of some form of weapon that remains dormant until initiated by the target. The use of mines by the Confederates during the Peninsula Campaign of the American Civil War was not fully accepted by either side as an introduction of a legitimate weapon. Nevertheless, as the war progressed, both sides fabricated mines, booby traps, and land torpedoes with some degree of effectiveness. These weapons were used almost exclusively in defensive actions and had the effect of slowing pursuit as forces retreated. The mine at Petersburg is often cited as an illustration of the use of mines in the American Civil War. It was simply a large chamber dug by miners from Pennsylvania under a salient in the Confederate position. The chamber was filled with explosive and detonated, opening a large gap allowing federal troops to breach the defense and threaten Richmond directly. The concept was brilliant. Execution of the "mine" was almost flawless. Unfortunately for the Union, the use of the mine as a weapon of war at Petersburg was a disaster resulting in thousands of dead and wounded soldiers. Incompetence in exploitation of the advantage provided undoubtedly was part of the reason for the fiasco,[12] but introduction of a new weapon and the need for developing tactics to exploit the advantage provided may have been factors. The employment of mines during the American Civil War cannot be used to make an overwhelming case either for or against them. The significant point is the war marked the introduction of explosives as a replacement for the potholes and sharpened wooden stakes of earlier times.

Mine use was limited in World War I. The origin of current mine warfare doctrine and practice really comes from the widespread use by all combatants in World War II. In the battle for Kasserine Pass in February 1943, mines placed by the U.S. Army had the desired effect of slowing the Axis advance, though only temporarily. One account of the battle states: "To Schmidt's right, infantry and engineers were on their knees in the mud, uniforms soaked black with the pouring rain, probing and stabbing with their bayonets. They looked for all the world as if they were cutting asparagus, he thought, rather than looking for the deadly mines lying beneath the surface of the mud and holding up the attack on the *Ami* positions beyond."[13] Similar examples can be found throughout both theaters. At El Alamein, Kursk, Normandy, Anzio, and literally hundreds of places, mines were used to defend with some degree of success. Where the threat of armor or other vehicles was low, as in the Pacific, antipersonnel mines were the predominant type used. In the European theater, the use of antipersonnel mines to deter breaching was common practice, as was the use of antihandling devices in secondary fuze wells on antitank mines. Flails, rollers, and plows were designed to mechanically breach minefields and protect the breaching force from antipersonnel mines and covering fires. These had some amount of effectiveness but were at best unwieldy to operate, and they were good only to conduct a breach; they could not perform a clearance efficiently.

In Vietnam, mines also had the desired effect. Perhaps one of the most commonly used weapons by American troops was the M-18 series antipersonnel mine, the Claymore. Around virtually every defensive position occupied longer than a short rest break, Claymores were positioned to provide protective firepower. They were particularly useful at night and during other periods of low visibility, and to cover terrain that could not be completely observed and covered by direct fire. When a unit moved, it reclaimed its Claymores for reuse. In fixed installations and base camps, other antipersonnel mines were used together with the Claymore, but they normally remained in place for longer periods. The Claymore mine was an essential tool of the infantryman.

The effectiveness of antipersonnel mines against dismounted soldiers is illustrated by literally thousands of examples from Vietnam. There was widespread use of mines and booby traps against U.S. forces. The use of antipersonnel mines against dismounted troops in Vietnam achieved the desired effect of delaying and inflicting casualties on the enemy while defending friendly positions. Estimates of mine casualties suffered by the United States are as high as one-third of the total, witness to the utility of mines and booby traps in insurgency situations.

In cases where mines have created a long-term barrier, they have rarely been challenged and have been effective. Barrier minefields have existed along many hostile borders—around Guantanamo Bay, in Korea, along the inter-German border, and on the Golan Heights, to name but a few places. There is little question they serve the purpose to maintain a separation line between opposing forces, and in some cases maintain isolation of one nation from another.

Other examples of the effectiveness of minefields used in various conflicts would lead to the same conclusion. Mines are an effective way for military forces to mold terrain to their advantage, they provide an economy of force measure to the user, and they destroy materiel and inflict casualties. Doctrine even includes the use of phony minefields. This is recognition that a minefield serves its purpose if the opposing force perceives its existence. Mines are but one piece of a complex assortment of weapons designed to work synergistically as part of a tactical and strategic plan. The purpose of any weapon of war is to confuse the enemy and impart an advantage to the user. Mines provide this utility. A question arises, though, about alternate means to achieve the same end.

Take mines away, and what is the result? If a commander is denied the use of mines, he must find another weapon or activity, with equal or greater effectiveness, to replace them. In January 1994, the International Committee of the Red Cross sponsored a symposium of military experts to examine the utility of mines.[14] They specifically looked at antipersonnel mines and a comprehensive list of alternatives, assessing each with respect to fifteen attributes. The conclusion is that "no alternative fulfills the military requirement in the way that antipersonnel . . . mines do," and that these mines are the "most cost-effective system available to the military."[15]

LESSONS LEARNED

It is thus evident that the military doctrine for the use of antipersonnel mines is clear. Furthermore, they perform their military purpose, as demonstrated by historical example, and while alternatives exist, they do not adequately fulfill the military requirement.

In conflicts between well-trained professional armies, the use of mines will most probably be according to doctrine and conventions designed to limit their effects to combatants. Because of the possibility of hindering the users' mobility, mines will be used sparingly and judiciously. There is a potential for inflicting casualties to civilians, but that possibility exists to some extent with all weapons of war. Depending on the tactical application, the mines used by a professional army may be a mix of scatterable mines, which self-destruct or self-neutralize, and conventional ones, which do not. In offensive warfare, most of the mines the United States will most probably employ will be scatterable and should pose no residual threat several months after dispensing.

In an insurgency situation, the mines used will be on the lower end of the technological scale and will most probably remain active until individually removed. Marking of minefields will be less likely in this type of combat, though local civilians may be warned of their existence. Use of improvised devices will be greater, as will the potential hazard to noncombatants. Mines are a prime weapon of choice by guerrilla forces and will continue to be, regardless of agreements concerning their use by governmental bodies.

The other item of battlefield explosive debris mentioned earlier merits brief examination at this point—unexploded ordnance. Modern munitions can consist of many small submunitions with an effect similar to that of mines against unprotected targets. While much attention has been paid to reducing the dud rate, it still is between 1 percent and 5 percent, depending on the type of munition. The dud rate was evident after Operation Desert Storm in 1991 because of the sparse vegetation in the region. Large areas of Kuwait and Iraq were attacked by coalition forces using submunitions from the air and the ground. As an example, the fully loaded Multiple Launch Rocket System (MLRS) has 12 rockets, each with 644 submunitions. Taking a conservative assumption that five hundred launcher loads of MLRS were fired in Operation Desert Storm, the number of dud submunitions resulting could easily fall within the range of 60,000–192,500. As another example, over one hundred thousand aerial-delivered scatterable mines were dropped on Iraqi territory. If the dud rate was 3 percent, over three thousand duds would be present on the battlefield after hostilities. The mines had a finite life of several months because of the limits of the reserve cell. Most other submunitions have no limitations on their lethality. Extrapolating from these two examples to include all munitions used in modern warfare, it is evident that the quantity and types of hazardous debris left on the battlefield are appreciable. Arguments about the hazards posed by mines are really an indictment of a lack of a countermine and area clearance capability. Solutions should be found to treat the complete problem posed by all hazardous explosive battlefield debris.

The Future

The near-term developments in mine usage are clear. The use of mines by well-organized, mechanized armies will continue to be significant. Maneuver warfare includes a recognized role for mines, mostly scatterable with a limited life. Unfortunately, the high cost decreases the probability that self-destructing or self-neutralizing mines will be used in low-intensity conflicts.

A trend has apparently developed to use mines with little metal content in insurgency operations. It is entirely understandable that mines will be employed extensively in these cases because of low cost and availability. The antitank and antipersonnel mines produced by the former Yugoslavia and marketed in the early 1990s are largely nondetectable. They are advertised as "antimagnetic," and the metal content is limited to thin foil disks. The antitank mines have secondary fuze wells sometimes, which, when fitted with an antihandling device, effectively make them a very large antipersonnel mine. The question then is, At what point does the antitank mine become an antipersonnel mine? Mine suppliers to the Third World are making no apparent effort to make their products detectable and, therefore, to decrease the hazards to noncombatants. This trend will no doubt continue unless agreement is reached on the absence of military utility of such items.

Nations spend money on military materiel to meet deficiencies in carrying out doctrine. As in any budgetary process, only high-priority items will be acquired. Mine warfare equipment is no exception; there are programs in development, and there are others not being pursued simply because of lack of money and priority. A useful way to look at land mine acquisition in the future, then, is by creating two categories: mines on the books as funded requirements, and improvements needed, though they currently may be no more advanced than an idea.

NEAR-TERM PRIORITIES

Scatterable mines, both antitank and antipersonnel, with self-destruct and self-neutralization features are recognized for their ability to meet tactical needs yet offer decreased hazards to friendly forces and civilians. Several Western nations are actively pursuing adding them to their inventories, though the procurement cost is high.

Wide-area and off-route mines, autonomously sensing, detecting, and destroying targets at ranges of one hundred meters or greater, are technically possible and are in various stages of development in several nations. Again, the acquisition cost is high. These mines will have self-neutralization and self-destruct capabilities, along with a command destruct feature.

A follow-on conceptual research effort is needed to develop intelligent mines and minefields with the capability to collect and use battlefield intelligence. These mines have the potential of being remotely cycled through many off/on sequences, as well as having the same features as wide-area mines.

There is an increasing capability to train with mines at large training centers, such as the U.S. Army National Training Center at Fort Irwin, California, and in computer simulations used to train combat leaders. This will lead to a realization of the importance of countermine activities and cleanup requirements after cessation of hostilities.

There is a smaller requirement for long-life conventional mines because of reliance on maneuver warfare. Still, some hand-emplaced mines (such as the Claymore) are needed for use by dismounted troops and in creating long-term barrier obstacles. Mines envisioned to meet this requirement will mostly come from existing inventories. Some development work is needed to update or replace older mines in arms stockpiles.

THE LONGER TERM

General Creighton W. Abrams, former Army chief of staff, is reported to have said, "The only trouble I had with logisticians was they always gave me what I wanted, not what I needed." Perhaps land mine developers and manufacturers are making the same mistake with their customers, for the category of modifications needed is a large one.

Electronically fused mines should include friend-or-foe identification technology, to prevent fratricide.

If nondetectable mines have little or no tactical utility, an international definition and agreement should be sought, and all mines should be made detectable—no exceptions. Enforcement of detectability standards is a problem that should be resolved in the agreement.

Improvements for conventional mines should include reliable and inexpensive self-neutralization mechanisms. There is no incentive in the form of funded government programs for any developer to pursue this course today.

Better ways are needed to mark, report, and distribute data on locations of employment of all explosive ordnance, including land mines. It should be possible, in conjunction with available means, like the Global

Positioning System (GPS), to generate maps of explosive hazards and give them to civil authorities at the cessation of hostilities.

Unexploded ordnance will become a greater problem because of the increased delivery capability of modern conventional systems. The use of submunitions to get larger target coverage simply increases the number of potential duds over single-warhead ordnance. Self-destruct fuzes are possible with almost all conventional ammunition and have been designed for several. However, even if they are introduced today, a large stockpile of non–self-destruct explosive ordnance will remain in inventory because of the very high cost of replacement. The Persian Gulf War highlighted the need to reduce dud rates in all explosive ordnance and to act on removal of the hazards remaining after combat ceases.

To this point, the discussion has focused on hardware and doctrine. One aspect touched upon perhaps too lightly may be the most important: how to address the impact of mines on noncombatants. It appears there are at least three communities involved in the issue. First are the professional military, who recognize a need to use mines responsibly, and try to do so in developing materiel and policy, but for some reason are only on the periphery of the solutions to problems of residual explosive ordnance from the battlefield after fighting stops. Second are the individuals and organizations who fully understand the consequences of unconstrained, irresponsible use of a weapon of war on innocent people and feel an obligation to correct the situation, perhaps by at least partially alleviating the problem through a ban on antipersonnel mines. And third are the leaders, fighters, and businessmen who allow the production and irresponsible use of mines by their associates to continue. The first two groups seem to have a common goal and could work together to provide increased emphasis on demining and the follow-on efforts to remove all explosive residues from the battlefield at conflict termination. Simply making a clearance plan a formal consideration for cessation of hostilities is a logical first step. Subsequent efforts could search for a way to completely address military and humanitarian concerns and give moral direction to those who now act irresponsibly.

Export Ban Implications

Beyond the political rationale and consequences of the U.S. export moratorium on antipersonnel mines, there are some military considerations. Scatterable (electronic) mine exports by the United States have been controlled and limited to NATO countries and other allies, like South Korea. While the technology the United States uses in scatterable mines is available to other countries, widespread production and use are not obvious. Other nations have not used these weapons in combat, perhaps because of economic considerations, or perhaps because the technology has not been widely adopted.

Though the mine production base in the United States is often portrayed as extensive, the number of manufacturers is actually quite small; many of the producers normally cited are subcontractors that make only components. Generally, with all mines, the nonexplosive parts are obtained from producers in the private sector, and explosive loading is done in government-owned facilities. If there is a requirement for conventional mines, the base can probably respond, since these mines do not require much more than a rudimentary production capability.

Scatterable mines, with their electronic fuzes, are another story. The designs are about twenty years old. In some cases, the components (for example, integrated circuits and capacitors) are unique or are no longer available. The assembly equipment is no longer state-of-the-art and was designed and acquired just to produce scatterable mines; industry may not retain it if no mine production is anticipated. A total ban on manufacturing antipersonnel mines in the United States may mean the country will not have the capability to manufacture the safest mines in the future, but will be capable of manufacturing only conventional mines. The small size of the base may limit competition and will possibly increase the procurement cost. It may be necessary to seek offshore sources for joint ventures in development and production; several electronic components of scatterable mines are now purchased from overseas suppliers. This is not a simple production capability that can be started or restarted in a short time just by spending money. If the production base is allowed to atrophy, time to reestablish it will be measured in years, not months, and the cost will be high. The result may be to deny U.S. forces the use of antipersonnel mines that have a documented need and utility while imposing no similar restrictions on opponents.

Conclusion

Mines have been a successful instrument of war, as many examples verify. While it is possible to cite cases where they have produced less than the optimal military result, it is not beneficial to claim mines are no good—to say so is irrelevant. The real problem is how to remove explosive residue from the battlefield after the fighting stops. Hardware and doctrine may need to be overhauled and new approaches found to change reliance on sources that now cause problems. The need is to frame a go-forward strategy focused on "the art of the possible." All responsible parties should be involved in the solution. Professional military and mine producers should be enlisted to assist in development of a phased plan with achievable goals and objectives.[16]

All nations have an obligation to provide their soldiers with the absolute best and most effective means to achieve decisive victory at the least risk to life when forced to fight. The need to balance this against risks imposed on noncombatants remains a far-reaching, complex issue. To rephrase a statement quoted earlier, when the soldiers move on, when the war moves on, the bombs should *not* remain.

3

The Humanitarian
Law Outlook

W. HAYS PARKS

The extent of the global land mine problem is abundantly, and painfully, clear.[1] It is equally clear that solving the problem will require changes in military doctrine, foreign policy, and international law.[2] An option within the field of international law is the law of war, sometimes called the law of armed conflict or international humanitarian law. The law of war has been defined as "that part of international law that regulates the conduct of armed hostilities."[3]

Former Nuremberg war crimes prosecutor Telford Taylor once observed that one may be an optimist or a pessimist about the law of war. The pessimist, seeing a hospital that has been shelled by artillery, would scoff at the value of the law of war. An optimist, observing that same hospital, would appreciate that but for the law of war, all hospitals would have been shelled.

As the nations of the world seek to address the land mine problem through amendment and strengthening of an existing law of war treaty, there has been some pessimism expressed regarding this process;[4] an argument can be made, however, for guarded optimism. The law of war is not the solution to the land mine problem, but it may offer a part of the solution.

National Defense and the Need for Land Mines

Plato's *Republic* acknowledges that the first responsibility of a government is defense of the state and protection of its citizens. This responsibility is recognized in the Charter of the United Nations, which codifies (in article 51) the inherent right of self-defense. Until we have eliminated war, and crime, this responsibility remains valid.

The military is a tool in discharge of this responsibility. Except in military-run dictatorships, the military does not exercise unlimited control over the development or acquisition of weapons; nor does it control the debate in international humanitarian law negotiations (such as are ongoing in Geneva). For example, development of guidance for the U.S. delegation to the Conventional Weapons Convention negotiations in Geneva is a deliberative process between the Department of State, the Department of Defense, and the Arms Control and Disarmament Agency.

Development and acquisition of weapons and weapon systems is an equally deliberate process, involving the military services, the civilian leadership of the Department of Defense, and the Congress of the United States. Weapons are acquired if, and only if, they contribute to national defense and if, and only if, their intended use is consistent with the law of war obligations of the United States.[5] The former is particularly true in this era of declining defense budgets. There is considerable competition for defense dollars, and it would be inaccurate to suggest that land mines exist simply because the military likes them.

Similarly, members of the U.S. military take an oath to defend our nation against "all enemies, foreign and domestic." They are obligated to do so within existing law, including the law of war. Those who fail to comply are subject to prosecution for their crimes. Investigation of alleged violations of the law of war and prosecution of violations is a cornerstone of the U.S. law of war program.

Informed military personnel agree that the law of war, the efficient use of military force, and the moral expectations of our nation are consistent with one another.

Cynicism does exist toward the efficacy of the law of war, usually in inverse proportion to an individual's knowledge of or experience with the military. One's cynicism may be related to expectations. If the objective is to prohibit war, or to prohibit a weapon that has military utility, one can expect disappointment. Various regimes put forth in the first half of this century failed to prevent war, and the history of the law of war reveals that no effective weapon has been banned.

At the same time, the nations of the world increasingly have been able to codify rules intended to provide greater protection for the civilian population and civilians not taking a direct part in hostilities. As they do so, there must be a balancing of the law of war principles of military necessity and superfluous injury (sometimes referred to as unnecessary suffering). Military necessity has been defined as permitting a belligerent "to apply any amount and kind of force to compel the complete submission of the enemy with the least possible expenditure of time, life, and money."[6] In the previous chapter, Richard H. Johnson has described the military necessity aspect of land mine use.

The prohibition on superfluous injury or unnecessary suffering is codified into law of war treaties. Article 23(e) of the annex to the 1907 Hague Convention IV, Respecting the Laws and Customs of War on Land,[7] prohibits employment of "arms, projectiles, or material of a nature to cause superfluous injury," while article 35, paragraph 2, of the 1977 Additional Protocol I[8] prohibits the employment of "weapons, projectiles and material and methods of warfare of a nature to cause superfluous injury or unnecessary suffering."

The test of unnecessary suffering must address two questions: first, whether land mines cause unnecessary suffering when used against combatants; second, whether certain use of land mines may cause unnecessary suffering for civilians not taking part in the hostilities.

In considering the first question, land mine use against combatants must be compared with injury to combatants by other weapons in use on the modern battlefield, such as small arms, artillery, armor, and aviation-delivered ordnance, as well as the customary practice of nations. The injury imposed on combatants by land mines, however severe, is no worse than that of other weapons in common use today; the law of war, in prohibiting unnecessary suffering, acknowledges that war entails necessary suffering. The customary practice of nations in this century clearly has been to employ land mines against combatants in armed conflict. In drafting and adopting the Landmines Protocol in the 1980 United Nations Conventional Weapons Convention, the nations of the world acknowledged the legality per se of land mines.

Addressing the second question reveals the present problem. Customary international law prohibits the use of any weapon against individual civilians not taking part in the hostilities or the civilian population. Paragraphs 1, 2, and 4 of article 51 of the 1977 Additional Protocol I state:

1) The civilian population and individual civilians shall enjoy general protection against dangers arising from military operations. . . .

2) The civilian population as such, as well as individual civilians, shall not be the object of attack. Acts or threats of violence the primary purpose of which is to spread terror among the civilian population are prohibited. . . .

4) Indiscriminate attacks are prohibited. Indiscriminate attacks are:
   (a) those which are not directed at a specific military objective;
   (b) those which employ a method or means of combat which cannot be directed at a military objective; or
   (c) those which employ a method or means of combat the effects of which cannot be limited. . . .

These prohibitions apply to any means or method of warfare. A review of the literature produced by Human Rights Watch reveals that the problem is not the indiscriminate use of all weapons of war, or necessarily one of land mine use in international armed conflicts, but primarily one of antipersonnel use against civilian populations in internal (or noninternational) armed conflicts by insurgent groups or developing nations with poor human rights records.[9] Human Rights Watch describes the problems in Angola, Cambodia, Iraq, Kurdistan, Mozambique, and northern Somalia as "perhaps the worst landmine disasters in the world, with the notable omission of Afghanistan," where the organization has yet to conduct a lengthy, on-the-ground investigation.[10]

Applicable Law of War

It is important to bear in mind that the law of war is negotiated, and nations become party to law of war treaties, on the assumption that there will be a good-faith effort toward compliance. That assumption must be balanced with the reality that there are some in the world who have no intention of respecting any law unless it is likely to operate to their advantage—which also is true with respect to domestic law. The effort internationally or domestically is to develop better law—and a mechanism for encouraging respect and enforcement when that fails.

With antipersonnel land mines, the problem is one of irresponsible use of an otherwise legitimate weapon, primarily (but not exclusively) in internal armed conflicts. The issues are the law of war's role in correcting the problem, and its potential shortcomings.

One part of the problem is a very distinctive split that exists within the law of war between the law applicable in an international armed conflict and that by which a nation is bound in a noninternational, or internal, armed conflict; the latter remains woefully undeveloped. As a result, a tragic irony exists, in that while it is illegal to employ land mines and other weapons of war against an enemy civilian population in an international armed conflict, the law of war appears not to prohibit their use against a nation's own civilian population, and appears to permit a government to leave land mines in place following an internal conflict, to kill or maim civilians in the peace that follows. The emphasis is on *appears*, as neither necessarily may be the case.

Internal conflicts are not new, and are very much a part of the wars of this century. Regrettably, some nations have placed the security of the regime in power on a higher level than the safety of the people, and most developing nations have been reluctant to apply the law of war to internal conflicts. In each of the four 1949 Geneva Conventions for the Protection of War Victims[11]—a total of 429 articles—only one article applies to internal conflicts.[12] A separate treaty[13] intended to expand and improve upon this single provision was negotiated during the 1974–1977 diplomatic conference that produced the 1977 Additional Protocol I. At the last moment in those negotiations, however, the developing nations "gutted" its provisions while raising the threshold for its applicability.[14]

A second part of the problem is that, historically, nations have assumed the responsibility for cleaning up the debris of war within their territory. The European nations did so (and continue to do so) following the world wars; the nations of North Africa did so (and continue to do so) following World War II; the Republic of Korea did so following the 1950–1953 conflict that ravaged its territory; Kuwait did so after the 1991 war to liberate it from Iraqi occupation; and at this moment, Germany is clearing the vast land mine field laid between east and west during the Cold War. Some nations, pursuant to the terms of conflict termination, have offered their assistance. For example, the United States cleared the naval mines from the harbors of North Vietnam in 1973; U.S. and British forces cleared naval and land mines from the Suez Canal area following the 1973 Arab-Israeli War; and U.S., British, and French forces cleared Libyan-laid naval mines from the Red Sea and Suez Canal in 1985.

As mentioned above, the law of war appears not to apply to the use of land mines against a nation's own civilian population, and appears to permit a government to leave land mines in place following a conflict. The prohibition on murder of civilians contained in article 3 common to the four 1949 Geneva Conventions may contradict this appearance, since illegal use of land mines or dereliction in their clearance could just as well be regarded as murder as placing a firearm to the head of a civilian and pulling the trigger. In correcting the land mine problem—and in considering amendments to current treaty law—it will be important to reexamine existing law perhaps a little more closely than might have been the case in the past.

Addressing the Land Mine Problem: The Conventional Weapons Convention

The land mine problem exists in part because land mines have been employed improperly by some nations, or opposing factions within nations, during internal conflicts, without subsequent cleanup. The various demining efforts under way by the United Nations, the United States, and others are intended to address this aspect of the issue.

Another part of the solution is applying the law of war to land mines. The law of war clearly applies to land mines, as it applies to any other weapon system; the issue is its specific application. Such application already exists.

In the course of the 1974–1977 diplomatic conference, several nations sought debate on particular weapons to include land mines. Because of the comprehensive and contentious agenda of that conference, issues relating to particular weapons were held in abeyance. The International Committee of the Red Cross (ICRC) hosted meetings of experts in 1974 and 1976, without reaching any specific conclusions regarding the improper use of land mines.[15] The fourth and final session of the diplomatic conference adopted Resolution 22, calling upon the UN General Assembly to convene a conference of government experts with a view to reaching:

agreements on prohibitions or restrictions on the use of specific conventional weapons including those which may be deemed to be excessively injurious or have indiscriminate effects, taking into account humanitarian and military considerations. . . .[16]

The UN responded affirmatively, holding preparatory meetings in Geneva in 1978 and 1979 before convening conference sessions in 1979 and 1980. Those sessions produced a treaty with a horribly long and inaccurately worded title[17] that, for brevity, is referred to as the Conventional Weapons Convention. The treaty consists of an umbrella portion and three protocols. Protocol I deals with weapons containing nondetectable fragments, a nonexistent weapon; Protocol II, with land mines and booby traps; and Protocol III, with incendiary weapons.[18]

In his contribution to this volume, Richard Falk criticizes the Landmines Protocol as inadequate. By today's standards, this may be correct because of its nonapplicability to internal armed conflicts and lessons learned since its promulgation. At the time of its negotiation, however, it was believed to meet contemporary needs. Neither the debates during conference sessions, the 1974 and 1976 ICRC-hosted sessions of government experts, nor the key literature of the time identified improper and indiscriminate use of land mines as a problem.[19] Resolution 22 of the 1974–1977 diplomatic conference noted "that there is a wide area of agreement with regard to landmines and booby-traps" because use until then generally had been responsible; the intent was to codify the existing law in international armed conflict. Although the effort to apply the Conventional Weapons Convention to internal conflicts was unsuccessful, a general view was that the same rules should be applicable in an internal conflict, as the codified rules not only were consistent with the customary practice of nations, but represented the most efficient use for land mines.[20]

PROVISIONS

The Landmines Protocol has been examined in detail elsewhere;[21] I will summarize its contents. After presenting scope and definition provisions, the Protocol repeats the prohibitions on attack of civilians and indiscriminate attacks contained in article 51 of the 1977 Additional Protocol I (quoted previously); follows the definition of proportionality contained in article 51, paragraph 5(b), and article 57, paragraph 2(a)(iii), of Additional Protocol I; and improves the definition of feasible precautions contained in article 52, paragraph 2, of Additional Protocol I.[22]

Article 4 restricts the use of land mines (other than remotely delivered mines, discussed in article 5) and booby traps, prohibiting their use in populated areas unless they are rigidly controlled by the party that laid them, or through measures (such as fencing or signs) to warn of their presence.

Article 5 establishes a precedent for the law of war, which is notorious for lagging far behind technology. "Remotely delivered" or "scatterable" land mines were an emerging technology in the 1970s, and were the subject of some concern in the course of the Conventional Weapons Convention debate because of a fear of their potential effect on civilian populations. The requirements for employment of remotely delivered land mines are the same as those for ordinary land mines, that is, subject to the customary international law prohibitions codified in article 3.

However, restrictions on use of remotely delivered mines differ from those of ordinary mines in that either the location of the former must be accurately recorded in accordance with article 7(1)(a), or they must contain a self-neutralizing device that will either destroy them or otherwise render them ineffective after a brief period of time.[23]

Article 6 restricts the types of booby traps that may be employed, and the circumstances in which legitimate booby traps may be employed. Article 7 addresses the recording and publication of the location of minefields, mines, and booby traps; article 8 provides protection for UN forces and missions against the effects of land mines and booby traps; article 9 sets forth in very limited terms procedures for international cooperation in the removal of minefields, mines, and booby traps upon cessation of active hostilities. A short technical annex provides guidelines for recording.

Article 6 of the umbrella portion of the Convention requires dissemination of the treaty and its protocols "in time of peace as in time of armed conflict" as widely as possible within each state party, and particularly within the military. The treaty contains no verification or compliance mechanism and, despite efforts by the United States, applies only to international armed conflicts.

The Convention has gained limited acceptance. As of mid-1994, it has 41 states parties—whereas the 1949 Geneva Conventions has 185 and the 1977 Additional Protocol I has 134.[24] In part, this is due to its lack of an active sponsor. The ICRC, as the de facto (and perhaps de jure) custodian of the 1949 Geneva Conventions and 1977 Additional Protocols, has campaigned aggressively for nations to ratify or accede to those treaties. By contrast, Conventional Weapons Convention's custodian, the United Nations, has undertaken no activity other than an annual nonbinding General Assembly resolution encouraging all nations to consider becoming a party; nor has any other agency taken any action on behalf of the Convention.

STEPS TOWARD REVIEW

And so, to the present, and reports regarding the use—and abuse—of antipersonnel land mines. On the basis of these disclosures, in December 1993 France exercised its right as a party to the Conventional Weapons Convention to call for a review conference, which any state party may do ten years after the Convention's entry into force.[25] The General Assembly followed with a resolution supporting France,[26] which was supported by a letter to the secretary-general from thirty states parties to the Convention.[27] The secretary-general, acting in his capacity as depositary for the Convention, established a group of experts, appointed by the states parties to the convention, with a view to facilitating preparations for the first review conference.[28] Governmental experts designated by states not yet a party to the Convention (such as the United States) and representatives of the ICRC may participate as observers.

The primary purpose for the review conference is to prepare concrete proposals for amendments to the Landmines Protocol for the purpose of

- strengthening restrictions on the use of antipersonnel land mines, particularly those without neutralizing or self-destruction mechanisms;
- considering the establishment of a verification system for the provisions of the Landmines Protocol; and
- studying opportunities for broadening the scope of this Protocol to cover armed conflicts that are not of an international character.

Preceding the UN experts' meetings, the ICRC hosted two meetings of experts to assist in defining the problem and considering possible solutions. The first, held in April 1993, was intended to provide as accurate a picture as possible of the actual use of antipersonnel land mines and the consequences thereof; to analyze the mechanisms and methods that exist to limit this use or alleviate the suffering of victims, as well as to identify the lacunae in such methods; to decide on the best remedial action; and to establish a strategy on how to coordinate the actions of different bodies involved in such action.[29]

The second meeting evolved from a recommendation made at the first meeting to seek the advice of military experts with regard to the military utility of antipersonnel land mines. This meeting was attended by invited military experts representing developed nations, developing nations, and former insurgent organizations, and by representatives of nonmilitary organizations with an interest in the issue.[30] The meeting's purpose was to set forth the military utility of land mines, identify alternatives to land mines and their effect, and consider possible control measures for antipersonnel land mines. It was intended to serve not as an argument for land mines, but a summary of information. Statements contained in the ICRC report were intended to be not an endorsement by the ICRC or nations or groups represented of ways in which antipersonnel land mines are used, but a recitation of facts. This is particularly true with regard to land mine use in an insurgent environment.

This meeting of experts reached five conclusions of note. First, antipersonnel land mines can play an indispensable part on the conventional battlefield. Second, the primary problem with antipersonel land mine use is their irresponsible, indiscriminate, and illegal use in internal armed conflicts. The ICRC report recognized a

> need to distinguish between conventional warfare, which is generally carried out in international armed conflicts where classical contemporary military doctrine prevails and where trained as well as disciplined soldiers are engaged, and that of civil war and counterinsurgency operations, where these conditions are not met.[31]

Third, when properly employed, antipersonnel land mines pose no greater risk to innocent civilians than other weapon systems in use on the modern battlefield. Fourth, present-day technology can contribute much to reducing the risk to innocent civilians. In direct response to the question of what would happen if land mines were banned, the conferees assembled a matrix that reveals that there is no complete substitute for land mines, and that alternatives would increase costs in manpower, ordnance, and equipment, in all likelihood raising the risk to civilian populations and friendly forces. Finally, a total ban on land mines would not be possible, as land mines are the weapon system most prone to field expedient alternatives—as U.S. forces learned in the Vietnam War.[32]

THE REVIEW CONFERENCE

From all the available data, and all the preparatory meetings, several issues emerge for the review conference to address.

Technology

Technologically, land mines have advanced as much as, if not more than, almost any other weapon system over the past twenty years. Land mines that are programmed to self-destruct or, failing that, have a "fallback" self-neutralizing capability already exist. It is foreseeable that land mines may be developed that can be predeployed (where necessary), but that can be "switched" on or off when required. Other devices may be possible that will make mines "intelligent" enough to discriminate the difference between, for example, a tank and other vehicles.

This technology would go a very long way to alleviate the primary mine-related problem of our day: mines that, once laid, remain until cleared or, worse, are tripped by a civilian years after the conflict has passed.

Should we prohibit all antipersonnel land mines that either are not detonated or controlled on command, or lack a self-destruction and self-neutralizing capability?

In limited cases, the latter may not be necessary and may add an unjustified expense. For example, the U.S. M-18 Claymore mine, a variation of which is made by several nations, is hand-emplaced above ground by individual soldiers for perimeter defense. It is command- or tripwire-detonated in proximity to military positions. When a unit moves its position, the device is made safe and taken with the unit. A self-destruct feature is not necessary for such a mine.

Certainly it would seem that we should be at the point that we can require that all other antipersonnel land mines (scatterable and nonscatterable) contain both a self-destruction and a self-neutralizing device. The issue is one of cost, in two ways. If it is technologically feasible to retrofit existing antipersonnel land mines with these devices, can advanced nations afford to do so? If it is not technologically feasible to convert existing antipersonnel land mines, how much would it cost to replace existing stocks? In an era of declining defense budgets, these are important questions.

Poorer nations view the question differently. As they see it, why should they buy (for example) self-neutralizing, self-destructing antipersonnel land mines for $30 or more apiece, when they can buy mines without those devices that will serve their purposes, but cost as little as fifty cents each?

A partial answer is that after the conflict, the high-technology land mine will have cleared itself, while the low-technology, inexpensive land mine will cost between $300 and $1,000 to clear—making the former the better buy in the long run.

At least one nation has discovered this "hidden" cost. Argentina, the United Kingdom, and the Falklands Islands government have reached agreement for Argentina to pay for a third party to clear some 30 thousand land mines (many Italian-made, remotely delivered mines lacking self-neutralization devices) laid by Argentina's forces in the 1982 Falklands/Malvinas War.[33]

But representatives of poorer nations have pointed out that this factor is irrelevant in their planning, as they assume they will be able to get the UN to clear their mines.[34] Hence any requirement to remove outmoded technology from the battlefield will encounter resistance from nations dependent upon low-technology mines and from manufacturers or holders of large stocks of older antipersonnel land mines.

The effort should be made, however, and can be made in two ways. First, at the time the Landmines Protocol was negotiated, producers and users were unsure which technology was better—that which "neutralizes" a land mine, or that which causes it to self-destruct. Experience has suggested that a self-destruct technology, with a simple passive self-inerting neutralization system as backup, is preferable. The trend definitely leans toward this philosophy, and article 5, paragraph 1(b), of the Landmines Protocol should be amended to reflect this trend.[35]

The second improvement includes two options. The simplest would be to amend article 5, paragraph 1, of the Landmines Protocol to eliminate subparagraph (a), which permits use of remotely delivered land mines if "their location can be recorded in accordance with article 7(1)(a)"—that is, recorded as a preplanned minefield on a map. This would permit only scatterable land mines equipped with a self-neutralizing device.

Another option would be to require that all antipersonnel land mines other than those that are command-detonated and under the direct control of the unit that laid them contain a self-destruct or self-neutralizing device.

Ancillary to this is the issue of failure rates of munitions. Generally, failure-to-detonate rates are 5 percent or lower. Requiring all antipersonnel land mines to contain a self-destruction device with self-neutralization backup lowers the failure rate. Modern electronic fuzing should make possible failure rates between one in 1,000 and one in 1 million. Should a percentage rate be incorporated into the Landmines Protocol as a criterion for a lawful land mine?

The recording provisions contained in article 7 are far too general, are related to outmoded methods, and do not take advantage (particularly with respect to remotely delivered land mines) of inexpensive, current technology such as the global positioning system.[36] Article 7 should continue the precedent of the Landmines Protocol by promulgating standards that exploit contemporary technology.

Opposition to these proposals is clear, and the reasons are obvious. Why should, for example, a manufacturer nation make a relatively expensive high-technology land mine when it still has inexpensive low-technology mines that sell? Why should, for example, a nation make antipersonnel land mines with self-destruction devices when its scatterable land mines lacking such devices sell? In this respect, we must observe the nature, and rules, of these negotiations: any change of the present Landmines Protocol will require approval by consensus. It is unlikely that holders of large land mine stocks will agree to changes that are not in their respective economic interests.

Demining

In postwar demining, detection of land mines is important. Land mines have gone through several phases, moving from metallic containers to synthetic or other nonmetallic (such as wood or concrete) cases. This was done in part to resist detection, though newer mines utilize plastic as much for its light weight and weather resistance as for its nondetectability. As scatterable antipersonnel land mines land on the surface, the issue of nondetectability is more important then it may appear, since mines fall into or become overgrown by vegetation, or become covered by drifting sand. To facilitate mine clearance, a requirement that each mine contain a minimum amount of metal would seem appropriate, if not essential. The issue, again, is economic rather than military.

Applicability to Internal Conflicts

Perhaps the most essential but by far the most difficult objective is to incorporate into Protocol II language that would make the Protocol applicable to internal conflicts. Efforts to this end, supported by the United States, were unsuccessful in the 1978–1980 negotiations. The states parties to the Conventional Weapons Convention include few developing nations. Participants in the review conference will be nations that are members of the United Nations and, again, voting will be by consensus.

Other Initiatives

Enforcement of the law of war is difficult, but not impossible. One easily can get trapped in a catch-22 argument: Why should we add punitive provisions to the Conventional Weapons Convention when no one is prosecuted for violations unless there is a total victory? The response is that a lack of punitive provisions makes prosecution more difficult if the opportunity presents itself. The Convention would be well served by addition of punitive provisions similar to those contained in the Grave Breach articles in the 1949 Geneva Conventions and the 1977 Additional Protocol I.[37]

Other enforcement alternatives should be considered. A premise added by the United States that goes a long way in establishing culpability is that the nation laying land mines is responsible for them, unless military exigencies (such as loss of territory in which mines are laid due to enemy action) prohibit exercise of that responsibility. Equally important, some sort of verification mechanism, such as the fact-finding commission established in article 90 of the 1977 Additional Protocol I, is essential. Collaterally, the land mine area is dynamic. The Conventional Weapons Convention may be a basis for establishing a commission that would meet periodically—perhaps every five years—to review the land mines environment and changes in technology, to recommend to states parties revisions in the Convention or other mechanisms.

Promoting Adherence

In conclusion, a word of caution is needed. Much can be done to make the Landmines Protocol better, but one involved in Geneva negotiations frequently hears the admonishment to exercise care not to allow the best to become the enemy of the good. A "perfect" land mines protocol will be of little value if few nations become a party, and fewer still actually implement it.

Thus arises the point of negotiation follow-up. A number of treaties are negotiated each year in New York, Geneva, and elsewhere. A state may become a party, sometimes because it believes in what has been negotiated, sometimes because doing so "looks good." Or it may participate in the negotiations but not become a party.

Too often, whether one becomes a party or does not, nothing else happens.

If there is a shortcoming in the field of international humanitarian law, it is in this follow-up, that is, promotion of adherence.[38] Article 6 of the 1980 Conventional Weapons Convention contains a requirement similar to that of other law of war treaties, obligating states parties to implement and disseminate the Convention. Without some program of incentive or enforcement, and perhaps assistance, however, this requirement is significant in its nonobservation.

By way of example, at the start of the 1990 Desert Shield operations, U.S. authorities had to inform the senior leadership of another state member of the coalition that it was a party to the 1949 Geneva Conventions. To their credit, those leaders sought U.S. advice on implementation of their responsibilities and followed those Conventions to the letter in their subsequent operations.

Much is spent on negotiation—the cost of running the experts' meetings in preparation for the Conventional Weapons Convention review conference could approach $1 million, with the U.S. portion coming to one-quarter of the total—yet nothing is spent on encouraging nations to become a party to international humanitarian law treaties and to respect them. This is a major failing in this field. As indicated earlier, the informed warrior sees the value of the law of war, and recognizes that its humanitarian values are entirely consistent with the efficient use of military force.

An international dissemination program will not prevent all violations; the bloodshed in Rwanda in 1994, for example, is a brutal reminder of man's potential inhumanity to man. We cannot stop all violations of the law of war, but a program to implement existing treaties and to ensure their respect would be of value. The ICRC has done much toward this end, but it cannot do it alone. The U.S. military implemented a major law of war program following (and as a lesson of) the Vietnam War.[39] In recent years, it has developed an "export version" of its law of war program that has provided law of war and human rights training to the military in several emerging democracies.[40]

In short, much more can be done to ensure responsible use of antipersonnel land mines and all other weaponry of war. But a fundamental change needs to occur in the way in which we do business. The Conventional Weapons Convention provides a mechanism to accomplish this change.

4

The U.S. Approach Toward Land Mines: A Realistic Policy for an Evolving Problem

THOMAS E. MCNAMARA

Over the past decade, the nature of the land mine problem has changed dramatically. Many belligerents, especially in civil conflicts in the 1980s, began using land mines indiscriminately as offensive weapons. They also began deploying high-technology, long-lived mines in vast numbers, using new scattering techniques. The total number of deployed land mines jumped from many thousands to the tens of millions. In short, the objective characteristics of the land mine problem changed in fundamental ways.

As the nature of the land mine problem has evolved, so have U.S. efforts to understand and address it. The development of U.S. initiatives is best understood in the context of a learning process. The United States was among the first to assume a leadership role in focusing attention on the problem and in allocating resources to address it. In the 1992 Defense Authorization Act, Congress asked the president to produce a report on international mine-clearing efforts in situations involving repatriation and resettlement of refugees and displaced persons. This task, delegated to the secretary of state, resulted in the report *Hidden Killers*,[1] the very first country-by-country, global survey of the land mine problem. *Hidden Killers* succeeded in helping to raise awareness of the problem in the U.S. government, in other governments around the world, and among many nongovernmental organizations, providing the baseline data that all could rely on and refer to.

It bears stating, however, that awareness and understanding of the problem have been very uneven around the world. Indeed, initial U.S. efforts to sensitize others to the growing land mine problem evoked little attention. As recently as 1993, most of the world did not take this problem seriously. Fortunately, that is changing, but the point is that just as the U.S. approach to the land mine problem is evolving, so is that of the rest of the world.

One event in particular highlights the evolving nature of international attitudes about land mines. In the summer of 1993, when the United States introduced a United Nations resolution calling on all countries to adopt export moratoriums similar to its own, the initiative won scant acceptance. Over time, however, there was an amazing turnaround. By December 16, 1993, the resolution had attracted sixty-six cosponsors and was adopted unanimously by the General Assembly. In fact, even more countries were lined up to be added as cosponsors when the list was closed so that a final vote could be taken. This dramatic turnaround is an indication of what leadership and education can do. The Clinton administration's initiatives and persistence have placed this problem high on the international agenda.

Comprehensive Strategy

Two fundamental realities of the land mine problem are particularly striking. The first is the immediacy of the problem. Land mines claim at least 150 casualties each week. Tens of millions of already emplaced antipersonnel land mines daily threaten civilian populations, virtually all in developing countries. In addition to the tragic human costs, uncleared land mines hinder refugee repatriation, impede economic development, and threaten political stability. These costs represent significant impediments to American foreign policy objectives in many regions of the world.

The second fundamental reality is the complexity of the problem. Given this complexity, no single approach will solve it in its entirety. A number of policy proposals impute a level of simplicity to the problem that is wholly unfounded. Proposals of an immediate ban on all land mines, for instance, fail to recognize the legitimate military utility that land mines can have when confined to the battlefield. In addition, irrespective of the intrinsic merits, it simply will not be possible to negotiate an effective total ban soon enough to have an impact on the problem of land mines.

Although the Clinton administration does not presume to have the complete answer, it is committed to seeking and implementing solutions that make an impact on all aspects of this crisis now. To this end, it has developed a comprehensive, four-track strategy to address short-, medium-, and long-term aspects of the problem.

DEMINING

U.S. demining efforts address the problem of mines that are already emplaced and threaten innocent civilians now. The United States is participating in ongoing demining assistance programs in Cambodia, Afghanistan, Nicaragua, and Mozambique. It is also working to support demining in Eritrea, Ethiopia, Honduras, and Costa Rica. Significant problems exist in Angola, Somalia, Rwanda, and Liberia, as well, but ongoing unrest in those countries has so far prevented the implementation of U.S. assistance programs. By the end of 1994, the United States expects to have conducted assessments in at least six other countries where land mines constitute a serious problem. These countries, combined, account for the great majority of the estimated land mine proliferation that has created this crisis. U.S. demining efforts are attempting to deal with the most serious cases.

American demining programs educate local populations about how best to cope with land mines until they can be permanently removed. They also help train personnel in effective, safe demining techniques. Such "train the trainer" programs have proved most effective because they enable land mine–plagued countries to address the problem themselves. Given current technologies, this is the most cost-effective way to approach the situation and the only way, in these countries, to bring to bear the numbers of deminers that are needed.

While this is a start, it clearly is not enough. With current technology and resources, it will take many decades to clean up already deployed mines. That is why the Departments of State and Defense have a research and development plan to develop new technologies in mine detection and clearance. Existing technologies that may be adapted to demining seem to offer the best options, if they can be successfully applied to solve many of the unique, complex difficulties that demining presents.

EXPORT MORATORIUMS

The United States has called on all countries that produce or export land mines to adopt moratoriums on mine transfers. In December 1993, the UN General Assembly unanimously adopted the U.S.-proposed resolution calling for moratoriums on exports of land mines that pose a grave risk to civilians. The United States is now working to persuade key countries to follow up their support for the UN resolution with concrete action. Already, a dozen other countries have declared moratoriums of their own, and several others have reported that they have controls in place that are tantamount to moratoriums. While several more are likely to declare moratoriums, the numbers are not good enough. The administration is continuing to press for others to respond.

INTERNATIONAL CONTROLS

A series of unilateral export moratoriums is a useful measure. It is, however, only temporary, and may best serve as a bridge to the third track of U.S. strategy: the establishment of a more permanent international control mechanism. The ease and extremely low cost of laying mines, coupled with the difficulty and enormous cost of detecting and removing them, dictate that strengthened preventive measures be a high priority. Hence, the administration is engaged in a fast-track policy review to develop a proposal for a multilateral antipersonnel land mine control regime. This systematic look at a broad range of options is guided by several basic principles.

First, the crux of the problem is civil unrest and warfare in the Third World. Land mines have become the weapon of choice in many developing countries where in the course of civil strife they are often purposely employed against civilians.

Second, achieving a regime that will actually save lives and limbs in the near term requires balancing a number of factors. The administration assuredly does not want to leave behind hazards that pose a continuing threat to civilians once hostilities have ended. At the same time, it would make no sense to pursue a solution to the land mine problem that increases the risk to American uniformed men and women, who rely on land mines for protection and for the achievement of national security objectives in various hostile situations, such as along the Demilitarized Zone between North and South Korea.

Third, some features of a desirable regime may not be negotiable. Since most of the problem stems from irresponsible use by those who have no regard for the safety of noncombatants, Washington does not want to give countries whose behavior it wishes to constrain an excuse to stay outside the regime. The administration also wants to avoid a negotiating process that takes years to produce results. The longer it takes to reach an agreement that can make a difference, the more additional mines will be laid, and the more innocent civilians will suffer.

U.S. proposals must be guided by feasibility and practicality. This is a classic case where the best may be the enemy of the good. The United States should not expect to establish a regime at the outset that will not need improvement or refinement over time. What is of utmost importance now is to get a good regime up and running. The U.S. experience with the Missile Technology Control Regime (MTCR)[2] is instructive in this regard. The controls in place today are much more stringent than when the MTCR was established. Although it is not yet clear what a land mine regime should cover, initial analysis suggests that some form of export control—perhaps patterned after the MTCR—holds considerable promise.

Besides strong support for the current export moratorium, the administration is working to fashion a more permanent arms control regime. Such a regime could restrict the export, production, and possession of antipersonnel land mines. In the opinion of the administration, measures to deny mines to irresponsible actors, to enhance transparency of stockpiles, and to encourage production of self-deactivating mines are the most immediately useful in ridding the world of this menace.

The administration is dedicated to building the international consensus necessary to bring about an international control regime in the shortest possible time, and is laying the groundwork in discussions with key countries.

STRENGTHENING EXISTING LAW

Finally, the United States is seeking to strengthen the 1980 Conventional Weapons Convention, in particular the Landmines Protocol. The president has recently transmitted the Convention to the Senate for advice and consent to ratification. This will help the United States to take the lead in pressing for substantial improvements to the Protocol, such as making it applicable to internal conflicts, requiring all mines to have a substantial metallic content, and requiring certain mines to be self-deactivating. (Further details of U.S. goals in this regard are presented throughout this volume.)

Conclusion

An effective policy to address the land mine problem must be sober-minded and comprehensive, including both corrective and preventive elements. It must also include a time horizon that begins immediately and extends through the far term. Although the present U.S. approach does this, it does not represent the ultimate solution. Just as the U.S. approach has evolved with a growing understanding of the nature of the land mine problem, it must continue to evolve as more is learned. That is the only way to assure that U.S. policies are tailored to address practical, real-world circumstances. The United States must avoid the temptation to opt for strategies that work only in an idealized situation. Only then will it be possible to address this problem in a time frame that is relevant to the millions who live and die with it every day.

II

SEEKING
SOLUTIONS

5

Walking the Tightrope of International Humanitarian Law: Meeting the Challenge of Land Mines

RICHARD FALK

The subject of land mines has risen to prominence in recent years among those concerned with the horrors of warfare. The evidence of mutilating injury, the persistence of lethal hazard long after the combat phase of war ends, and the sheer magnitude of the problem help to explain this crescendo of concern. The cheapness of land mines, their ease of acquisition, and the expense, danger, and difficulty associated with their removal complicate the task of legal regulation, the objective of which is to safeguard the civilian population.

Against this background, momentum in support of a campaign to ban the use of land mines unconditionally is growing. Sen. Patrick Leahy has spearheaded an effort to impose a legislative moratorium on the U.S. export of land mines, with the avowed goal of eliminating land mines from the battlefield. In this volume, notable calls for a ban come from Cyrus Vance and Herbert S. Okun, and from the secretary-general of the United Nations, Boutros Boutros-Ghali, individuals of exceptional stature who rarely raise their voice in relation to unresolved controversy. Recently, also, a series of nongovernmental organizations (NGOs) have lent support to the campaign for banishment, most significantly, Human Rights Watch, especially by way of its published study *Landmines: A Deadly*

Legacy, and, more cautiously, the International Committee of the Red Cross (ICRC), through a series of meetings on whether such a ban would be acceptable to governments.

The media, too, have joined in to make a larger segment of the public aware. *Time* had a cover story, and numerous features have appeared in print and visual form, detailing the horrors of land mine use and endorsing the call for a ban.

And yet, for such a campaign to succeed, two major obstacles must be overcome: the resistance to a ban by the professional military must be softened, if not eliminated; and the extent of the ban must reach all political actors, including revolutionary movements and governments that lack the resources to rely upon more sophisticated and expensive combat alternatives to land mines.

The Role of International Law: An Overview

International law has long been dogged by allegations of ineffectiveness, especially in relation to war. It is not enough to favor a ban on land mines if the behavior of belligerents is unlikely to be altered. In this chapter, the issue posed is whether the main regulatory effort should be made on behalf of an unconditional ban or should focus more modestly on strengthening existing legal constraints on land mine use.

With notable exceptions, international humanitarian law has not been successful in sparing the civilian population from the torments of war, especially to the degree that modern military strategy has been extended to treat the civilian infrastructure of "the enemy" as an integral part of an overall war effort. In this regard, the logic of military necessity has prevailed, and continues to prevail, over deference to civilian innocence, and cannot in most instances be effectively challenged directly through law. International humanitarian law can generally contribute positively only if the political preconditions for regulation have been met, which at present is not yet sufficiently the case with respect to land mines, despite some encouraging developments along these lines. The emergence of a worldwide civil campaign during the last several years with a strong abolitionist flavor does satisfy an important political precondition—namely, repudiation by moral authority figures and a significant segment of the public—but this pressure has not made sufficient inroads on the professional military ethos to create the basis for effective law.[1]

International humanitarian law has always been subject to two types of failure that seem opposed, but actually feed off one another. The first type of failure arises when moral concern about tactics and weaponry relied upon in warfare generates strong societal pressures that exceed the operational imperatives of military necessity as battlefield commanders and strategists understand them. Any effort to regulate behavior in these circumstances is likely to be disregarded in practice as "legalism," and result in creating a permanent gap between the claims of law and patterns of state practice.[2] Acquiescence in the existence of such a gap can be more damaging to the credibility of law than is the gap itself.[3] Law in many circumstances, including in otherwise well-governed societies, fails to deter or punish violative behavior, but those in positions of authority make good-faith efforts at enforcement. This kind of gap between legal standards and social behavior now describes several areas of criminal law, such as drug enforcement and various types of white-collar crime. To the extent that the gap is believed to result in large part from police corruption, it tends to discredit government, but not the law itself. In the setting of war, the gap is understood differently, as evidence of the futility, even the frivolousness, of supposing that legal standards could challenge the pursuit of military victory by whatever means belligerents deem effective.

When the gap between law and practice persists without even ruffling the feathers of those in authority, it is extremely discrediting to the legal enterprise, and gives rise to the other common error, which is equally serious, that of dismissing international humanitarian law altogether as a hopeless and naive endeavor. This dismissal seems the opposite of legalism, but should be regarded as its twin. Along this line, cynics contend that the potency of the Clausewitzian logic of absolute war undermines every legal and moral attempt to constrain the pursuit of victory on the battlefield. Such a scornful rejection of primal humanitarian impulses confirms cynicism of an extreme sort, implying that the very notion of international humanitarian law is tantamount to a jurisprudential oxymoron. Such cynicism is as unwarranted by experience as is legalism.

To a serious extent, the discussion of the contemporary land mines challenge has tended to ignore these twinned dangers of legalism and cynicism, and their implications for identifying the most constructive policy initiatives that might be used to reshape battlefield behavior in beneficial directions. My attempt here is to walk a tightrope, acknowledging the dominance of militarist perspectives in wartime, yet claiming practical relevance for the principal goals of international humanitarian law, namely, the achievement of the maximum possible protection of the civilian population consistent with the pursuit of war aims.

To take account of the limited possibilities of international humanitarian law in relation to land mines requires that we understand when and why legal restraints in war have been respected, and when and why they have failed. International humanitarian law tends to be effective only when two sets of conditions are present.

First, there must exist some degree of perceived mutual interest that supports moves to limit or eliminate reliance on particular tactics or on a given type of weaponry; in effect, the legal claims need the support of a structure of reciprocity of the sort that has induced antagonistic combatants, in most circumstances, to respect legal standards governing the protection of prisoners of war and the sanctity of hospitals and medical facilities.[4] There is implicitly here an acknowledgment that, at least in some respects, terrorizing the other side is not legitimate or effective in war and should be eliminated by agreement, and that violations should be punished severely.

Second, there exists a widely shared view that certain tactics and weapons are at odds with the basic dignity and self-esteem of the military profession, and should be shunned. Arguably, reliance on biological and chemical weaponry, and on torture, engage these professional taboos, which are themselves to some degree descendants of premodern ideas of chivalry in war that influenced military behavior in medieval Europe and underlie the more secular drive of modern times to develop legal restrictions on military behavior. The influence of this professional ethos is more likely to inhibit behavior if there is no extensive record of military use and the weaponry or tactic is not regarded as useful or necessary in battlefield situations.[5]

These general observations apply with anguishing relevance to contemporary efforts to control land mine use, particularly as it occurs in internal wars. During internal wars, military operations do not generally take the form of large-scale battlefield encounters. Often, virtually the entire country is treated as a combat zone, and the outcome of the war can turn on the relative ability of the government or the insurgent side to win over the hearts and minds of the people, and satisfy their basic needs for protection, food, shelter, and health care.

This chapter seeks to show why prospects for imposing humanitarian controls *directly* on the use of land mines either by improving the application of existing legal standards or through agreement on a total ban remain difficult, despite the public campaign. Further efforts to impose more effective constraints on use may yield some limited positive results, and for this reason the effort is probably justified, although risky, because of the disillusionment likely to follow upon further failures to make serious inroads on battlefield behavior. Mainly for these reasons, it seems reasonable to give greater weight to an *indirect* approach, that is, trying to influence the availability and design of land mines and their postcombat clearance, rather than focus exclusively on what combatants do by way of deployment and use.

The discussion also specifies steps before and after land mine use that might reduce the quantity and character of suffering, and the role that international humanitarian law could play in this process. The pedagogy of war itself receives particular attention. Such an emphasis may seem inappropriate, but it is a response to the recognition of the professional military ethos as posing the most formidable obstacle in the context of any proposed moves to cut down on the use of land mines or to establish a regime of partial or total prohibition. As such, this pedagogic effort seeks to challenge dominant, yet far from unanimous, views of military utility and combat tactics, and engage the military professional in moral, political, and legal dialogue. The conviction underlying this line of argument is that prevailing views of military necessity in various combat settings fail to take into sufficient account the adverse consequences for a war effort if the population affected by the war is being alienated by the inhumane way in which the war is being waged.[6] It is precisely because the security of civilian society is often what such wars are ultimately about that disregard of the well-being of the citizenry can be a fatal "military" error. Such disregard is manifest in many patterns of land mine development, production, sales, deployment, and tactical use.

Military specialists often stress that recent patterns of irresponsible deployment of land mines can be attributed mainly to insurgent forces operating in Third World settings. A further contention is that governmental use of land mines tends to be overwhelmingly, and increasingly, "responsible," that is, relying on maps, employing self-neutralizing devices, and being confined to genuine battlefield roles associated with legitimate military targets. Such self-serving claims, while having some merit, are also misleading. Leading states often are the suppliers and allies of insurgent forces that are guilty of irresponsible behavior, as was the case extensively in Afghanistan, Central America, and southern Africa. Also, it is the high-technology societies that have introduced plastic mines, explosives with low metallic content, which cause inoperable injury.

More substantively, the governmental side in these internal wars often controls the air and enjoys overwhelming firepower advantages that are used in indiscriminate applications. If the insurgent is to be induced to forgo its most accessible weaponry, land mines, then the governmental side will likely have to reciprocate in some equivalent manner that extends beyond land mines to cover other dimensions of battlefield behavior.

.

Constraining the Use of Land Mines: The Direct Approach

There are two complementary efforts involved in the direct approach. There is, as discussed below, reliance on the general frameworks of the law of war that appears to set humanitarian limits on weaponry and tactics of a sort applicable to the design and deployment of land mines. A second effort entails the more focused type of direct approach in which legal treaty norms are negotiated to apply explicitly to land mines.

GENERAL FRAMEWORK

The contemporary law of war takes the form of multilateral treaties that have been negotiated among leading states, but it rests upon, and explicitly incorporates, the very general principles of legal constraint embodied in what is known as customary international law. This unwritten law continues to provide the normative structure that is specified in greater substantive detail in the two overarching law-making ventures, the 1899 and 1907 Hague Conventions, focusing on the modalities of combat, and the 1949 Geneva Convention, along with the 1977 additional Protocols, addressing the protection of individuals (whether soldiers or civilians) caught up in war.

At this level of the law of war, as set forth in general provisions, tactics and weaponry are forbidden unless they satisfy the following principles:

• principle of discrimination: the tactic or weapon must discriminate between civilian and military targets in concept, but especially in application;
• principle of proportionality: the tactic or weapon must not inflict harm that is disproportionate to the military utility being achieved;
• principle of necessity: the tactic or weapon must not inflict harm unless necessary for the achievement of military objectives; and

• principle of humanity: the tactic or weapon must not cause injury or death in forms that are cruel or cause gratuitous suffering, especially with respect to noncombatants (civilians).

Specialists may dispute the precise wording given to these general principles, or prefer to rely on the formulations of these norms that have been reproduced in the form of treaty provisions. Article 1(2) of Protocol I to the 1949 Geneva Conventions contains language that incorporates the famous de Martens[7] clause:

> In cases not covered by this Protocol or by other international agreements, civilians and combatants remain under the protection and authority of the principles of international law derived from established custom, from the principles of humanity and from dictates of public conscience.

It would seem that such a grounding for international humanitarian law would make it applicable to all forms of "armed conflict," at least in its most abstract expression as a series of principles designed to limit belligerent discretion.

Protocol I additional to the 1949 Geneva Protocol Relating to the Protection of Victims of International Armed Conflicts, signed in 1977, contains provisions that borrow from the earlier formulations of the Hague Conventions to carry forward the generalized legal commitments to impose humanitarian limits on the conduct of war. For instance, article 35(1) sets forth the central earlier restrictive idea: "In any armed conflict, the right of the Parties to the conflict to choose methods or means of warfare is not unlimited." Of course, without operational content, such a legal guideline is no more than a reminder to leaders to acknowledge limits on their capacity to inflict destructive harm. Article 35(2) says: "It is prohibited to employ weapons, projectiles and material and methods of warfare of a nature to cause superfluous injury or unnecessary suffering." And article 35(3) declares: "It is prohibited to employ methods or means of warfare which are intended, or may be expected, to cause widespread, long-term and severe damage to the natural environment."

Other provisions of a kindred character can be found. It can also be persuasively argued that such generalized legal directives apply to all forms of belligerency, at least where the parties to the conflict are states. Protocol II additional to the 1949 Geneva Conventions, also adopted in 1977, is concerned about protecting victims in "non-international armed conflicts," that is, those between the armed forces of a state that is a party to the treaty and "dissident" or "organized" armed groups "which, under responsible command, exercise such control over a part of the territory as to enable them to carry out sustained and concerted military operations and to implement this Protocol."[8]

Part IV of each protocol contains provisions for the protection of the civilian population, with those in Protocol I being far more detailed and specific. Article 51 of Protocol I is especially relevant, as it imposes a series of duties designed to protect civilians against indiscriminate methods of warfare. Article 51(4) explicitly prohibits "indiscriminate attacks," defining these as "(a) those which are not directed at a specific military objective" and "(b) those which employ a method or means of combat which cannot be directed at a specific military objective."[9] Even Protocol II declares, in article 13(1), that "the civilian population and individual civilians shall enjoy general protection against the dangers arising from military operations" and, in article 13(2), that "acts or threats of violence the primary purpose of which is to spread terror among the civilian population are prohibited."[10]

Ah, the charm of words! And the enticement of the legal craft! Any normal reader would suppose that these general directives would clearly challenge even the most hard-nosed militarist, given the overwhelming evidence of disproportionate damage that land mines are causing to civilians as a result of all recent patterns of use, as well as the degree to which their deployment interferes (in many cases, deliberately so) with the survival needs of society (especially in poor agricultural countries, where most of the people live in the countryside). In addition, the generalized condemnations of land mine use coming over the last decade or so from the media, and the public more generally, and given expression by world leaders with especial moral authority seem to build a strong case against legality of *any* use. But legal language of this sort, at least in the context of war, particularly warfare carried on in a Third World country, is mainly a kind of moralistic charade that pretends to pay heed to humanitarian concerns. It is not taken seriously in the context of weapons design, military planning, or belligerent practice. The patterns of disregard are so pronounced and widespread as to invite the most cynical view of the role played by international humanitarian law.

The overwhelming evidence suggests that virtually all political and military leaders, however situated, rely on whatever methods and weaponry appear useful to achieve military advantage, and that where the nature of the war encompasses the allegiance and morale of the civilian population, inflicting suffering and trauma on civilians is treated not as "incidental," but as a central objective. In this regard, land mines widely dispersed in the countryside are especially valued precisely because they terrorize civilian society both by their presence and by the mutilating forms of harm they cause. It is not only land mines, but bombing and artillery attacks, free-fire zones, plant-killing chemicals, and the plowing of forests (causing flooding of agricultural areas) that manifest recourse to indiscriminate warfare. The entire course of warfare in this century has embraced indiscriminate tactics, as well as implicitly accepted that the civilian population is a legitimate object of attack to the extent that destroying its morale contributes to victory, and represents a way, often the prime way, to inflict damage on "the enemy." In this regard, characteristic types of modern warfare have become inherently terroristic.[11]

Where does this line of analysis lead? It puts in context the inability of the generalized norms of international humanitarian law to inhibit reliance on land mines despite their apparent incompatibility with widely endorsed legal standards. Such standards have not even inhibited the design of land mines to any appreciable degree, given the availability for use and export of mines with plastic explosives and the failure as a matter of course to include self-neutralizing mechanisms. Not only is a military logic at work that appears to regard the terroristic dimensions of certain weapons as useful, but a fiscal discipline seems to influence production and development priorities by reference to both market considerations and matters of cost-effectiveness. Cheap, sinister mines remain premium weapons, despite their demonstrated impacts on civilians, for military establishments throughout the world.

This failure of the generalized framework of international humanitarian law has led, in the instance of land mines, toward a more focused substantive approach. When international humanitarian law attempts to get more specific, negotiation is taken more seriously, and the emergent agreement may be expected, under certain conditions, to involve the acceptance of a contractual relationship to the agreed-upon legal standards. The hope is that such specificity will ensure a significant behavioral impact or, by the loopholes embedded in the treaty, give clearer hints that no serious regulatory goals are being pursued. As mentioned earlier, specific regimes of prohibition have achieved impressive results in relation to biological and chemical weaponry, unconditionally prohibiting use, possession, development, and sales, and addressing problems of verification and compliance in a manner that generates confidence among states that compliance is expected and that evidence of noncompliance will induce a harsh response.[12] These prohibitions have been respected, by and large, but with varying explanations of why.

On the other side of the ledger are tactics and weaponry of warfare—

such as involving air power, submarines, and nuclear weaponry—that characteristically ignore the generalized injunctions about indiscriminate attack, and at the same time are not made the object of specific regimes of prohibition. Why not? These patterns of behavior are clearly regarded as critical military options for major states and, as such, are not susceptible to meaningful regulation. This aura of regulatory futility is so manifest in relation to such critical weaponry that no attempt is even made to move from the general to the specific.[13]

APPLYING THE LAW TO LAND MINES

Land mines as potential objects of regulation are located in an intermediate zone. Their use is not so critical to leading states as to nullify the regulatory impulse in the face of the severe suffering being caused, but land mines continue to be perceived as having legitimate military uses that are valuable in certain belligerent settings. Furthermore, their use is integrated into military thinking and practice, and their properties as weapons (unlike those of biological or chemical weapons) do not directly challenge the vocational ethos of the professional military. The situation is further complicated by the public pressure, augmented by influential action by respected NGOs, to oppose the use and publicize the civilian harm caused by land mines. From this line of analysis, the expected result in relation to land mines, given the history of international humanitarian law, would be the establishment of a specific regime that *appears* responsive to the moral concern, but that is so configured as to have little or no impact on behavioral results.[14]

The regulatory response to the land mines challenge has, in fact, been precisely what one would expect, given these antecedent conditions—namely, a specific treaty instrument, the Landmines Protocol, with no appreciable regulatory bite, and indeed setting forth a normative framework that can be understood as more deferential to military logic than was the generalized framework it was supposedly superseding so as to impose greater regulatory control. As pointed out in a detailed legal analysis of the preexisting generalized norms, "the logical result of these provisions is to ban the use of landmines altogether."[15]

Let me be clear. The Landmines Protocol advances some laudable objectives, identifying land mines as requiring attention, as well as restating the customary international law duty to protect civilians from indiscriminate mine warfare. Article 3(3) of the Protocol specifically forbids the "indiscriminate use" of land mines, but article 3(4) conditions this injunction by insisting only on "feasible precautions . . . which

are practicable or practically possible taking into account all the circumstances ruling at the time, including humanitarian and military considerations."

Article 5 takes a similar approach to "remotely delivered mines."
Their use is prohibited unless in "an area which is itself a military
objective or which contains military objectives." But articles 5(1)(a) and
(b) allow further exceptions, to the effect that use is legally acceptable if
accurate recording is undertaken and the mine contains "an effective
self-neutralizing mechanism." These guidelines seem reasonable enough
until it is appreciated that high-technology land mine deployment is
being validated even where no military objective is located, a formula
that assuredly subjects the civilian population to severe dangers over
extended periods of time and expanses of territory, and authorizes
indiscriminate warfare. The same hortatory tone is found in article 9,
which admonishes states and international organizations to enter into
agreements to facilitate mine clearance operations.

The Protocol provides no procedure for complaints, no mechanism
for verification, no consequences of noncompliance of even a flagrant
character, no extension of coverage to noninternational conflicts, no
effort to reconcile high- and low-technology priorities. The Protocol has
remained on the shelf, and behavioral patterns rarely have even made
the pretense of abiding by the guidelines contained within its provisions.
This sorry record was compiled as a consequence of battlefield pressures and military mind-sets, and not mainly because many leading
states, including the United States, that drafted and signed the Protocol
have not as yet seen fit to submit the treaty for ratification. The
appalling pattern of land mine use over the last decade has been primarily a reflection of the relevant political consensus that land mines
remain weapons of choice for variously situated belligerents regardless
of effects on civilian society. Can these defects in the Protocol be overcome? My short response would be, not significantly without the support of the military experts in the leading governments in the North,
and that does not seem to be forthcoming, except on marginal matters.

The way this distinction is drawn between what is prohibited and
what is accepted as an inevitable part of war can help us understand
why it may be difficult, if not impossible, to obtain an effective specific
regime in relation to land mines, yet why at the same time the impulse
to restrict use is stronger here than in some other areas of warfare. My
claim is that an effective repudiation of weaponry will occur only when
the representatives of the professional military in the leading governments of the North approve or at least acquiesce, and that neither

prospect now exists with respect to land mine use. The intensity of the public campaign has had some impact, as probably have the evidence of the high incidence of civilian casualties (estimated at 80 percent of all deaths), the difficulties associated with demining in poor countries, and land mine damage done for many years after the guns have fallen silent. That is, there is a greater willingness to propose a ban on land mines as a result of these pressures being mounted by various forms of agitation in civil society, but it is not nearly sustained or widespread enough to push land mines into the domain of potentially prohibited weaponry and tactics, given the continued insistence by representatives of the military that if mines are used properly, they remain an important battlefield weapon and a legitimate one.

The military position consists of several strands. First, land mines as explosives are seen as no worse than other kinds of weapons and tactics that do heavy civilian damage, yet are relied upon more, being widely posited as "necessary." Second, being so widely produced, deployed, and relied upon, land mines have become habitual weapons in warfare; their proscription would thus have to overcome entrenched patterns of behavior, and be that much more difficult to challenge. Third, although a high-technology society could configure all land mines under its control with self-detonating or self-neutralizing devices, or even get along without using mines at all, this is not nearly so feasible for low-technology belligerents, who are not in a position to rely on more sophisticated mines or to give mines up in combat situations. Fourth, since low-technology revolutionaries and belligerents are dependent on cheap land mines and are likely to ignore legal restraints, their high-technology counterparts do not feel any strong pressure to uphold applicable legal standards.

This assessment of the overall situation would lead one to expect opposition from military circles to any proposed full-fledged ban on land mines, combined with support for a tighter arms control approach that would preserve high-technology land mine uses while disallowing low-technology patterns of use. Given these asymmetries of attitude, one should not anticipate more than minimal impacts of international humanitarian law on battlefield practices in relation to available land mines.

Underlying this assessment is a wider conception of the modalities of modern warfare, and the artificiality of constraining land mines while air war and artillery fire remain unrestricted, despite their tendency to inflict cruel punishment and even higher magnitudes of casualties on civilian populations.[16] In this regard, military professionals treat land mines as one more dimension of the complex and "synergistic" (a favorite word in military jargon these days) technological landscape of modern warfare.

Also influencing and reinforcing this professional resistance to moving more drastically is an underlying sense of futility of the wider regulatory enterprise, given the anticipated unresponsiveness of "the other side," namely, the low-technology revolutionary adversary. Specialists widely assume that such an adversary will refuse to restrict operational discretion to use land mines freely, given these weapons' strong economic and combat appeal in the context of a long internal war where the advantages of military materiel and scale are generally weighted heavily on the counterinsurgent side.

The report of the January 1994 ICRC high-level meeting of military experts strongly confirms this conclusion.[17] That is, the professional military establishments of leading governments resist any generalized ban on land mines, although they are willing to condition use on some generalized guidelines (involving recording and marking the location of minefields) designed to take "all feasible precaution . . . to protect civilians from the effects of mines."[18] This welcome sensitivity to humanitarian concerns is offset, however, by a failure to propose enforcement mechanisms, and by several disturbing acknowledgments of tactical advantage to be derived from widespread reliance on land mines under the heading "Conventional Forces Engaged in Counterinsurgency": "The casualties caused by the use of landmines is particularly effective as opposition forces lack the medical infrastructure to care for their wounded." The report also accepts without question reliance on widespread use of land mines to disrupt control over territory that has fallen under the control of the insurgent, thereby implicitly endorsing the military logic that produces a terroristic impact on civilian society. In discussing antipersonnel mines, the report says that a "further important impact of anti-personnel mines is the psychological effect of injured soldiers on their comrades and the logistical burden involved in treating casualties." The report, as expected, arrives at an unqualified endorsement of the military utility of land mines for combatants: "In summary, the military do not regard alternative systems [to antipersonnel mines] as being viable."[19]

In fairness, it should be appreciated that the mandate of the report was to fulfill an ICRC undertaking, which was to obtain the views of experts on military utility, rather than the solicitation of views on how to protect civilian society. Nevertheless, it is revealing that despite the extraordinary scale of use and civilian injury, these military experts showed no disposition to examine current patterns of land mine use that are responsible for disproportionate civilian casualties or whether the level and nature of the harm being caused might justify a break with past views of how to define military necessity in relation to land mines. Perhaps more disturbing was the acceptance, although veiled, of uses for land mines that can only be described as "terroristic": burdening of primitive medical capabilities of the insurgent side; disrupting societal control as insurgent authority over a country expands.

Aside from the direct humanitarian concerns such a conception of military necessity provokes, such views blur any feasible distinction between military and civilian targeting, and incorporate a logic of total war. If that logic prevails on the richer, high-technology side, proposing a more restrictive logic to govern the generally far poorer, low-technology side is mere posturing, with no expectation of response. It is this fundamental contextual circumstance that makes the recommendations of the ICRC experts so dubious from the perspective of strengthening international humanitarian law vis-à-vis land mines. Where legal standards on belligerent operations have had some impact on warfare is where the total war logic has been rejected, as in relation to torture, the treatment of prisoners, collective reprisals against civilians or captured soldiers, and the repudiation of chemical and biological weapons. In these instances, arguments from the perspective of military utility have been rejected or qualified, and treated as either unpersuasive or unacceptable. As yet, this humanitarian logic has not been able to challenge successfully the logic of military utility within professional circles as applied to land mines.

Despite the activation of NGOs and public opinion on the land mine issue, it will not be possible to move ahead very much, if at all, unless this professional resistance to a more fully implemented regulatory regime can be overcome, or at least eroded. Of course, international humanitarian law, by its nature, challenges to varying degrees, with varying rates of success, prevailing conceptions of military utility. The history of this experience suggests that the challenge will not succeed behaviorally unless it *actually* convinces the military professionals to redefine military necessity in a narrower, more restrictive way, with appropriate adjustments in battlefield tactics and weapons procurement plans. There is no indication that this is likely to happen in the near future with respect to the *use* of land mines. Of course, if the public campaign gathers more steam, and heads of important states join the campaign, then it becomes more plausible to override the views of military commanders and their advisors.

Regulating the Before and After Phases of Land Mine Use

The premise here is that the most promising, near-term regulatory prospects are in the nature of indirect constraints on land mine use that make no claim to impinge on battlefield assessments of land mine use, and yet seek to diminish the harm inflicted on civilians. In some respects, this approach resembles attempts to control nuclear weaponry: no serious legal challenge has been mounted against possession, development, even deployment by nuclear weapons states, but a major effort has been made to discourage proliferation and deter use.[20] Here the argument is that land mine use is subject to a legal regime of limitation that has proved to be essentially unworkable, failing to take account of low-technology priorities in internal wars and not appreciating the extent to which military planners conceive disrupting civilian society to be an essential war aim in conflicts where land mines are most extensively relied upon and where harm to civilians from land mines tends to be greatest. Shifting the regulatory focus to the before and after phases of combat removes most considerations of military utility from regulatory policy, and may thus weaken professional military objections.[21]

BEFORE COMBAT

Several interrelated steps require careful consideration. The objective would be to influence the type of land mine available through arms sales. What I would propose is a suppliers regime that sets minimum design standards, emphasizing self-detonating or self-neutralizing mechanisms in every mine that are timed to avoid risk after relatively short time periods, measured in months, not years. Technology should be shared, and technological assistance, including economical mapping techniques, should be available to any supplier or purchaser. The most serious difficulty with this proposal is that it would likely interfere with competitive forces and raise the market price of mines, thereby leading low-technology buyers with limited resources to develop their own primitive production facilities or to purchase cheap mines outside the suppliers regime.[22] Could this difficulty be met, in part, by subsidizing the less-destructive mines or by supplying low-technology combat forces with easily insertable self-destruct devices?[23] If the regime was not tilted too grossly toward high-technology users, then it might be possible to persuade virtually all suppliers to participate, and to reduce civilian casualties and long-term effects by orders of magnitude.

Such a regime would need to be reinforced with some kind of verification process that could generate complaints about noncompliance, and appropriate responses. It would also be useful to embody agreed-upon design constraints in export controls and sanctions that were common to all or most supplier countries, and tie the licensing process at the state level with an unconditional duty to report to the UN arms registry all sales of land mines.

Given the magnitude of the suffering being caused, and that likely to continue, as well as the relatively small dollar amounts in the land mines market, it might be possible to highlight the humanitarian urgency of the undertaking. The military professionals are not likely to openly oppose such an effort because it would not reduce their combat options.

AFTER COMBAT

Here the obvious focus is on mine clearance. Perhaps, the same regime that would be formed to regulate design and sales could also assist existing UN efforts in clearance, providing experts and state-of-the-art technology. Further, if the country where the mines are located is unable to pay for their removal, then the financial burden of removal could be borne by the regulatory regime, with assessments based upon an agreed formula, or somehow correlated with an estimate of relative market shares at the sales end in relation to the particular combat area.

Here again, the military experts should have no serious objections. In postcombat settings, humanitarian concerns emerge in their most poignant form, as mines continue to inflict horrifying mutilation and death almost exclusively on civilians after "peace" has been reestablished, and to maim the most innocent of all victims—children at play. The only governmental resistance that is anticipated would involve costs, and an equitable means to share the burden. Demining entrepreneurs and specialists, in conjunction with the UN program on mine clearance, would be needed to shape the regime in the most efficient manner.

Conclusion

Of course, this emphasis on the before and after phases of land mine use does not even purport to reach the core of the problem—namely, relying on land mines to wage war by means that do not respect civilian innocence, and that cause widespread injury and death, leaving behind

many maimed reminders of the war and projecting war danger indefinitely into the future. At present, the criterion of military utility is
almost impossible to challenge effectively, as the whole history of warfare in this century abundantly demonstrates. At stake, in the end, and
not only in relation to land mines, is whether civil control over battlefield behavior could be established in accordance with the generalized
mandates of customary international law. To the extent it could, the
rationale for an unconditional ban on land mines would acquire immediate feasibility as a political project.

With land mines, there is room for debate as to military utility. Some
military experts question the standard wisdom that land mines are useful for defensive purpose relative to their overall cost (including the
political impacts of damage to civilians and the financial cost of clearance). In the background are unresolved issues about how best to relate
to the civilian population in an internal war situation, but surely experiences in Somalia demonstrate that it can be crucial to the success of
"the mission" not to alienate the civilian population. Evidently, various
military forces, including those of the U.S. government, have been at
times used in a nation-building mode, in Third World countries, and
to operate without weapons to convey peaceful intentions to the population. In other words, it seems important to engage the military professionals in discussions about prevailing assumptions of military utility in
many of the settings where land mines are widely used.

In this spirit, it is also a matter of urgency to extend the reach of
international humanitarian law to noninternational armed combat situations, and to draw all belligerents into the overriding effort to minimize
civilian suffering. At least, it would seem essential to represent the concerns and viewpoints of low-technology belligerents in meetings of
experts of the sort convened by the ICRC.

The most cherished goal of international humanitarian law is to reconcile the conduct of war with consistent deference to civilian innocence.
The record has been generally disappointing, exhibiting a willingness by
belligerent forces to use weaponry that is perceived to give battlefield
advantages even if indiscriminate in its impact. What is disclosed, as has
been the subject of much commentary on modern war, is an encompass-
ing conception of war that makes the enemy civilian infrastructure a military target. Furthermore, extending "the law" contributes little to up-
holding civilian innocence in wartime unless the appropriate political
forces are willing to implement or, at least, are subject to challenge in the
event of noncompliance. The gap between legal rhetoric and actual

behavior usually diminishes respect for the seriousness of the regulatory effort, although it can in some situations help NGOs to exert pressure on belligerents that discourages the worst violations.

There will be no quick fixes when it comes to land mines. Whether the current mobilization of concern eventually can be translated into tangible results depends, at least in the short run, on finding ways to reduce harmful effects without depending on either the conversion of military professionals or their views being overridden by political leaders.

6

Land Mines: The Arms Control Dimension

M ost of the debate about the control of land mines focuses on
international law, especially the degree to which the use of
these weapons is already prohibited under customary humanitarian law.[1] Relatively little attention goes to a different issue: the
potential pertinence of arms control agreements and regulations to restrict the development, possession, or use of land mines.

In any effort to constrain or ban particular military capabilities by
international agreement, humanitarian and arms control law face a sim-
iliar dilemma. A generalized norm of law aimed at eliminating particular
weapons or their use is rarely sufficient to achieve the specified objective. In a contest between normative and military imperatives, the latter
will almost always overshadow the former. Indeed, there is reason to be
cautious about crafting regulations that cannot be widely supported and
credibly enforced. Weak agreements, like weak laws, invite cynicism and
fatalism.

No current international arms control law or even enduring norm is
directly applicable to land mines. No voluntary regime, international
treaty, or any other type of mechanism regulates the production, possession, or transfer of land mines internationally. Indeed, customary

The author is indebted to Stephen Goose for his generous assistance in preparing this chapter.

international humanitarian law and the Landmines Protocol of the 1980 Conventional Weapons Convention apply only to *use* of land mines, and they do so imperfectly. The experience of the past decade, which has witnessed a steady growth in the use—and abuse—of land mines, demonstrates that attempts directed at regulating only use of these weapons are inadequate. To be credible, restraints on land mines need to be governed by a verifiable arms control regime that covers production, stockpiling, and exports, as well. Humanitarian and arms control objectives coincide in this matter, as any efforts to prohibit the employment of land mines are likely to be effective only if accompanied by comprehensive restraints that stigmatize all activities related to these types of weapons. A comprehensive ban on the production, possession, trade, and use of antipersonnel land mines, however difficult an objective this may prove, has pragmatic advantages over reliance on humanitarian law rules attempting to restrict mines on normative grounds.

If a total ban were embraced as a common goal for a large number of countries, it would be easier to stigmatize land mines as an illegitimate instrument of warfare, relegated to the scrap heap of history along with other inhumane weapons, like biological or chemical weapons. The control of land mines, in fact, may be feasible only if these weapons are delegitimized internationally, which is unlikely to occur if some uses remain acceptable under partial controls.

Despite the precedents for a comprehensive, global ban on land mines, however, the political and technical complexities of reaching such an agreement suggest the need for interim steps as part of a longer-term strategy.

Precedents

Efforts by the international community to control the spread of nuclear, chemical, biological, and certain advanced conventional technologies have been part of the diplomatic landscape for decades. These include formal treaty regimes, such as the 1970 Nuclear Nonproliferation Treaty (NPT); multilateral or bilateral supplier cartels designed to limit the export of key technologies useful for weapons development, such as the Australia Group, established to restrict access to materials needed for chemical weapons, and the Missile Technology Control Regime, which controls the trade in ballistic and cruise missiles; and domestic legislation or unilateral measures prohibiting national exports of certain weapon or weapon-related technology.

Several international agreements have banned whole categories of weapons considered to pose intolerable harm, and these measures could be seen as precedents for a land mines ban. They include the St. Petersburg Declaration of 1868, prohibiting the use of certain explosive or inflammable projectiles; the Hague Agreements of 1899, banning use of "dum-dum" (expanding) bullets; the Geneva Protocol of 1925, which prohibits use of asphyxiating gases and bacteriological warfare; the 1972 Biological Weapons Convention, which bans production, stockpiling, transfer, and use of biological and toxin weapons; and the 1992 Chemical Weapons Convention, banning development, production, possession, and use of chemical weapons.

The majority of control regimes derive from a common perception that particular military capabilities are inherently destabilizing or immoral. This kind of categorization depends on several considerations, including the degree of risk a certain military capability poses to noncombatants because of its indiscriminate effects (nuclear, chemical, and biological weapons); normative concerns about the way in which a weapon inflicts injuries or casualties (death by poison gas or biological toxins is viewed as more horrible than by conventional means); and a perception that a system is particularly useful for preemptive, offensive operations that could prove regionally destabilizing (ballistic missiles).

Determining which weapons become subject to international prohibitions is a fairly subjective exercise, but it depends most significantly on the military value accorded to particular capabilities by states that possess them. Chemical and biological weapons, because of their operational limitations, have never been central to developed countries' military doctrines, and thus have proven relatively less difficult to renounce. Nuclear weapons, meanwhile, have served as the core of the superpowers' security paradigms for decades, and even despite a strong taboo on their use, only recently has it become possible to even discuss serious reductions in nuclear arsenals—let alone the more remote prospect of nuclear disarmament.

Reduced utility is sometimes the result of military innovation, when a particular weapon is rendered technically obsolete by a more advanced capability and is therefore seen as less valuable. The more common challenge for arms control (and international law), however, is to alter the balance between the perceived utility of a weapon and the potential political costs incurred by its use or misuse. For weapons seen as indiscriminate in their effects and posing undue hazards to noncombatants, for example, any increment of military utility achieved thus would have to be weighed against other factors, including the international opprobrium directed at the user.

An agreement to control antipersonnel land mines, as such, would require agreement from military professionals about the relative disutility of these weapons in light of their inadvertent risks. The conventional wisdom that mines are vital for defensive purposes would have to be calibrated with the political and economic costs of maintaining such a military option, including risks to civilians, the dangers of continued global diffusion of mine technology absent any international regulation, the socioeconomic disruption inflicted on societies where mines may remain long after the cessation of a conflict, and the disproportionate economic burden of clearing minefields.

For the United States, in particular, eliminating reliance on weapons that pose indiscriminate effects is consistent with the type of intervention most likely to involve the American military in the future. Traditional military conflicts are likely to give way to intervention to help restore order or distribute aid in places where sovereign authority or agreed borders have broken down. Somalia and Bosnia demonstrate that legitimacy and political neutrality are far more central ingredients of operational effectiveness in such situations than are calculations of relative firepower and lethality.

Conflicts involving internal instability or the breakdown of recognized sovereignty may also prove uniquely unsuited for the defensive use of land mines, which requires the ability to delineate clear enemy zones and emplace mines accordingly. Chaotic and rapidly changing conditions would seem to preclude confidence in identifying military positions and installations without also posing risks to noncombatants. This limitation would be especially acute in conflicts in which the United States is not fighting an immediate or identifiable enemy, but attempting instead to protect innocents in civil strife.

The use of mines by states in conflict, moreover, may increasingly impinge on the ability or willingness of the United States or other countries to intervene in such areas, including for humanitarian reasons. The American public has shown that it has limited tolerance for casualties in warfare, and apparently even less so when it comes to ventures where U.S. national interests are not crystal clear. Given the low cost and wide diffusion of land mines, therefore, they could serve as a cheap countermeasure used to deny or certainly to complicate U.S. interventionary options.

This is another area where the interests of the military and humanitarian organizations coincide. In a growing number of cases of intervention, humanitarian workers and military professionals are working together to accomplish similar missions. The military risks the former are increasingly encountering in conflict areas is a key concern, especially to the U.S. military. The U.S. Army, for example, has undertaken joint training exercises with nongovernmental organizations (NGOs) such as the Red Cross, both to teach NGOs about coping with armed threats and to learn about operating effectively in conflicts where there is no obvious or traditional adversary.

Difficulties of Achieving an Agreement

There should be no doubt about the political and technical difficulties of negotiating, achieving, and implementing a land mines arms control agreement, even if the political will exists and the objections of the military of various nations can be overcome. Indeed, a prerequisite for attempting such an agreement is an honest assessment of the enormous technical and political complexities of such a task. Among the major challenges are these:

- The sheer number of mines diffused worldwide, along with the growing number of producers and exporters. Over 200 million antipersonnel land mines are said to have been produced over the last twenty-five years. Antipersonnel mines continue to be produced at a rate of 5–10 million a year by approximately fifty nations, of which at least thirty are exporters;[2]
- The emergence of new suppliers of land mines in the Third World that have significant stakes in the land mines market—including China, Egypt, and Pakistan;
- The ease with which these weapons can be produced and transported, given their size and weight, including through a highly competitive black market;
- The degree to which national militaries and insurgents value these weapons as part of their military strategy;
- The likelihood that even with a comprehensive ban, there will be violators, including some rogue nations that will continue to produce and export mines, and some armies, rebel forces, and terrorists who will continue to use them.

The precedents of successful agreements for bans on certain weapons, however, faced no fewer complications. For instance, chemical weapons were renounced by the large powers despite their valued role as an integral part of NATO and Warsaw Pact military strategy over several decades. Chemical weapons also are easy and cheap to produce, are readily concealed, and serve as a valuable form of currency in the international black market. Indeed, any country with a pharmaceutical industry can achieve some kind of chemical weapons capability. These obstacles did not prevent 157 countries from signing the 1992 Chemical Weapons Convention. Although implementation still presents challenges, the broad consensus is that the world will be a safer place if the number of chemical producers is reduced from dozens to a handful, and the number of users is further reduced to those who are willing to risk widespread international condemnation and sanctions. This obviously would pertain to land mines, as well.

Steps Toward a Ban

Short of a ban, a wide range of arms control options could help build the foundations for such an agreement in the long term. As these steps are considered, however, it is important to remember that the articulation of the long-term objective of a comprehensive ban may be a crucial ingredient of success for even modest measures. Failing to embrace a ban even as a distant goal would open the way to many of the same problems faced in other partial control regimes, such as the NPT. A key weakness of the nuclear regime is that it is aimed at controlling the spread of nuclear weapons capabilities to additional states, not at delegitimizing them as instruments of power among the declared nuclear powers.

Four near-term options could be undertaken internationally: prohibitions on the design and sale of especially indiscriminate types of mines; an export control regime; measures that promote international transparency in national arsenals and international commerce; and technical consultations about what would be required for a more comprehensive ban.

PROHIBITIONS ON CERTAIN TYPES OF MINES

One interim measure could focus on restrictions or prohibitions on the design, production, possession, and transfer of mines that pose the most severe risks to noncombatants. One version of this would be a suppliers regime that sets minimum design features emphasizing self-detonating and self-neutralizing mechanisms in all mines, while providing technical and financial assistance to poorer states to modernize their stockpiles and to help in demining. In addition, prohibitions on other kinds of particularly indiscriminate mines could include devices that are not detectable (that is, plastic and minimum-metal mines); mines with antihandling or antidisturbance features; and remotely delivered ("scatterable") mines.[3]

CONTROLLING EXPORTS

Initial steps aimed at controlling land mines have focused on export restrictions, and progress has been considerable in recent years. In 1992, the U.S. Congress imposed a one-year moratorium on the export of antipersonnel land mines; as of late 1993, the moratorium was extended for another three years.[4] At least six other countries have announced a halt to their mine trade: France, Belgium, the Netherlands, Germany, Greece, and South Africa. The European Parliament passed a resolution in 1992 calling on member states to enact a five-year export moratorium. In November 1993, the United Nations General Assembly passed a U.S.-sponsored resolution calling on states "to agree to a moratorium on the export of antipersonnel land mines that pose grave dangers to civilian populations."[5]

Export controls are likely to be the focus of U.S. executive branch policy, as well. State Department officials have indicated that their priority over the next four to five years will be to pursue an international export control regime. Discussions have centered on a voluntary supplier-oriented regime similar to the Missile Technology Control Regime or the Australia Group.

No matter how strong and carefully crafted an export control agreement may be, clandestine commerce in land mines is likely to continue, with rogue states and subnational actors engaged in illicit production and trade. Still, limiting the commercial availability of land mines clearly makes sense. Most of the nations with the worst problems relating to land mines—including Cambodia, Afghanistan, and Angola—do not produce mines indigenously, but are supplied by other countries.

TRANSPARENCY

In a world in which the information revolution has made it increasingly difficult to disguise military behavior, measures to formally promote transparency could be a helpful, albeit modest, step toward a comprehensive land mine agreement. Developing a mechanism to generate and exchange information at the international level about production, stockpiles, and exports of mines would be one measure. In keeping with the spirit of the UN Register on Conventional Arms, which requires nations to report on major weapon systems only, nations could be encouraged to register the number and type of antipersonnel land mines produced, and report to the UN any transfer of such devices.

TECHNICAL CONSULTATIONS

All successful arms control agreements have been preceded by extensive formal and informal consultations to define the scope of negotiations, the character of the weapons being subject to control, and other technical matters. These technical consultations form the foundation for a regime, and even provide momentum toward an agreement when the subject matter is otherwise too sensitive to address head-on. Years of technical exchanges went into the formation of the terms for the Strategic Arms Limitation and Strategic Arms Reduction Talks, for example, helping to define a common vocabulary for negotiations and to permit the United States and the Soviet Union to engage indirectly about their respective nuclear arsenals.

A consultative mechanism among like-minded states, possibly under the aegis of the UN Committee on Disarmament or a similar body, could be readily organized to discuss the many issues pertaining to a multilateral agreement to ban mines. These could include the following:

• Technical definitions of what constitutes an antipersonnel mine, a production facility, dual-use componentry, and mine delivery systems. In this regard, special attention needs to go to the blurred line between antitank and antipersonnel mines, and the question of submunitions and other ordnance that can function similarly to land mines;
• Ways to devise a routine and enduring verification regime, which could include declarations of stockpiles and on-site inspections to ensure confidence in compliance;
• Whether a special challenge inspection regime, of the kind incorporated into the Conventional Weapons Convention, would be feasible;
• What a protocol and agreed mechanisms for the destruction of stockpiles in a specified time period might require, including provisions for international verification of destruction;
• What sanctions should be considered in the case of noncompliance;

- What national legislation and enforcement mechanisms might be needed to support the terms of the multilateral agreement;
- The degree to which certain mine-related activities should be allowed, such as research for the improvement of demining equipment, mine countermeasures, and protection of troops;
- Improved strategies for funding and implementing comprehensive mine clearance programs.

In addition, engaging military professionals in consultations about mine warfare doctrine, the relative utility of mines in various contingencies, and which of the various restraint measures under discussion might least impinge on perceived security interests could be an important way to build consensus. These discussions should include a frank appraisal of the military legacy of mine warfare—that is, the degree to which mines have actually proved decisive in battle relative to the human and political costs of civilian casualties and the level of resources now urgently needed to clear mines around the world.

A Comprehensive Ban

The potential effectiveness of the interim steps discussed above has clear limitations. An effort to place restrictions on the design of mines, for example, would raise a risk that less-advanced and cheaper mines would become more commercially competitive and flood the market with sales to countries still committed to offensive (and "unsafe") land mine use. Partial bans, especially supply-side controls among the larger powers, also pose political problems. Smaller states often see agreements of this kind as a form of great power discrimination that is insensitive to regional security concerns. If some land mine production and export is considered legal, as such, there may always be inconclusive debates as to what constitutes a violation worthy of penalty or whether the regime as a whole is legitimate. Without a clear and compelling stigma, in other words, many countries may see no particular interest in restricting their production, sales, or use of mines.

Rather than wishing for panaceas, however, one should view interim steps as tools to advance the discussion from normative to practical considerations. Even with imperfect measures, the development of a clear taboo can be encouraged by this process, which in itself can begin to serve as a deterrent against the misuse of mines.

An international agreement providing for a comprehensive ban on antipersonnel land mines should be the common goal of all civilized nations. Arms control law has clear precedents for a ban on indiscriminate weapons that inflict unconscionable harm on noncombatants as well as soldiers, including the Biological Weapons and Chemical Weapons Conventions. Arms control provisions might conceivably be incorporated into the Conventional Weapons Convention of 1980 during the 1995 review conference, but it is more likely that a separate international agreement, convention, or treaty to address arms control issues will be needed.

Achieving controls on conventional weapons has always proven an elusive objective of diplomacy. Despite periodic attempts to craft international guidelines to restrain exports of conventional arms, no formal or enduring agreement has ever emerged. During the Carter administration, negotiations with the Soviet Union on arms sales restraint did include an effort to define and prohibit a class of weapons that posed undue risks to civilians and in which neither government had a significant military stake. Known in the trade as "weapons of ill repute," these included various incendiary weapons, man-portable air defense systems, fuel-air explosives, and long-range surface-to-surface missiles. The talks foundered in the politics of the Cold War, and this proposal was never formally discussed.[6]

An effort to control land mines, as such, could be seen as a reasonable starting point for reconsidering a regime to restrict a larger category of indiscriminate weapons. Stressing incremental, technical measures that would be of minimum controversy could help minimize the political burden that any initiatives would bear at the outset. This could help buy time to develop the fundamental infrastructure—political, military, and diplomatic—needed to institutionalize permanent bans on weapons whose marginal military utility and high human costs should long ago have rendered them unacceptable to civilized society.

7

Land Mines:
A Political-Moral
Assessment

J. BRYAN HEHIR

I n a speech to the Senate on the suffering caused by land mines, Sen. Patrick Leahy expressed his conviction that the elimination of land mines was "a moral issue."[1] In exploring the meaning of Senator Leahy's statement, we must bear in mind that the resolution of the problem of land mines will require a multidimensional effort; the moral argument for policy is one piece of a much larger picture. Moral arguments, based on ethical principles and rules, seek to restrain power and to provide direction for it in the complex domain of international politics. But such principles and rules never function in isolation. An ethical argument has its own intrinsic meaning, logic, and influence; but particularly in the world of social and political affairs, the ethical argument must be woven together with perspectives of politics, strategy, law, and economics. This chapter will address both the ethical and the political-strategic dimensions of the land mine problem.

The first observation to be made is the difficulty of sustaining an ethical argument in the arena of world politics. Professor Stanley Hoffmann of Harvard University has highlighted the traditional case: the absence of a central political authority and a law that binds all actors, combined with the cultural diversity of the international system, makes international ethics the most difficult terrain for moral discourse in all of human affairs.[2] The paradox, of course, is that the absence of effective political and legal authority is precisely the reason why ethical restraints on power are needed in world affairs. Moral arguments are designed to influence two levels of decision making. First, they should be used in the policy debate of a society, seeking to bring policy under public scrutiny. Second, moral arguments are directed to the conscience of individuals—citizens, soldiers, diplomats, opinion makers—to aid in their decision making. At each of these levels, moral principles can be used to judge and direct policy even if positive law does not exist on certain questions. Positive international law does exist on the land mine question, but it is fragile and limited; a broader and stronger moral argument can serve as a bridge between law and policy at the national and international levels.

The policy question posed by the use of land mines is one dimension of the broader issue of the ethics of military power. In the language of an earlier generation of moralists, the study of land mines is an exercise in ethical casuistry—that is, the study of a "case" in the ethics of war. To address the case, it is necessary to establish a framework for analyzing the moral use of force, then to look for the distinctive features of the problem of land mines.

The Nature of the Ethic: Legitimate and Limited Use of Force

In any moral assessment of the use of force, the starting point of the analysis influences the shape of the moral argument at each step. In the historical debate about the morality of war, three quite different starting points can be identified.

First, the stance of the moral abolitionists: this is the classical position of nonviolence, or pacifism, whether it is argued in religious or philosophical terms. The essential affirmation of the position is that the use of lethal force cannot be morally justified. While the prohibition on the use of force is absolute, this ethic is not passive in the face of injustice. It seeks to oppose injustice through nonviolent means. In its contemporary versions, the nonviolent ethic is often joined with a powerful social ethic, calling for profound social change, but always in a nonviolent fashion.

Second, the position of the realists: I use the term here in the way Professor Michael Walzer of the Princeton Institute for Advanced

Study employs it.[3] In this sense, the term asserts that there is no room for moral analysis or moral discourse in the domain of politics and war. Not all realists would espouse this view, but Walzer is correct in identifying such a position as part of the historical debate on the ethics of war. In this sense, realism distinguishes between the "normal" politics of peace, which affords room for moral considerations, and the time of war, when the stakes of the outcome are so critical to the life of nations that no restraints are to be imposed on what is done in the name of survival and security. The logic of this starting point gives free rein to strategy and tactics; no limits exist for either the statesman or the soldier. Realism eliminates the moral point of view.

Third, the view of the moral architects: this position legitimates some uses of force, but not all uses. The moral architects are committed to a structure of principles and rules that is used to assess each resort to force on a case-by-case basis. The essential position of the moral architects is that any legitimate use of force must be a limited use; limitation is imposed by the ends sought, the means allowed, and the intention that guides the policy. This position of "legitimation with limitation" is the Just War ethic. It is the position that will be used in this chapter to assess the problem of land mines.[4]

THE JUST WAR ETHIC

The Just War ethic begins with a presumption against the resort to force; in that sense, it reflects the basic position of the abolitionists. Unlike the abolitionist position, however, it does not hold the presumption against force as an absolute rule; it envisions exceptions, morally justified cases in which the presumption is reversed and force is used in the name of moral values. The logic of the presumption-exception reasoning is reflected in the phrase "Just War"; one goes to war in defense of the value of justice. Even when this occurs, however, the presumption against the use of force continues to exercise influence in moral decision making; Professor James Childress of the University of Virginia argues that the overridden presumption leaves "moral traces" on the rest of the decision.[5] In the Just War ethic, these moral traces continually place the burden of proof on those who are resorting to force, imposing restraints throughout the war.

Building upon the presumption-exception model, the Just War ethic uses three questions to determine when a justifiable exception exists. The "why" question asks what reasons or purposes will justify the use of lethal force. The "when" question asks under which conditions force can be employed. The "how" question seeks to limit the means used in warfare.

Professor Ralph B. Potter of Harvard University helpfully summarizes centuries of reflection upon the why question, categorizing the narrow range of causes that can justify resorting to arms. They are to protect the innocent from unjust attack; to restore rights wrongfully denied; and to reestablish an order necessary for decent human existence.[6] These reasons do not exhaust the circumstances that bring nations into conflict with each other, nor do they approximate the wider range of issues that bring individuals and groups into conflict within states. But the three just causes are regarded as the limit situations in which the line between politics and war can be crossed. The reasons are purposefully defined in extreme terms, citing *only* those cases when all peaceful remedies seem to be incapable of addressing the injustice being perpetrated.

The why question must be satisfied before any others can be raised: without just cause, no resort to force can be contemplated. Even in the face of just cause, however, the influence of the presumption against resort to force is felt. The when question produces additional criteria, designed to prevent precipitous decisions to undertake war; the when criteria presume a serious reason for war exists, but they probe whether violence is the best answer to the problem. The criteria that flow from the when question illustrate the multiple moral limits placed on the unpredictable instrumentality of force in politics. The five criteria involve issues of political legitimacy (asking who is the proper authority to invoke the use of force); they test the intention driving the policy; they ask whether all other means of redressing injustice have been tried (last resort); they probe the relationship between ends and means in the policy (possibility of success); and they ask whether resort to force will produce more harm than good (the proportionality test).[7] These diverse moral questions seek to prevent needless incidents of violence. The perennial danger for the Just War ethic is that its intended goal of distinguishing between just and unjust uses of force will be distorted by states or others who seek legitimation of their policies, but have no intention of setting limits on them. The when questions examine the use of force from quite distinct angles of moral vision. They test the role of the propriety of the moral agent, as well as both the intentions and consequences of the policy being pursued.

Passing the why and when tests legitimates the decision to go to war (*jus ad bellum*); when war is undertaken, the how question is pursued by two distinct tests, noncombatant immunity and proportionality.

Taken together, these principles shape moral conduct in war (*jus in bello*). The strength of the ethic is rooted in the different kinds of restraint embodied in the two principles. The noncombatant immunity principle is deontological in character; that is, it determines right or wrong conduct in terms of the character of the action judged, not in terms of the consequences produced by the action. In more technical terms, it defines the right apart from the good. The principle forbids all consciously (directly) intended targeting of or attack on civilians. The fundamental assertion of the principle is that war against a whole society can never be legitimate war. The moral logic of the principle flows from the very heart of the Just War ethic. Since the only justification for the use of force is to prevent aggression against human life, human rights, and human dignity, *only* those who are perpetrating such acts are open to attack. Both the nature of modern war (engaging the resources of the entire nation) and the developments in the technology of warfare (allowing direct attacks on the center of the adversary's society) have challenged the distinction between civilians and combatants. In the face of the challenge, the moral architects have struggled to maintain the barrier, knowing that the collapse of this principle would endanger the entire structure of restraint built in to the Just War ethic.[8]

The deontological test of noncombatant immunity is the first restraint placed on the means of warfare. This principle has primacy in the ethical argument. If a policy cannot ensure protection of civilians from directly intended attack on them, it cannot be ethically pursued. Even when this principle is satisfied, however, the Just War ethic uses a second means test: the principle of proportionality. This is a consequentialist test; that is, it assesses the rectitude of an action in light of the consequences it produces. Again, in the technical language of ethics, proportionality defines the right in terms of the good. The proportionality principle presumes that noncombatant immunity is being observed. It then raises questions about the kind of material and human damage a given strategy or tactic will produce. Much of the debate about the bombing policy during the Persian Gulf War was a proportionality debate. The enormous damage to Iraqi society, in spite of a stringent policy of not targeting civilians, raised moral questions and generated severe critique of the policy on the grounds of proportionality.

The issue of land mines will be primarily a means question, to be assessed in light of both the deontological and the consequentialist perspectives of the Just War ethic.

Before making that assessment, one other characteristic of the ethic of war needs to be analyzed. A moral theory exercises influence by its appeal to conscience, both the public conscience of a society and personal conscience. The Just War ethic has had two audiences in mind, particularly in a democracy. On the one hand, as Jesuit theologian John Courtney Murray argued, the primary value of the Just War ethic has been "its capacity to set the right terms for rational debate on public policies bearing on the problems of war and peace in this age characterized by international conflict and by advanced technology."[9] This is the appeal to public conscience, the attempt to join the political-strategic arguments about the use of force with an ethical argument about the moral purposes and moral limits of warfare. Historically, the Just War ethic has been primarily a policy ethic, designed to address the public responsibility that statesmen and citizens assume when a society goes to war. The primary method of imposing restraint on the use of force is to build the restraints directly in to the instructions issued through channels of command and control, and in to the strategy and tactics of the war effort.

The second restraint on force is, to adapt Murray's terminology, to set the right terms for personal conscience and choice. This appeal becomes particularly important if the public arguments go unheeded. If the policy being pursued is violating clear standards of moral restraint, those responsible for the ethic of war must appeal directly to citizens, soldiers, diplomats, and others to refuse cooperation with the policy. Obviously, when this stage of the argument is reached, a civil crisis exists in the society. The appeal to personal conscience places the individual at the intersection of the political and moral order, and it invokes the higher obligation of obeying moral principle by refusing the commands of civil authority. If the public moral arguments are effective, and policy is shaped by moral principles, then the individual citizen or soldier is spared this extreme test of conscience.

To summarize the ethical argument, the Just War ethic establishes a framework of principles and rules that both legitimates *some* use of force and places limits on *all* uses of force. The ethic is designed to guide both policy choices and personal choices. As a framework of principles, it can be set forth on its own terms, but to engage the actual issues of policy and personal choice, the ethic must be related to the fabric of policy discourse. That is the task to be undertaken in the assessment of land mines.

Land Mines: The Challenge to the Ethic

In assessing the nature of the land mine challenge, the first step is to define the ethically relevant characteristics of land mines. The most comprehensive analysis of the contemporary problem of land mines is found in the volume *Landmines: A Deadly Legacy*, jointly produced by the Arms Project of Human Rights Watch and Physicians for Human Rights. Drawing on the research of this volume and on an assessment of contemporary international politics, it is possible to isolate two defining features of the land mine problem: the character of the weapon and the political context in which it is used.

CHARACTER OF THE WEAPON

The primary characteristic of land mines is that they are inherently indiscriminate; more precisely, as they function today, land mines are indiscriminate in terms of time and targets. The opening page of *A Deadly Legacy* captures this double challenge of land mines concisely and eloquently:

> Landmines are blind weapons that cannot distinguish between the footfall of a soldier and that of an old woman gathering firewood. They recognize no ceasefire and, long after the fighting has stopped, they can maim or kill the children and grandchildren of the soldiers who laid them.[10]

Some might argue that a description of land mines as "inherently indiscriminate" seeks to prove too much. It is conceivable in principle to argue that land mines should be deployed as a defensive weapon only in a well-defined theater of operation, that the area should be precisely mapped, and that the party deploying the mines should accept responsibility for removing them after the conflict is over. Under these conditions, and assuming that no other weapon fills the defensive function of land mines, it is possible to imagine a discriminate use of land mines. Discrimination means that only combatants are targeted and that the mines are defused within a specific time period.

In the case of land mines, however, the argument in principle does not correspond to the facts of their use in most cases. Land mines are not limited to defensive purposes, they are not deployed only in battlefields, they are seldom identified by reliable maps, and they are most frequently not defused after a conflict ends. Again, the Human Rights Watch volume summarizes the actual pattern of use of land mines today: "They have shifted from being primarily a defensive, tactical battlefield weapon to an offensive, strategic weapon often aimed deliberately at civilians in order to empty territory, destroy food sources, create refugee flows, or simply spread terror."[11]

It is important to grasp that land mines are indiscriminate regarding targets *because* they are indiscriminate in time: because they are never defused, they cannot be targeted only on combatants; they immobilize societies long after their military function is over. Strewn across large areas, they pose an ongoing, ill-defined threat to the civilian population, which often has neither the resources nor the requisite skill to remove them.

The indiscriminate character of the weapons is complemented by the kinds of conflict where they are most often used. The end of the Cold War has had the beneficial effect of drastically reducing the danger of nuclear war. It has had the less-happy effect of releasing the discipline imposed on the international system by the very danger that super-power nuclear conflict threatened. The immediate effect of the nuclear danger was to create a zone of common interest between the two super-powers; while deeply divided ideologically, they found their mutual vulnerability a reason for restraint. A second-order consequence of the superpowers' prudence was the restraining influence they exercised upon or imposed upon other actors in the international system. The Yugoslav case may be the best example. The superpowers had a common interest during the Cold War in keeping Yugoslavia stable and unified; in this sense, they reinforced the authoritarian rule of Tito. His death and the collapse of superpower discipline opened the arena for resurgent nationalism and ethnic animosity in Yugoslavia. Bosnia exemplifies the kind of conflict that characterizes the post–Cold War era: internal conflict has gained primacy over interstate war; conflict is driven by ethnic, national, or religious divisions; conflict erupts against a unified state or begins when a state collapses.

In this kind of war, the rules of war are least likely to be obeyed. The war engulfs the entire nation; the battlefield is coterminous with the society as a whole; clear lines of command and responsibility are often difficult to identify or to maintain. Land mines are frequently the weapon of choice because they are cheap, devastating in their effect, and relatively uncomplicated to use. The result is that in the most probable kind of conflict of the day, the "deadly legacy" of land mines finds multiple uses:

> [M]ines are used principally as area denial weapons, useful in overcoming the low force-to-space ratio typical of such conflicts. Consequently, in wars today, mines are frequently placed in areas of high civilian concentration rather than being confined to discrete battlefields of limited size. Mines are laid in vast quantities across whole zones, and are often aimed directly at civilians.[12]

This passage captures the central moral problem of land mines: they violate the principle of noncombatant immunity and thus strike at the very heart of the principle of limitation. The fundamental test of limitation in the ethic of war is the ability to preserve noncombatant immunity. It is the only principle in the framework of the Just War ethic that places an absolute barrier on the kind of force that can be used in a morally justified way. The categories of last resort, moral possibility of success, and proportionality all have a contingent character about them, inevitably generating different moral assessments of the same factual data. The prohibition of direct attacks on civilians constitutes an absolute standard in the ethic of war. Because of the way land mines are used, particularly in intrastate conflicts, they encounter the full force of the noncombatant principle. These are indiscriminate methods of war.

POLITICAL CONTEXT

Arguments against land mines should focus on their indiscriminateness for two reasons. First, it is the heart of the contemporary Just War ethic; an age of technological warfare has brought this principle to the core of the effort to limit the consequences of war. Second, there has been a remarkable evolution in the United States understanding of the ethics of war regarding the protection of noncombatants. In the last fifty years, this principle has moved from a norm that was violated with impunity during World War II to a standard that was a central concern of the policy debate during the Persian Gulf War.

Two works capture the experience of World War II. During the war, Father John Ford, a Jesuit theologian, wrote his classic article "The Morality of Obliteration Bombing," in which he argued that the Allies were engaged in a just war against the Axis powers, but were pursuing the war with unjust means. In a detailed analysis of the bombing policy, Ford demonstrated that it clearly failed the test of noncombatant immunity.[13] At the time Ford's article was published, it was hardly noticed. Testimony to this fact is provided by McGeorge Bundy's perceptive and comprehensive history of the nuclear age; Bundy's detailed narrative of the debate leading to the use of the atomic weapons on Hiroshima essentially argues that there was little resistance to a direct attack on a city because that barrier had been crossed much earlier in the war. Regarding the atomic bomb, Bundy says: "No one ever said simply, do not use it on a city *at all.*"[14] He cites Michael Walzer's post-factum indictment of the attack on Hiroshima, but then says: "Walzer's is a powerful argument, but it runs as forcefully against incendiaries as against nuclear bombs."[15] This, of course, was precisely the logic of the John Ford article in 1944. Ford knew nothing of an atomic capability in U.S. hands, but he did know and say that direct attacks on civilian centers were murderous actions, not justifiable warfare.

The learning curve for policymakers and the American public on the principle of noncombatant immunity has been steep; the principle was not observed in Korea and attracted attention during Vietnam only after 1966. But its centrality in the nuclear deterrence debate of the 1980s, along with the post-Vietnam debate on the ethics of war, brought renewed attention to the principle in policy debates and among the public as a whole. During the Persian Gulf War, it was clear that the description of the allied bombing strategy was cast in terms designed precisely to protect it from a critique based on noncombatant immunity.

It is on this foundation that the policy argument about land mines can be constructed. In contrast to the situation during World War II, there are now precedents in the policy debate on which to build a case against weapons that primarily endanger civilians. That is the principal charge that should be brought against land mines; both the moral power of the principle and its salience in the public arena highlight its centrality to the land mine issue.

Can any other moral perspective be brought to bear upon land mines? The answer is yes, but the argument is both more complex and less definitive than the one based on noncombatant immunity. The "moral traces" left by the presumption against the use of force include the criterion that weapons should not inflict unnecessary suffering upon the human person, whether a combatant or a civilian. This restraint is reflected in both legal and moral policies about warfare. In the twelfth century, an effort was made to ban the crossbow, while the nineteenth century focused its attention on the dum-dum bullet. In both instances, the argument was based not on the weapons' indiscriminateness, but on the suffering they caused even if used with discrimination.

This argument has a primary (but not exclusive) relevance to combatants. In this sense, it is more complex in character and less definitive in its prohibition than the noncombatant case against land mines. Combatants, of course, are not immune from attack, and in the debate leading up to the Persian Gulf War, while many moral arguments of restraint were invoked, no one, to my knowledge, made a case against land mines in the theater of operation. Land mines were deployed in preparation for the expected land warfare in Kuwait. If a case is to be made against land mines used in this way, it will have to rest on an extension of humanitarian concern to combatants. In fact, this theme has been one of the legacies of the Persian Gulf War debate. In a conflict where the public record shows a serious concern for observing noncombatant immunity, the moral arguments in the post–Persian Gulf War period have focused on proportionality standards, applied to both civilians and combatants. The loss of civilian life during and after the war due to the bombing of the infrastructure of Iraqi society raised the most serious proportionality issues—a topic yet unresolved in the political-moral argument. But the large-scale combatant casualties also drew attention; this fact is notable since it has so seldom been an issue in the ethics of war. Precisely because it has not often been invoked, there is little consensus as yet how to weigh proportionality as it applies to combatants. If an argument about land mines were to be made in terms of combatants, it would have to be some combination of the proportionality criterion and humanitarian concerns about the kind of injury inflicted by land mines. This argument would clearly be a secondary one to the noncombatant immunity critique, but in support of a total ban on land mines, a concern for the status of combatants could reinforce the more precise deontological case.

Both of the how criteria, therefore, can be used in the critique of land mines. Both principles function in casuistic fashion to create a case against these devices. This precise argument, aimed at the specific character of the weapon and the way it is used in contemporary conflicts, must be the foundation of the moral argument. It needs to be supplemented, however, by a broader assessment, one that is rooted in the judgment found in *Landmines: A Deadly Legacy*. Having described how land mines are actually used today, with their consequences for the general population of a country, the report concludes that land mines "take on certain features of strategic weapons."[16]

This characterization opens up a different possibility for political-moral analysis—that is, to make an evaluation of land mines that is analogous to the one made of weapons of mass destruction (chemical, biological, and nuclear weapons). The goal is to make a "macro" argument against them, to stigmatize them as a class of weaponry that should be placed beyond the pale of any notion of war as the extension of rational political activity. This kind of macro analysis is less focused on precise aspects of a given use of a weapon than it is designed to delegitimize a particular class of weapons. It creates an enormous burden of proof that any potential user of the weapon would have to overcome in the eyes of the international community.

Using the analogy of weapons of mass destruction, one can distinguish two strategies that flow from the macro analysis of a category of weapons. The first objective would be to build upon moral stigmatization of the weapons to a legal ban on their production, deployment, export, or use. The model here is the 1972 Biological Weapons Convention; as in other areas of international politics, one seeks a moral argument that is then translated into positive international law. The moral and legal foundations provide the basis for the political actions of states.

A second strategy that can build on a moral critique of land mines is the more limited one that has developed incrementally regarding nuclear weapons. In this case, a total ban has never been possible, but a combination of arguments have been used to create a "nuclear taboo," a sturdy barrier against resorting to nuclear weapons even though they remain in the arsenals of states, ready to be used. A taboo has neither the legal force nor the comprehensive scope of a ban, but it clearly has had an effect on the nuclear policy of states. It has built a psychological-political-moral barrier against resorting to nuclear weapons that survived the deep ideological divisions of the Cold War. It must be admitted that creating a taboo for land mines will be more difficult on two counts. On one hand, the danger of the weapon will be evaluated differently from that of nuclear weapons. The specter of escalation to an uncontrolled nuclear exchange always hung over the consideration of using nuclear weapons. Land mines threaten less-catastrophic dangers. On the other hand, the nuclear taboo did not eliminate the functional role of nuclear weapons. They acted as a deterrent even in spite of the taboo. Land mines will not so readily serve a deterrent function if an effective taboo is created regarding their use.

The challenge of land mines should, however, evoke a moral critique, arising from both their character and the way they are used in war today. The resources of the Just War ethic provide both specific principles and a perspective to bring land mines under review and to form the basis for further political-legal action to contain them. The moral argument is a fundamental aspect of effective action to restrain and eliminate the legacy of land mines, but it must be joined with other resources in an effective political strategy.

The Challenge of Land Mines:
A Political-Moral Response

Fashioning an effective strategy to restrain land mines will require returning to the opening observation of this chapter, the fragility of ethics in the world of international politics. The restraints of ethics must be joined with a knowledge of international politics and with lessons learned from arms control theory and practice. An effective strategy must focus on two levels of action: the international system as a whole and the policies of states.

At the systemic level, the effort to restrict land mines has been focused on the 1980 Landmines Protocol, which is annexed to the UN Conventional Weapons Convention. The Protocol addresses the protection of civilians, and its method is to restrict use without trying to ban all use. Forty-one countries are parties to the Protocol, which is designed to apply customary humanitarian law to the problem of land mines. The Human Rights Watch assessment is that after a decade in force, the Protocol must be judged a failure in theory and in practice.[17] The reasons for this harsh judgment are that the Protocol fails to address the effect of land mines after a conflict ends, it is focused almost entirely on interstate conflict, and it did not interpret customary humanitarian law stringently enough in its restrictions on land mines. More generally, because the Protocol seeks only to restrict use, it has had no effect on the development of land mines over the last decade. The Landmines Protocol does not even attempt the kind of ban imposed by the Biological Weapons Convention of 1972, nor does it approximate the more modest restraints of the Nuclear Nonproliferation Treaty. Its goal of systemic restraint is quite limited, and its fabric of restraints is fragile. Effective strategy at the systemic level will require a more ambitious conceptual framework; a much greater number of signatories to a successor protocol; and an enforcement strategy to prohibit production, use, and transfer of land mines. In 1994, there is little movement to provide this kind of comprehensive, rigorous regime, except for a proposed review conference to assess the Protocol. The review conference mechanism is useful, since any ultimate solution to this problem will require systemic restraints, but the short- to mid-term agenda will have to concentrate on the policies of states.

The analysis here will focus on U.S. policy; in this area, as in so many others, the policy of the United States is both significant in itself and a precedent for others in the international system. U.S. policy regarding land mines produces a mixed picture. On the one hand, the United States has signed but not ratified the Landmines Protocol; on the other hand, the United States has undertaken initiatives that move beyond the existing pattern of international restraints on land mines. U.S. policy can be evaluated in two steps: the unilateral initiatives already undertaken constitute an "ethic of restraint"; the broader policy that is still needed points to an "ethic of advocacy."

In terms of the ethic of restraint, the centerpiece of U.S. policy is the

Landmine Moratorium Act of 1992. The act, extended in 1993 for another three years, "imposes a one-year U.S. moratorium on the sale, export or transfer abroad of anti-personnel mines."[18] Sponsored by Senator Leahy, the moratorium imposes tighter restrictions on exports than any international obligation does, and it envisions a U.S. effort "to seek verifiable international agreements to further limit the use, production, possession and deployment of anti-personnel landmines."[19] In other areas in arms control, the major powers, particularly the superpowers, have been behind the curve of international opinion, often being pressured to do more; in this area, by contrast, the U.S. policy is ahead of what international consensus has produced. In Senator Leahy's view, the policy of restraint can be the foundation on which to build efforts to address the three principal weaknesses of the Landmines Protocol: lack of compliance features; minimal restraints on antipersonnel land mines; and lack of international support.[20] This definition of policy objectives, particularly accepting leadership for building international support, moves the design of policy from the ethics of restraint to the ethics of advocacy, but it also opens a new frontier of questions for U.S. policy.

The questions arise from the content of U.S. policy on land mines, .but they point to deeper and wider themes in the post–Cold War international system. They are reflected in the speech Senator Leahy made in the U.S. Senate when he introduced the Landmine Moratorium Extension Act on July 22, 1993. The dominant tone and theme of the speech was the urgent necessity for the United States to play a leadership role in addressing the land mine problem; the central feature of the legislation was a moratorium on export or transfer of these weapons abroad. Included in the speech, however, were these words:

> The landmine moratorium does not affect U.S. manufacturers, or use of landmines by U.S. forces. Nor does it affect exports of anti-tank mines. But I would have introduced the moratorium even if it did, because we have to do more than just talk about this problem. The moratorium has given momentum to a global campaign to put limits on anti-personnel landmines, or to ban them altogether.[21]

The public record leaves no doubt about Senator Leahy's leadership on the land mine question, nor about his final objective, which he expressed in a later article: "Ultimately, our goal should be to ban landmines outright, as we have done with biological weapons."[22] Short of this objective, however, there is a severe tension in U.S. policy. The United States will not sell or share land mines with others but will retain the right to use them. This proposition entails a double problem. First, it is difficult to generate support for the idea that a certain weapon is so destructive or uncontrollable that it should be placed in a special classification, beyond possibility of use, while maintaining the right to use it on an interim basis. This is particularly the case when the key countries to be recruited into the effort argue that land mines are a necessity for them precisely because they do not possess the range of weaponry available to the industrialized powers. Rather than an act of self-restraint and leadership, the moratorium can be interpreted as an effort in the short term to deny to others—on moral and legal grounds—an option the United States continues to maintain.

The second problem with this policy is that it can be related to other arms control issues, particularly nuclear proliferation, to depict an emerging two-tiered world. With the Cold War order dissolved, it is yet unclear how the structure of power will take shape. One aspect of it, however, could be that the model of the Nuclear Nonproliferation Treaty is repeated in a variety of policy areas. It will be increasingly difficult to maintain a structure of power in which one argues for restraint for most of the nations of the world and possession of certain weapons for a few. There is a fragile logic in this case, which can be used for nuclear weapons because of the nature of deterrence. But the argument can hardly be extended in a convincing way. The world of international politics, conceived in terms of power and influence, is inherently unequal because nations of different size and strength compete in the same arena. But seeking to reinforce such inequality through treaty obligations that require voluntary restraint from nations that see their strategic options already restricted is a policy doomed to fail. Current U.S. land mine policy exercises self-restraint in export but not use, while asking others to refrain from possession or use. For the United States to lead as a policy advocate toward a world banning land mines in toto, more restraint will have to be exercised across the board as the price of leadership.

The price should be paid, the role of leadership should be creatively and energetically assumed because the "deadly legacy" of land mines is an affront to a humane order of politics. It should not be allowed to threaten yet another generation of children and civilians.

8

The Use of Mines and the Impact of Technology

PATRICK BLAGDEN

ven though their horrific effects on civilian populations are now
well documented, antipersonnel mines continue to be featured in
the inventories of "responsible" armies, such as those of NATO
and its allies. But even with these armies' claim to act "responsibly" in
their use of mines, one has to ask whether they manage to do so in
every case, or whether in the heat of battle mines are sometimes left
unmarked, unfenced, unrecorded, unmapped, and above all uncleared.
This very likely is the case. At a symposium hosted by the International
Committee of the Red Cross (ICRC), it was agreed (by the army representatives at least) that there was no substitute for antipersonnel
mines, and we have to accept that this is true.

It could well be that the continued stated need for mines derives to
some extent from the continuation of existing doctrine. Minefields,
though a major hazard in war, are rarely if ever featured realistically in
major military exercises in peace. This means that after any war, real-
time experience of the difficulties and constraints of working in a mined
environment soon pass away. Comments on recent wars[1] clearly point
out how antipersonnel minefields have caused many casualties to their
own troops rather than to the enemy; how restrictive such minefields
became if forward units needed to change their positions; and how fear

of minefields caused patrols to default on their objectives, losing their power to control the ground in front of them. Such information should be required reading for anyone involved in the formulation of doctrine for the use of antipersonnel mines, and advice from those with practical experience should be incorporated into that doctrine.

These points are not intended to lead to the unilateral removal from responsible armies of an effective weapon system, but to open up informed discussion as to how antipersonnel mines can best be used, taking into account the lessons learned in the past. From a mine clearance point of view, some types of antipersonnel mines are more acceptable than others. For example the M-18 Claymore fragmentation mine is in military terms highly effective; it is extremely lethal, with a wide damage area and the capacity for both victim and command actuation. It is easy to emplace, easy to remove for later reuse, and, even if left behind, easy to clear because it is surface-laid (though easily hidden) and contains a great deal of metal. If more reliance could be placed on this type of weapon rather than on the small buried plastic blast mines that are so difficult to locate and remove, it would save civilian casualties later, when the fighting had moved on or ended, as well as money and time during the postwar clean-up.

It is surprising that the army units who lay or authorize the laying of such mines receive little or no training in the postconflict effects of antipersonnel mines on the civilian population. In the thirty-four years this author spent in the British Army, the subject was never mentioned, let alone taught as part of the mine warfare syllabus. This could and should be changed, and the effects of uncleared antipersonnel mines should be included in the teaching at the staff colleges and engineer training schools in all responsible armies.

How Technology Can Help to Make Mines Acceptable

Although little or no money has been spent on research into clearing mines, many millions of dollars have been spent making mines more effective, more wounding per unit cost, and more difficult to clear. Some consider that antipersonnel mines can be made more acceptable by fitting them with self-destructive fuze mechanisms. Such a capability has military advantages, although several of the national military delegations at the Red Cross symposium did not want any limit placed on the active life of their self-destruct mines, and many wanted the conventional non-self-destructing types as well. Self-destruct mines have their problems: they will be relatively expensive to produce; they will be unlikely to achieve the reliability needed for mine clearance (99.95 percent or more); and although they will be "fail-safe" (inert when their batteries have run down), the sight of even a failed mine will be enough to stop villagers from returning to their houses or fields. Where self-destruct mechanisms fail, although the number of mine accidents will decrease, areas contaminated by failed self-destruct mines will have to be cleared just as rigorously and expensively as normal minefields. Fear of mines can be as restricting as the mines themselves; in Kuwait, a special team drove fifty miles to remove what turned out to be a fuel tank cap from the entrance to a small farm. The fear of an unidentified minelike object had kept that part of the farm unused for twelve months.

How Technology Can Help Mine Clearance

In 1993, UN-funded programs cleared about 80 thousand mines, a minute fraction of the 2–3 million thought to be laid each year. These figures give an indication of what needs to be achieved in the future in quantitative terms. In real terms, a fiftyfold increase in mine clearance capability may well be necessary just to stabilize the mine situation: such an improvement must be looked for by the year 2000, with the goal of a further doubling by 2005. Even if all wars miraculously ended today, and mine laying stopped immediately, with existing technology, we would still be left with a twenty-year mine clearance program, even at the projected clearance rates for 2005. These targets may sound ambitious, but their achievement is essential if the mine clearance problem is to be solved, and should provide reasonable achievement benchmarks in our search for technological solutions to the mine problem.

We should not forget that many other types of lethal munitions are left behind after wars. Perhaps none are as dangerous as mines, because these devices are specifically fuzed to be victim-actuated, whereas most other munitions need deliberate or inadvertent mishandling before they become dangerous. The term "mine clearance" as used here should be taken to include the removal of unexploded munitions of all kinds.

A technological solution to the mine problem is necessary for two further reasons: cost of clearance, and danger to clearance staff. To achieve a fiftyfold increase in capability using current conventional mine clearance methods would involve training and deploying 170,000–200,000 mine clearers worldwide. Even a locally recruited mine clearer costs $6,000 per year to field, so this strategy implies costs of $1.02–$1.2 billion per year. Obviously, a technological solution giving a fiftyfold increase in capability is going to be expensive, but this level of cost is probably unsupportable. The goal should be a tenfold improvement in cost-effectiveness—that is, a fiftyfold increase in output coupled with not more than a fivefold increase in cost.

Manual mine clearance is dangerous, and accidents happen at a rate of one out of every 1,000–2,000 mines destroyed. A fiftyfold increase in manual mine clearance would probably cause a death and injury toll among these mine clearers of about 2,000 per year, a rate that in the long term may not be supportable. Minefield accidents are difficult to control, because mines are optimized to kill human beings, and human beings are by nature fallible. Only a technological solution can fully remove the hands, feet, and eyes of mine clearers from the vicinity of the mine, or give them adequate protection, and thus reduce the horrific toll of death and injury. Weapons are normally designed not to explode by mistake or misfire at a rate of more than one in 1 million; the benchmark for mine clearer injuries should be the same, or better.

If technology is obviously so important to mine clearance, it is astonishing that so little research into mine clearance technology has actually taken place, and that clearance techniques have advanced so little since 1942. Some part of the reason must lie in the fact that mine accidents get little public notice, possibly because they happen singly, and usually in Third World countries. Another reason for the lack of new technology is the confusion that exists in the minds of many between the military act of minefield breaching, which has attracted many millions of research and development (R&D) dollars, and the civilian act of minefield clearance, which has not. One country with major equipment development expertise that has a mine clearance research program is South Africa, because of the many mines laid within its borders during the internal struggles in Zimbabwe and Mozambique. As a result, it produces what is possibly some of the best mine clearance equipment in the world.

Practical Problems with Mine Clearance

It might help at this point to consider some of the practical aspects of mine clearance. Mine clearance involves detection of mines and their removal. Detection can be divided into general area detection (the finding of minefields and mined areas), and the detection and location of each and every mine in a mined area. Removal can be divided into the defuzing or neutralization of mines so that they can be moved for destruction elsewhere, and the destruction of mines, either by actuating the mine system or by setting off some or all of the explosive filling.

One begins with a general area survey, based on available mine maps; then on word-of-mouth information from the warring factions and local inhabitants; and on information from a limited ground inspection over as wide an area as possible, looking for fenced minefields or other signs of mining activity. Such surveys are currently carried out by small teams of trained staff, covering as much of the country as possible and submitting the results to a central collection agency.

At some point, the individual mined areas have to be located and defined. At present, this is done in two stages: a minefield survey and marking team identify the boundaries of each minefield; then, with great accuracy, they mark and locate its edges with respect to prominent identifiable objects on the ground, such as trees or buildings. This task relies on manual prodding, magnetic detection, and the use of sniffer dogs. In general, fewer than 50 percent of the total mines have to be located, but the edges of the minefield have to be well defined, to prevent unnecessary clearance efforts on uncontaminated ground.

Before each mine can be destroyed, it needs to be located to an accuracy that depends on the method of destruction. Careful prodding with a metal rod or use of a metal detector can locate a mine to within one centimeter. Small blast antipersonnel mines are typically about 4–8 centimeter in diameter, although even smaller versions exist. However, the process takes time, as it requires great delicacy.

The last phase of mine clearance is destruction of the mine. This can be done in many ways, but actuation either by pressure or by sympathetic detonation is the preferred method, because it totally destroys the target mine, and when properly done is completely safe. However, this method has certain disadvantages, as described later in this chapter.

Existing Mechanisms and Technologies for Mine Clearance

Many mechanisms have been explored for destroying mines, but mostly in the context of minefield breaching. Almost all have followed one of three main routes: neutralization, most likely leaving the mine to rot in place; removal, with destruction at a later stage; actuation, by pressure, heat, or other methods. So far, none of these has managed more than about 80 percent clearance in actual minefields. Plows merely move the mine from one place to another, where it still has to be located and destroyed by hand; the flails so far used are expensive (from $300,000 to $1.4 million), weak, unreliable, and inefficient; experiments with sand sifters, crimpers, burning, bullet impact, and air or water blast have all failed. Rollers were used with limited success in flat areas against antipersonnel mines in Kuwait; Soviet tank-mounted rollers were used in Angola, but abandoned. The explosive hoses and fuel-air pressure charges used in minefield breaching are about 100–1,000 times as expensive as hand clearance, and unreliable in their effects.

Certain mechanical clearance methods have shown some success. Where limited areas are known to be mined, mines can be dug out with rakes mounted on armored excavators. This method has been successful in South Africa and Kuwait, but only where the approximate mine locations were known. The same machinery can be used for "pressing" antipersonnel mines to make them explode, a method of destruction that is appropriate for mines that old age or environmental extremes have rendered unsafe and unstable. The combination of digging and pressing can be very effective. This is much safer than hand clearance and is relatively inexpensive, but for large areas has to be limited to surface-laid minefields. Efforts were made to press the bigger antitank mines, but no materials were available to make a pressing head that would tolerate the repeated physical and thermal shock of a large explosion. After many experiments, most organizations working in mine clearance have been forced to return to the slow process of destroying mines individually by sympathetic detonation.

Limitations on the Use of Technology

Any new technologies proposed for mine clearance are likely to face a number of problems. The first problem is terrain. Most designers of mine clearance equipment seem to imagine that minefields are flat, open, and sandy. This is true in parts of the Middle East and southern Africa, but untrue in much of central Africa, the Far East, Europe, and Latin America. Mines are laid wherever soldiers can fight—on the sides of mountains, in rice paddies, in banana and tea plantations, on bare stony hills, in bogs, on riverbanks, in jungles, or in forests. This may prevent the use of aerial or vehicle-mounted equipment and require, instead, reliance on hand-held equipment, with all its limitations in power and weight.

The next problem is climate. Most mechanical mine clearance

equipment is not designed to work in wet ground, bog, marsh, or peat, or among closely growing trees or bushes. Much equipment, being metal and not air-conditioned, gets very hot in desert countries, and operations in extreme heat or cold can place great stress on mine clearers, who are already under great physical and mental pressure because of the dangers of the job. Ideally, equipment must be designed for the climate in which it to be used, to reduce operator stress. In addition, the climatic conditions reduce the effectiveness of some technologies. Infrared detection systems are less effective when the daily temperature changes are very slight; wet ground affects the responses of radar and neutron backscatter; heavy rain and low cloud cover affect radar and optical surveillance.

Mine clearance also has to be tailored as far as possible to the capability level of the local population. The UN concept of mine clearance is to generate within the mine-contaminated country the capacity for indigenous mine clearance. This involves instructing local people, mostly soldiers or ex-soldiers, in the techniques and equipment used in mine clearance. Thus, the techniques and equipment have to be tuned to the educational and cultural status of the people. This need not diminish their capabilities as mine clearers; even when working with illiterate ex-soldiers, once the local mine clearers understand the hazards facing them and the techniques to be used, they are often reliable, hardworking, and stoical. It does, however, place limitations on the use of high-technology equipment, unless this equipment is specifically developed to be operated and supported by unsophisticated users. This is not just philanthropy: as mentioned earlier, it costs about $6,000 per year to field a trained local mine clearer; it can cost up to $180,000 per year for a trained expatriate.

The Goals of New Technologies

What should these new technologies achieve, in terms of performance, safety, and cost, in the fields of general and minefield survey, mine location, and mine destruction? General survey is currently done by teams of trained operators; typically, an organization of six to ten teams will survey 600,000 square kilometers in three months at a cost of about $1.5 million. To replace them, we would probably need an aerial or satellite sensor system, capable of detecting at least 25 percent of the mines, and locating them to an accuracy of more than fifty meters. It would need to be able to detect plastic and shallow buried mines with a detection resolution of four centimeters. The sensor systems would still have to cope with hilly and vegetated terrain, and poor weather conditions. Airborne survey would be safer than ground, although no casualties have been reported from general survey teams to date. No method would be acceptable that increases the hazard to the operators. A fifty-fold increase in speed might not be so important, especially if survey costs could be contained to their present level of 400,000 square kilometers per $1 million.

Minefield survey is also done by teams of trained operators. The costs are about $45,000 per square kilometer, and teams can typically survey 1,300 square meters per day. Detection is currently done by eye, assisted by mine detectors and sniffer dogs (who are by far the best mobile biosensors available today).

All the current methods for locating individual mines have their drawbacks. Prodding is slow, confusing, and dangerous, especially when the mines are laid in hard-packed or stony soils, or when they are fitted with antidisturbance fuzes. Metal detection works well with metal-cased mines, but plastic has increasingly replaced metal in modern mines, and soon mines will not be detectable by their metallic content. Dogs can detect the vapor coming from the explosive filling of mines, but they are temperamental, require long training, and tire quickly. Individual location takes time, given the delicacy of the task. The actual detection of a mine may take as little as a half-minute, but digging down to the mine to expose it for identification and destruction may take three to fifteen minutes. It must also be remembered that every empty tin can or piece of shrapnel has to be investigated with the same care, and there may be as many as fifteen false alarms for every mine. Typically, a team of thirty men can cover 2,330 square meters in one day, at a cost of $500.

To improve the individual location of mines, we need a highly accurate sensor system, probably vehicle-mounted, that can locate 99.95 percent of all mines, plastic or metal, to an accuracy of one centimeter or less. Such devices would enable mine clearers to achieve an output fifty times greater than a hand clearance team, that is, 120,000 square meters per day or a 3-meter strip 40 kilometers long.

The last phase of mine clearance is destruction by causing the target mine to explode by sympathetic detonation. The same method and equipment can also be used for destroying many other forms of explosive ordnance. However, individual destruction by current methods is expensive in explosive and time. The process requires about 125 grams of plastic explosive, costing about $2–$3, and fifteen minutes for each mine, and the site has to be cleared of workers when the destruction is in progress. A small shaped charge fired into the body of the mine is far more likely to set it off, and has the advantage that it can be fired into the mine through earth cover or from a small standoff distance, so the chances of touching the target mine or actuating a disturbance fuze are greatly reduced. Shaped charges also use less explosive than bulk explosive charges.

Any technologically improved mine destruction equipment should be integrated with mine location equipment. A dispenser for small shaped charges, attached to the mine clearance vehicle, would safely destroy any mines, provided that the vehicle and its sensors were protected against mine blast, and that its mine-locating and mine-destroying components were coordinated to within one centimeter.

Both antitank and antipersonnel mines were destroyed in Kuwait using a relatively lightly armored, driver-operated, commercial excavator costing around $200,000. This does not hold up as an ideal system, but is one that the author has used with success, and is mentioned only to indicate that achieving the technological cost and performance goals may not be impossible. Safety goals will be achieved, because the driver will be in a cab, above ground level, and protected against blast and noise, as they were in Kuwait. The difficult goal to achieve will be the accuracy of the sensors.

Although a high proportion of minefields can be accessed by a highly mobile tracked vehicle such as a bulldozer or an excavator, some will remain that can be reached only by foot. For that reason, efforts must continue to develop mine detection, location, and destruction equipment that is light, portable, safe to use, and economical on power, so that hand mine clearance can continue, especially in isolated and inaccessible areas.

Use of Robotics

Many people commend the use of robots in minefields, but the practical difficulties are many, and the advantages are few. Robotic vehicles are expensive to operate and maintain, especially for Third World staff. Remote vision, even with the best cameras available, cannot match the accuracy and discrimination of human sight, making accurate remote operation very difficult. Above all, robots are not necessarily safer for their operators than are properly mine-protected vehicles; indeed, recovering an injured and immobile robotic vehicle could be more hazardous to the recovery crew than a manned vehicle. Robot designs should be considered for development only if their operating capabilities are shown to be significantly, more cost-effective than those of manned vehicles.

Use of Military Equipment and Technologies

It is often suggested that the answer to the lack of mine clearance technologies is to make greater use of military expertise and resources. The problem is that fundamental differences distinguish the military act of minefield breaching from the civilian/humanitarian act of minefield clearance. Minefield breaching involves punching a hole through a minefield, usually by the quickest possible means, clearing at least 80 percent of the mines, often pushing the mines to one side without detonating them. Cost is rarely a consideration in minefield breaching, and much equipment is tank-mounted or involves expensive explosive devices.

Minefield clearance involves precisely locating all sides of the minefield, and carefully removing over 99.95 percent of the mines as cost-effectively as possible. Although some equipment, especially hand-held mine detection equipment, can be used for both, mechanical breaching equipment can rarely be adapted for clearance use.

Environmental Effects

Mine clearers, like those who laid the mines in the first place, have so far not been able to show much concern for the environment, possibly because they consider that the environmental improvement caused by removing lethal explosive mechanisms from the ground has always outweighed the possible pollution to the earth or atmosphere caused by the detonation of a quantity of explosive. No instance has ever been reported in Afghanistan or Cambodia of reduction in fertility of fields cleared of mines; indeed, the enforced period of lying fallow may have rendered them more productive rather than less. Nevertheless, a study needs to be made of the toxic effects of mine destruction, but probably at a priority lower than that assigned to finding a successful method of mine clearance.

What to Do Next

The immediate need is for a review of the technologies currently avail-able. There is also need for a database, to hold information on what and where the main mine clearance problems are, what mine systems are be-ing used, what clearance techniques are being employed to remove them, and the cost of removal. The United Nations is setting up a suitable mines database, and preparations are in hand for collaboration with the U.S. Department of Defense. The development of a database, though necessary, serves merely to clarify the problem, and not to solve it. What needs to be clearly defined is the mechanism by which these new tech-nologies will be researched and developed, and then fielded for use by mine clearance staffs worldwide. Above all, we need to establish a mech-anism by which new technology R&D will be monitored, coordinated, and funded.

Research on technologies such as infrared detectors, ground pene-trating radar, neutron backscatter detectors, and other potential systems is taking place in many areas—in academe, in private and government R&D laboratories in many countries, and in industry. There is overlap, duplication, competition, and potential waste; above all, there is no mechanism for drawing together the researchers, even within one coun-try, to achieve collaboration. The United Nations, in conjunction with the United Nations University, is funding a literature survey into the state of available technologies, but in many cases, the information will be incomplete because of national security or commercial confidential-ity. This is not good enough. If mine clearance technology is to be addressed sensibly, a technology review program needs to be formu-lated, funded, and started by the end of 1994 (the end of the General Assembly season). This program needs to establish achievable goals, and state how and in what time frame they are to be reached. Unfortu-nately, no mechanism exists for launching or funding such a program and until one does, the technology review is unlikely to take place.

The technology review program should be followed by a period of intensive R&D along a strictly limited number of technological avenues, identified as those most likely to produce fieldable equipment by the end of the year 2000, in accordance with a phased program with identi-fied goals, milestones, times, and costs. To get the best results from the scattered resources available, this needs to be centrally coordinated, possibly in the United Nations, if the resources for such a coordinating agency can be funded and staffed. Again, mechanisms are lacking for setting up either the coordination or the funding to promote the R&D.

It is unlikely that mine clearance can derive all the technologies it needs from military research, or that military R&D agencies would be the best focus for a mine clearance program. They have their own minefield breaching research programs; it might not be fully productive to divert money from these military programs into a humanitarian clearance research program, especially if both sets of programs were to be run simultaneously in the same R&D establishment, using the same staff. Most NATO armies cannot provide experienced feedback to their own R&D staff, because their soldiers are not permitted to enter live minefields. Fresh thought is urgently needed, by engineers and scientists who are not involved with other programs, and who can be supported by the real experience of practical mine clearers.

Conclusion

The mine clearance problem is grave, and getting rapidly worse, and to arrest the deterioration, we need to make a quantum jump in our capability to locate and remove land mines swiftly and cheaply. In practical terms this cannot be achieved by making a commensurate jump in the numbers of mine clearers; for reasons of economy, practicability, and safety, improved technologies must be found. We are learning more about these technologies and their potential for mine clearance. Now a concerted effort is needed to establish mechanisms for technology development and funding so that we may put these technologies to work as soon as possible.

9

Technology Beyond the Probe

THOMAS R. EVANS

There was a time when the land mine was directed almost exclusively against military fortifications and forces. The mine exploded by Union forces during the siege of Petersburg in the American Civil War was typical of the uses conceived for such weapons. Beginning in World War I, mines became accepted as area denial weapons. As a result, their effects became less confined to the military forces and spread into the civilian population that surrounded the conflict. In recent years, the mine has become a widely used tool in conflicts where political considerations lead to attempts to control or terrorize the civilian population as a way to conquer established governments and their military forces.

This last use of mines has dramatically changed the scale of the demining problem. Where once only a few mines would be encountered in a limited area, now 85–100 million mines are estimated to be in place worldwide.[1] Sadly, this situation is not stable but continues to deteriorate. In the former Yugoslavia alone, the number of mines deployed grows at about fifty thousand per week. The density and distribution of this enormous mine population results in the denial of civilian use of the land of several countries. In Cambodia, for example, it is estimated that

4–7 million mines render almost half of the country unsafe for use by the civilian population.

Clearing mines in the numbers now deployed imposes a crushing burden in many Third World countries. According to one estimate, clearing the mines now in place in Cambodia would require ten times the country's annual gross national product. With the techniques now available, the cost to find and render safe each mine is between $300 and $1,000. Thus, clearing the 85 million mines deployed worldwide would require $30–$85 billion. The time required for the process (estimated in terms of decades in many areas) would likely result in lost economic opportunity and human injury costs of equivalent magnitude.

The substantial advantage now held by those who implant mines results from major capital investments in mining made worldwide over recent years. The mine has become the weapon of choice in many circumstances. As a result, mines have been mass-produced, materials used in manufacture have been improved to decrease cost, and extensive engineering has been dedicated to systematically reducing the detectability and vulnerability of emplaced mines. Further, mine delivery and emplacement have been automated.

No commensurate capital investment has been made in the clearing process because military sources have expressed no substantial demand for countermine technology. As a result, the classic approach of probing for mines remains the most reliable method of locating mines for removal in areas where explosive clearing is not acceptable. The best response to the mass-produced mine is, therefore, a craft approach, in which highly skilled individuals called sappers practice an art rather than a science. Clearing remains a dangerous, manpower-intensive process that can provide only slow search and clearance. While modern mining systems can deploy thousands of mines over thousands of square meters in an hour, the sapper, searching carefully, can clear only about 50–70 square meters in a day.

Military forces throughout the world are continually improving countermine capability for selected military applications. Until recently, this work was heavily devoted to penetrating established minefields by subjecting limited areas to clearing by explosive cutting techniques, rapid overpressure events, armored bulldozing, and sapper teams. Speed of penetration was the primary goal, and 80–90 percent clearing success was acceptable. Modern forces saw the clearing of anti-armor devices as the primary task. If these devices were substantially negated, the effects of antipersonnel devices would be minimal on troops transported through the field in armored vehicles. Mines outside the breach area were thought to be removable later and at a slower pace.

Since the mid-1980s, this picture of the mine problem as a purely military matter has been overwhelmed by events. The low cost of mines and automated dispersal methods developed and proven by the United States and the Soviet Union have resulted in wide distribution that pervades the battlefield and the civil space that surrounds it. Investments in demining have been insufficient to reverse the imbalance between mining and demining capabilities in this new regime.

Recent military demining efforts have, however, established the technical ground upon which a new effort to improve civil demining can begin. Most nations' military forces are equipped with blast breaching machinery consisting of linear charges, fuel-air explosives, and packaged countermine charges that are quick and effective. Mechanical sweeping devices such as plows, flails, and rollers mounted on armored vehicles, both heavy and light, have been in use for many years and continue to be refined and developed. The classic prodding and sapper search techniques have been upgraded by improved hand-held mine detectors and armored truck–mounted detection systems that clear some portions of the field and reduce the threat to the individual sapper beginning the search.

Interest in capability to respond to rapidly laid mines has been increasing. The U.S. Army is now involved in the development and fielding of the Airborne Standoff Mine Detection System (ASTAMIDS), which searches for area minefields that have been deployed by aircraft or artillery fire. Vehicle-mounted mine detectors, now in use to clear roads, have been substantially improved, and efforts continue to improve hand-held detectors for use in the final clearance by the man on the ground. Experiments have been conducted in the United States and Europe to locate buried mines by neutron bombardment of the weapons in place, to electromagnetically stimulate the weapon fuzing to explode mines remotely, to use radar surface scanners for detecting freshly dug holes and subsurface penetrating radars for underground imaging of mines, and to locate mines by biosensing of the chemicals they emit. These efforts have been relatively constrained and have not been integrated in a structured process to solve the mass mine problem. As one knowledgeable worker in the field has observed, none of these technologies supplies a "silver bullet" to counter the modern mine problem.

What must now be done is to refocus efforts to develop demining techniques that facilitate clearing large areas with success rates approaching 99 percent and with minimum damage to the local environment. If the civil demining problem is to be solved, it will be necessary to establish two parallel programs focused on improving demining capability for the world. In the first, a relatively short-term program, the focus would be on transferring the maximum demining capability from the military to the civilian sector. In the second, a long-term program, the goal would be to apply the widest possible range of recent technological advances to provide an integrated solution to the civilian demining problem.

The Short Term

Over the years, the military has invested a substantial amount of money in demining approaches that failed to completely satisfy its requirements but that could be, over the short term, very useful in ameliorating the civilian problem. Therefore, in a short-term program, technology would be selected that is, to the extent possible, simple, transferable, and applicable to increasing the rate of return of labor efforts in demining. The program depends on an effective technology transfer from the military to the civilian sector, involving consideration not only of the degree of technological sophistication, but also of the complexities and the techniques of retraining a local work force to employ the new technologies. While this program will offer some benefit to the immediate situation in countries that have available a large low-cost work force, it will not deal with the entire problem. Neither will it offer an approach to the greater problem of land mine clearance worldwide, since the large number of widely dispersed mines would require an unacceptable amount of time for clearance with the short-term technologies.

In particular, the following military techniques recommend themselves to the short-term activity.

The Mine/Countermine Information System (MCIS), developed and maintained by the U.S. Army, can be used to train the civilian demining work force about mines that may be encountered. MCIS is a flexible and relational database containing information on mines, fuzes, countermine equipment, and mine emplacement equipment, as well as relevant bibliographic references. The database contains unclassified information on mine- and countermine-related equipment on a worldwide basis. It contains data on approximately 750 mines, 610 fuzes and detonators, 60 pieces of mine emplacement equipment, 250 pieces of countermine equipment, and 11 pieces of protective equipment.

MCIS, as presently operated, can be used to accomplish the following:

- Provide immediate access to a central repository for the most accurate and up-to-date mine information.
- Provide customized reports on land mines, tailored to the specific threat expected, so preparations for clearing may be more efficient.
- Provide a means for identifying unfamiliar devices.

The army has also made significant investments in optical reconnaissance systems that can be mounted on airborne platforms for detecting mine fields. These systems can be integrated with a global positioning system (GPS) to geographically locate mined areas. In the short term, video cameras and reconnaissance photographic equipment that uses film sensitive to both ultraviolet and visible light are commercially available. This equipment, along with a GPS to mark the mine field locations, can be mounted on a commercially available aircraft. The optical systems offer sufficient resolution at low altitudes to identify even small antipersonnel surface-laid mines. The initial system will, of course, have some limitations. It must have optical access to the mines for detection, it detects only clues to buried mines (for example, freshly dug holes), and it will not precisely locate each mine. In addition, some areas requiring demining may not be suitable for low-altitude flying. Experience suggests, however, that an initial civil capability could be obtained.

To refine the output of the airborne system, there will be a continuing need for vehicle-mounted and hand-held detectors. A vehicle-mounted system has several advantages over hand-held detectors. First, the detected path width and rate of advance are greater. For two people operating hand-held mine detectors side by side, the rate of advance for a path of detection 8–10 feet wide is one-tenth to one-fifth of a mile per hour. A comparable path width for a vehicular detector could be accomplished at one-half to one mile per hour, a 250–500 percent improvement.

Vehicular systems also have much less severe volume and weight restrictions. Thus, a single platform may use more sensors, additional displays, and greater processing power, all of which lead to improved system performance. A vehicular system affords an additional margin of safety for equipment operators because undetected mines may occasionally be detonated. The chance of injury to the operator is considerably less with a vehicular system and could become vanishingly small with the use of a remotely controlled vehicle—a technology that exists.

An electrically powered, remotely controlled "all-terrain" vehicle is available as a demonstration unit. This includes a visual display, communications, and control station. Such a system was tested with a sensor suite consisting of a metal detector and a neutron moderation detector in a limited field test in December 1993. Other remote-control packages also exist for application to a near-term civilian demining demonstration system.

The additional weight and volume available in a lightly armored vehicle would allow the use of any of several detection systems that have shown promise in early testing but have not been taken to full military standards. The following mine detection sensors are included in this category.

LOW-FREQUENCY METAL DETECTORS

Numerous low-frequency metal detectors are available off the shelf, including the PSS-12, which is a U.S. Army–fielded hand-held metallic mine detector. This unit is the Schiebel standard mine detector model AN 19/2, the standard hand-held metallic mine detector used by the military in at least ten countries. It has a proven probability of detection of greater than 92 percent for standard military metallic mines and mines with low metallic content. However, in operational environments in which metallic clutter is present, the AN 19/2 is not recommended for use in detecting mines with ultralow metallic content.

PASSIVE INFRARED AND ULTRAVIOLET

These technologies are highly effective in mine detection in many environments. Passive infrared (IR) is effective in detecting surface mines and the distinctive thermal signature of buried mines. Off-the-shelf IR imagers have demonstrated effectiveness in detecting mines with standoff distances of up to fifty feet. The performance of these detectors decreases with increasing vegetation that reduces optical access and in areas with high traffic. In addition, they are less effective when the land mine and surrounding soil are at the same temperature, as occurs for about two hours each night, when the mine and surrounding soils are cooling at different rates.

Existing ultraviolet (UV) detectors offer advantages of increased target contrast for surface mines as compared with visible and IR detectors. In addition, UV detectors can enhance the performance of thermal viewers during the thermal crossover period.

Thermal imagers and UV cameras are commercially available from a number of sources. Some mine detection software also exists for near-term use.

GROUND PENETRATING RADAR

Ground penetrating radar (GPR) radiates energy that penetrates materials that do not conduct electrically, but is effectively reflected by highly conducting materials. Several GPRs are available for application to mine detection. Although a number of these devices were developed for other ground-probing applications, some have been developed or modified specifically for mine detection. These GPRs typically operate in the frequency range of one-half to four billion cycles per second because of the trade-off between signal attenuation in the earth (which becomes worse with increasing frequency) and resolution (which improves with increasing frequency). The use of GPRs is constrained to areas of dry soils or sand, where the electrical conductivity of the medium is low. Candidate GPRs for the short term include a continuous wave radar and at least two impulse radars. Specific mine detection software is available for these GPRs.

NEUTRON MODERATION

Because the explosives contained in mines have a higher concentration of hydrogen than do typical soils, techniques that detect hydrogen have been used in mine detectors for dry soils. A system using a small neutron source has been subjected to limited field tests. The results indicated a probability of detection of 0.95 to 1.0 in very dry soils; the performance degrades significantly as the soil moisture rises above 5 percent by weight. Thus, this technique should be considered very effective for dry soils but not applicable to wet soils.

TECHNOLOGIES ON THE HORIZON

The U.S. Army has begun examining several new detection technologies that could be available in a somewhat longer time frame. These include photon backscatter, forward-looking radar, and forward-looking infrared.

The photon backscatter approach uses a pencil-thin beam of X rays projected into the soil. These X rays penetrate the surface, are backscattered from objects below the surface, and are collected by panels of detectors located on either side of the beam. The detected X rays are used to form high-resolution images of buried objects. As the vehicle moves forward, the X ray beam is scanned along its width, allowing for full width detection in front of the vehicle. Laboratory tests of this technique have demonstrated that high-resolution images of buried mines are achievable for a number of soils and burial depths. An X ray source suitable for integration on a field-tested system is being fabricated.

Conventional wisdom has held that forward-looking radar is not a promising approach for mine detection. Recent laboratory results, however, indicate considerable promise for this technique. Field tests scheduled for late 1994 should verify these results, in which case this technique could comfortably fit into the demining scenario in seven to ten years.

Ongoing work in the area of forward-looking IR, especially algorithm and signal processing developments that enable the signal of interest to be separated from noise inherent in the measured signal, is expected to enhance the performance of these systems by increasing standoff detection and extending operation to environments not achievable with the short-term system.

The Longer Term

If significant improvements are to be made that will redress the imbalance in the mining-demining contest, a major shift in philosophy must occur. Focus must be shifted away from efforts aimed at improving the capability of single sensors to find single mines or increasing the power of brute-force clearing machines, and toward efforts aimed at producing efficient clearance of ensembles of mines at reduced cost. The new philosophy must recognize that land mines today are a carefully engineered weapon system that can be effectively countered only by applying modern system engineering techniques to the development and production of a countermine capability at affordable cost.

Owing to technological advances in many areas, the time is ripe for such a shift. For example, the ability to accurately determine the position of a sensor at the time of detection of a mine has dramatically improved as a result of worldwide availability of signals from the GPS and improved inertial navigating systems. Similarly, the successful development of advanced signal processing techniques utilizing computers now allows the use of sensors at increased sensitivity levels where previously, the occurrence of noise (false signals) would have masked any useful data. These two advances alone offer hope that accurate maps of a mined area can be produced that provide high confidence indications of not only the location of mines, but also safe unmined areas in the field.

The creation of an accurate map giving location and classification of mines throughout the mined area will allow the systematic development of a strategy for area clearance that can consider personnel risk, cost of clearance, reduction of collateral damage, and the effectiveness of environmental remediation activities made necessary by the clearing process. Development of such a strategy will benefit significantly from the advances in computer process control that have occurred in numerous industries.

The possible cost benefits of developing such a strategy must not be overlooked. When substantial areas of the mined field are determined to be clear, the effort previously required to examine them can be redirected or saved. Such savings can be either realized in decreased clearing cost or, as necessary, reallocated to reduce risk or environmental damage during clearing. Shaped charges might, for example, become an economically acceptable tool for in situ mine disposal if the present labor-intensive search and clearing process could be simplified. Implementing this new philosophy, and grasping the economic benefits it offers, requires a systematic approach that exploits the technology now available.

The industrial powers must undertake a program to improve the world's long-term ability for civil demining. This program would focus on three critical aspects of the problem. It would develop new mechanisms for the search process, concentrate research to improve safe mine removal, and devise ecological remediation techniques to restore areas damaged by mine extraction. A new set of goals would need to be addressed in each of these areas.

For the search problem, the goals of the program should be to do the following:

• Increase search rates 100- to 1,000-fold. Mapping of 150–200 acres per man-day should be a long-term goal.
• Increase the probability of automated mine detection to 95 percent in the near term, and to 99 percent in the long term.
• Decrease the occurrence of false alarms to 0.01 per square meter surveyed in the near term, and to 0.001 per square meter surveyed in the long term.
• Improve the ability to classify emplaced mines by type to facilitate planning of mine extraction.
• Decrease human exposure in the search process.

As for improving the safety of mine removal, the program should seek to do the following:

- Develop techniques that "dud" emplaced weapons.
- Provide devices that confine explosive events.
- Minimize the need for human actions at the point of extraction.

In the area of ecological remediation, the program should do the following:

- Develop accurate estimates of the environmental impact of alternative clearing strategies.
- Devise economical techniques to minimize hazardous by-products of destroyed mines.
- Improve the mechanical capability to treat damaged soils in situ.

With these goals in mind, it is possible to offer a broad outline of research approaches in each area.

MINE SEARCH AND MAPPING

In numerous applications, for both civilian and military purposes, the use of improved mathematical correlation techniques with multispectral sensor data has significantly improved mapping capability. Experiments have shown that applying advanced signal processing and computing techniques to the data produced by multiple sensors can result in major improvements in map accuracy while attaining substantial savings in time and cost. The lessons of this approach indicate it would be prudent to undertake the following practical, and feasible, steps:

1) Test existing mine-sensing devices against known mines in place in a range of soils, terrains, and covers. Develop a library of responses by each sensor to the mine stimuli in terms of detection and false alarm probability. Focus on measurements made at maximum instrument sensitivity.
2) Use modern computer simulation to evaluate the utility of combinations of sensors against each mine and site combination. The output of the simulation should indicate the probability of true readings and false alarm levels of various sensor combinations, the search rate of each multisensor package; and the capability of each multisensor package to provide classification of emplaced mines.
3) Develop computer processes to integrate multisensor data from the selected multisensor packages. Navigation and mapping processes should be coupled to the sensor package output.

4) Fabricate prototype multisensor packages and operate them in field conditions against known mine deployments. If simulation results are replicated, move to limited production of operational sensor packages.
5) Develop remotely operated systems. Install multisensor packages on unmanned aircraft, air cushion vehicles, and small ground crawlers as appropriate. Apply computer control to optimize area search coverage and speed.

At this point, the developed system should be tested. A trial in a mined area should be conducted, and a map of observed mines prepared. Then the area should be searched by classic sapper methods. On the basis of the truth established by prodding techniques, the utility of the system can be established. If the agreement between truth and system experiment results is good, the proven field systems should undergo a manufacturing engineering design review to ensure greatest reproducibility and lowest unit cost.

A feasible way to use this type of system is to have it operate at maximum sensitivity with a minimum of filtering and signal processing, so that false signals are included in the detection process. Thus, on a first pass over an area with one or more sensors operating on the platform, nothing is missed. The next step involves "separating the wheat from the chaff." Here, as multiple passes are made along different paths, the amount of filtering and signal processing of noise associated with the data taken by the sensors increases. The different paths result in signals at specific locations that coincide with signals taken from previous passes. Such coincidences increase the probability of detection of an actual mine and enable the system to filter out the false signals. In addition, increased filtering of noise enables the detection algorithms to reduce the false alarm rate to almost zero.

There is good reason to expect that the program outlined above will succeed. The basic approach has had considerable success in locating embedded munitions in military weapons impact areas. As an example, the Arete Engineering Technologies Corporation of Arlington, Virginia, offers the GeoDAPS mapping system that will scan an impact area at the rate of 8–10 acres per day and produce a map of weapons below the surface with an accuracy of location on the earth surface better than one meter and of depth better than one-tenth of a meter. The data presented classify observed targets as small, medium, or large, and can be interpreted to yield dimensional estimates as needed. Field tests indicate the probability of detection of buried twenty-millimeter rounds to be about 95 percent. This capability has been achieved by integrating the output of two sensors and coupling the results with positional data derived from commercial GPS receivers. The sensor ensemble is carried through the area by an operator, and the derived data transmitted to a recording van for processing. The rate of search is limited by the speed of movement of the human operator and the integrating time required by the GPS receiver.

In the future, a significant increase in search rate could be obtained for such systems by incorporating an inertial navigating system, similar to those used in commercial aircraft, to produce accurate track descriptions between occasional GPS fixes. This would allow movement of the sensor set at speeds of 3–10 meters per second and would make it practical to use a remotely piloted vehicle, such as a small air cushion device, to map areas of 50–100 acres per day.

MINE DISPOSAL

An effective capability to map mine location would allow focused effort on the highly dangerous task of rendering mines safe. In the near term, efforts should be concentrated on developing improved countermine charges and on blast-confining shields to be used by the man in the field.

In the area of countermine charges, two avenues should be followed. First, the capability of automated production now supporting the mining process should be tapped to produce shaped countermine charges in large numbers. With care, the cost of the countermine charge might be reduced to levels near those of present mass-produced mines.

Second, once mass-produced counter charges are available, steps should be undertaken to maintain their usefulness if new mines employing insensitive explosives are fielded. Tailored biological agents that attack explosives should be exploited in a combined system that uses the shaped charge to break the mine case in the ground, for entry by the biological agent.

In the longer term, particularly as mines with microchip-controlled antidisturbance features become widespread, the focus must be on removing the man from the mine site. This, too, requires that two avenues be pursued. Remotely operated machines should be developed that will enter the mined area, seek out the mapped mine, and either envelop it in a blast-confining structure or excavate the entire weapon in situ for transfer to a "safe" detonation area. Meanwhile, a remotely operated vehicle should be developed that can enter a mined area, proceed to a mapped mine location, and irradiate the mine in situ with focused beams of subatomic particles or microwave radiation to disable the fuze, cook the explosives in a low-order burnoff, or otherwise render the explosives inert. Experiments in the United States and Europe indicate that neutron bombardment and microwave radiation may be effective in this effort.

Quite remarkably, particle beams have been used at Massachusetts General Hospital to treat pituitary tumors that are difficult to remove by conventional surgical techniques. Here, a subatomic beam of particles is precisely aimed at the small tumors on the pituitary gland. The velocity, and hence the energy, of the particles is adjusted so that practically all the energy is deposited into the tumors, thereby destroying them while the rest of the gland is protected. In much the same way, the energy of a particle beam might be tuned so that it penetrated the soil and deposited most of its energy in the conventional explosive inside a mine to disable it.

DAMAGE REMEDIATION

The availability of accurate maps of mines in the local terrain opens the possibility of obtaining an integrated approach to the clearing process that considers environmental effects. With knowledge of the location and type of mines in a clearing area, computerized environmental assessments can be made to evaluate the impact of alternative clearing schemes. This will become critical if future demining efforts become more dependent on explosive or low-order burning of the charges in emplaced mines. Such actions will increase the impact on fragile environmental areas and will require substantial improvement in remediation capability.

The United States and other Western nations are beginning to develop useful remediation techniques in response to heightened environmental concerns. In the United States, the Department of Defense is paying particular attention to remediation of artillery impact areas and ordnance test sites. Testing is under way on new technologies that reduce the damage to soil and water at the point of explosive detonation. Substantial progress has been made in developing bioremediation techniques, which are particularly tailored to biological organisms' breakdown of explosion by-products in place. The U.S. Navy Civil Engineer Laboratory, in Port Hueneme, California, has demonstrated the effectiveness of this approach in several field sites. A review of these technologies should take place, with the goal of identifying promising candidates for technology transfer to developing nations.

Moving Beyond the Probe

Patrick Blagden, the UN mining expert, has rightly observed that today, the most effective method of mine clearing is a skilled sapper equipped with a probe. If that appraisal is to be changed in the future, the technological capabilities of the developed countries must be put to the task of providing affordable improvements.

In the near term, modest investments in the transfer of low-technology systems developed by military forces can produce high return in the Third World. With proper training, and access to an extensive labor pool in the countries to be demined, significant increases in clearing rates might be obtained. The investment of a few tens of millions of dollars could have major results in this area.

In the longer term, much more substantial investment will be required to significantly enhance demining capability in the face of ongoing improvements in mines. It would not be unreasonable to expect that expenditures of hundreds of millions of dollars will be required to realize a solution to the mine problem. This cost, while high, must be seen against the $80-billion problem now facing the world. Failure to act will involve costs that transcend monetary measures: the loss of lives, homelands, and hope.

10

The Medical Lessons of Land Mine Injuries

CHRIS GIANNOU, M.D., AND
H. JACK GEIGER, M.D.

The central medical lesson of land mine injuries is an old one, reflected in the long history of epidemics afflicting large and impoverished populations: Medical responses that focus on individual treatment, trauma management, or rehabilitation, though essential for the individual, are insufficient to address root causes and thus to contain or end an epidemic.

The disciplines involved in attempting first to limit and then to end the worldwide epidemic of land mine injuries focus fundamentally on military, political, legal, ethical, human rights and humanitarian, economic, and technical issues. To these must be added the approaches and disciplines of public health.

Rationale for the Public Health Approach

Several aspects of the mine problem point to the need for public health approaches. First among these is the sheer magnitude of the devastation already wrought by land mines and the extended time period over

The authors acknowlege the assistance of Eric Stover in the preparation of this chapter.

which that devastation will continue. The U.S. State Department estimates that at least 85–100 million antipersonnel and antitank land mines are deployed and threaten civilians in sixty-two nations;[1] the United Nations Working Group on Mines has estimated that worldwide, 800 people die from mine-related wounds every month, and a much larger number are injured and permanently disabled.[2] Though no precise casualty count is available, the worldwide total over the last few decades is probably in the hundreds of thousands. In Cambodia, it is estimated that one in every 236 people has had an amputation because of a mine injury; in Angola, one in 470, and in northern Somalia, one in every 1,000.[3] Rates of this magnitude persist, furthermore, even after formal hostilities end; without self-destruct mechanisms, land mines pose a threat for decades to come.[4]

A second factor favoring a public health approach is the multiple levels at which land mine injuries are devastating. In many contemporary conflicts in which land mines have been used extensively, civilian populations have been specifically targeted. The purpose has been to disrupt families, depopulate areas, prevent the return of refugees to their homes, and shatter the productive life of communities by making it life-threatening to plant and harvest crops, gather firewood, graze livestock, or travel between villages. Cambodia, Afghanistan, Angola, Mozambique, and Somalia demonstrate variations on a theme: mines are scattered across pastoral or farming lands, hidden near water holes or in rice paddies, and placed along roads linking villages with each other and with central markets. The cumulative effects are on a national level, hampering economic reconstruction and social reintegration. For generations to come, peasants will have to beware while planting rice paddies, tilling the soil, herding flocks, gathering firewood, or simply sending children out to play.

Third, the need for public health approaches and disciplines stems from the very nature of land mine wounds, the complexities and costs of medical treatment and rehabilitation, and the structural problems that limit effective medical care.

Caring for Mine Wounds

After land mine injury, the problems begin with the simple dilemma of evacuation.[5] Transportation through mountains and paddy fields is difficult even during peacetime in the desperately poor countries where mines have been used extensively. The number of people who die of hemorrhage, gangrene, or (in largely nonimmunized populations) tetanus infection before reaching first aid or hospital facilities is unknown, but there is every reason to believe that it is substantial. Many of these deaths are not clinically inevitable; they could be averted, were the roads practicable and, where roads exist, were the means of evacuation available and affordable. Ignorance of proper first aid takes a further toll. Even when an injury is limited to foot or ankle level, the inappropriate application of a tourniquet—without release for twenty-four hours or more during transport to hospital—can cause gangrene of the whole leg and force the surgeon to amputate above the knee, at or above the tourniquet.[6]

At the hospital level, poverty and the dislocation that accompanies war can severely limit care.[7] Most hospitals in developing countries are poorly equipped and staffed. Underpaid or unpaid volunteer medical staff often lack appropriate training; few, if any, orthopedic surgeons or general surgeons have extensive experience treating blast-related injuries.[8] Essential medicines are scarce. Shortages of anesthetics, X ray film, antibiotics, and surgical supplies are common. Patients with mine blast injuries often require twice as much blood as those wounded by other munitions. A study of the use of blood in the hospitals of the International Committee of the Red Cross (ICRC) found that, overall, for every 100 wounded, 44.9 units of blood were required, while every 100 mine injuries required 103.2 units.[9] Studies by Physicians for Human Rights in Cambodia, northern Somalia, and Mozambique found that hospitals were often in critical need of blood.[10] In societies not acquainted with blood donation, and where blood is often imbued with mystical qualities, providing blood for acutely anemic patients can be a frustrating experience. Many patients who survive operations and then succumb could have been saved by an adequate blood supply.

The formidable nature of land mine injuries intensifies these deficiencies of resources, staffing, and training. Mine wounds are dirty and contaminated. The blast not only tears through tissues,[11] burns, and coagulates; it also drives soil, grass, metal, or plastic fragments of the mine and pieces of shoes and clothing up into the leg, burrowing between tissue planes and often causing severe secondary infection. These same foreign materials, plus bone fragments of the shattered foot, can also be blown up into the patient's genitals, buttocks, or arms. Damage is frequently caused to the other leg, the chest, and the face. The shock wave from an exploding mine can destroy blood vessels far up the leg, necessitating amputation much higher than the site of the primary wound. The blast may cause irregular contusions and contamination of the muscles of the leg.

Multiple operations—at least two, often more—are required to treat mine wounds. A first operation aims to transform the irregular, soiled traumatic amputation stump of the leg into a clean, properly molded one. All traumatized tissue must be cut out. The wound edges are left open, for fear of infection. Several days later, the patient must undergo a second anesthesia and operation to close the wound, but if contamination or traumatized tissues are present, further operations are required.[12] Victims of mine blasts are more likely to require amputation[13] and are likely to remain in the hospital longer[14] than those wounded by other munitions. In Cambodia, for example, a typical land mine victim will be hospitalized for three weeks and require two operations.[15] In 1991, surgeons in Cambodia performed between 300 and 700 amputations a month; although the number had dropped by more than half in 1993,[16] the need for these procedures will likely continue for decades. One estimate is that 2 million active mines remain to be destroyed, and the costs of demining will approximate $12 million a year for 5–10 years.[17]

Children face particularly difficult problems. As a child ages, the bone of the amputation stump will grow more rapidly than the surrounding skin and soft tissues. The child may need revision of the stump length and undergo reamputation after several years, sometimes repeatedly, as the bone grows out through the soft tissues, causing sores, pain, infection, and an amputation stump incapable of supporting an artificial limb. Even without repeated operations, according to the ICRC, a prosthesis for a growing child should be replaced every six months, and for an adult every 3–5 years. A ten-year-old child with a life expectancy of another forty or fifty years will thus need twenty-five prostheses, at a total cost of approximately $3,125, in his or her lifetime.[18]

Social Effects of Mine Use

The staggering costs for direct medical care and rehabilitation are, in turn, dwarfed by other, less-tangible but equally important social costs. The widespread use of land mines in impoverished agrarian societies, in which family and community survival are dependent on subsistence farming, creates multiple crises: psychological damage, social ostracism, and economic hardship of amputees; loss of productivity of family caretakers; removal of hundreds of thousands of acres of arable land from safe use for decades; and disruption of transportation and agricultural markets.

In the technologically developed countries of the West, amputee victims of land mines would be described as "physically challenged" or "disabled." Less-charitable persons would use the word *handicapped*. In the bleak poverty of war-ravaged societies of the Third World, no euphemism is possible. These people are seen (and see themselves) as cripples; they have been mutilated. They cannot help their families eke out an existence, or provide food or the fuel for its cooking; the children cannot even play.

In many societies, these wounds are also a cause of social ostracism. A family's attempts to come to terms with the social and emotional trauma of a land mine victim can have catastrophic consequences. A patient who has already had a foot or part of a leg blown away by a land mine needs surgery. Before that can happen, however, in places like Afghanistan or Somalia, the family must confer among themselves, delaying the operation. Even if the family members accept the operation, they may point out the level at which they wish the surgeon to cut, in the belief that the operation should "save" as much of the leg as possible. All too often, their preferred level is not high enough to remove all of the damage tissues, and amputation there would cause infection or gangrene, or would make the fitting of an adequate prosthesis impossible.

Secondary Costs

In countries where health facilities are inadequate even in the best of times, the war-wounded place an inordinate drain on resources, both material and human. Often, several operations are performed—after the operations to amputate are completed—in a desperate attempt to save the other leg, also damaged or infected. Repeated dressings, prolonged use of expensive antibiotics, and increased blood transfusion needs are the result.

UNICEF estimates that nearly 9 million children under age five die each year—approximately 24,000 each day, one thousand each hour—from *preventable* disease.[19] The burden of land mine injuries consumes curative care facilities (the per case cost of repeated surgical procedures and prolonged hospitalization far exceeds that of treating malaria or most infectious diseases) and preempts preventive investments. In every nation in which mines have been placed in significant numbers, they are thus a driving force in the maintenance of high maternal, infant, and childhood mortality rates. The total of disease and deaths caused by land mines is therefore far higher than the number of direct victims of these weapons.

Thus, in terms of human health and survival, the greatest secondary cost of land mine warfare is the diversion to direct and rehabilitative medical care of money, personnel, and effort from primary care and preventive and public health measures that are the priorities in developing nations with inadequate health facilities—immunization, sanitation, protection of water supplies, nutritional supplementation, and environmental and biological control of disease vectors.

The Public Health Response

If all manufacture, sale, and placement of antitank and antipersonnel mines were to end today, these dreadful consequences would nevertheless continue through much of the next century. A problem of this complexity and duration has no simple "solution," but many efforts at limitation and amelioration can have a prompt and significant effect. While the proliferation of mines is, at its core, a political problem that has very little to do with medicine, it may be useful to consider such mitigating efforts and responses in the framework of the classic public health trilogy of prevention.

Primary prevention means preventing the occurrence of disease or injury (for example, immunization against infectious disease). Secondary prevention involves early detection and intervention, in order to limit or reverse the progress of a condition or injury. Tertiary prevention means minimizing the effects of disease and disability by interventions aimed at restoring function and preventing complications and further deterioration.[20]

PRIMARY PREVENTION

In the long run, primary prevention is the task of the international political, military, and legal communities: to establish a total and effective ban on land mine use or, more broadly, on the production, stockpiling, transfer, and use of such weapons. A more modest goal is to update the Landmines Protocol amended to the 1980 UN Conventional Weapons Convention, to bring it into conformity with international humanitarian law, to extend it to internal conflicts, and to develop effective verification procedures.[21] These challenges confront the three

UN experts' meetings to be held in preparation for a 1995 review conference on the Convention. They require resolution of the conflict between two sets of claims: Military sources claim that mines are necessary tactical weapons, posing no threat to civilian populations when used by professional armies in a professional manner, and that their use should never be wholly banned or greatly restricted. Humanitarian groups, meanwhile, assert that in recent decades, those armies that have used mines extensively and indiscriminately are unprofessional forces that have totally disregarded the distinction between military and civilian targets and in some cases have deliberately employed these weapons to kill and terrorize civilian populations.

In the short run—and that is a span of many decades—primary prevention means reducing the incidence of mine-related injuries—traumatic contacts between people and weapons, even in the presence of large numbers of mines. It is here that increased mobilization and use of public health specialists—epidemiologists, health educators, and community organizers—can make a significant contribution to present efforts. The most effective public health strategy, obviously, is to promote active and thorough mine marking and clearance efforts. Epidemiologists can help deminers at the initial and essential survey phase. When most humanitarian demining groups arrive in a country, they begin by trying to identify the most heavily mined areas—a basically epidemiological task. Yet humanitarian or UN-sponsored mine clearance teams, composed mostly of former military ordnance personnel, often fail even to consult with local health officials, to utilize data they have collected, or to seek their collaboration.

So far, of all the organizations involved, the Mines Advisory Group and Halo Trust (both U.K.-based) have undertaken the most systematic, survey-based approach. For example, Halo Trust dispatches small teams to survey villages and collect limited hospital data to identify the most heavily mined areas, which will then receive priority in mine marking and clearing efforts. Public health professionals could bring greater rigor to these efforts and extend them to cover wider areas. Most important, however, national public health organizations and local health professionals—where they exist—should be encouraged to participate in the data-gathering phase and to train local workers in the simple survey, recording, and analytic methods required.[22]

Public health educators and community organizers have an equally important contribution to make to the second strategy of primary prevention: promoting awareness, among local populations and returning refugees, of mine locations and types through culturally appropriate use of radio, film, leaflets, comic books, and other print media, with special attention to mothers, children, and schools. Resources will always be limited, but such campaigns are essentially no different than the public health risk reduction efforts familiar to the citizens of developed nations.

SECONDARY PREVENTION

Secondary prevention involves all the problems described earlier in rapidly evacuating and appropriately treating and transfusing land mine victims. Here, the range of potential contributions includes the specific skills of public health and medical care administration—the creation of simple, regionalized systems of first aid posts, transportation, treatment resources and supplies, and referral. It includes training surgeons in standardized operative techniques, training general physicians in emergency procedures, and—again with the use of public health educators—training local citizens in first aid techniques.

This is a familiar set of roles for international health organizations and has parallels in numerous targeted campaigns against specific disease problems. In many of these areas, the ICRC has already played a major role, especially during periods of active conflict. Once a war ends, however, the ICRC's role diminishes, and the importance of involvement of national and local ministries of health and hospitals in coordinated efforts increases.

TERTIARY PREVENTION

In the context of land mine injuries, tertiary prevention is essentially the provision of prostheses and physical therapy for rehabilitation. Here, too, the difficulties are complex. There is active debate between partisans of local manufacture of prostheses, using locally available labor and materials such as wood and leather, and those who favor importing (or training local technicians in the high-volume production of) more modern, lighter and longer-lasting prosthetics of plastic and aluminum. The lesson of myriad public health campaigns in developing nations over the past half century is that (as in the case of prostheses themselves) it is simply not true that "one size fits all." Aside from the technical choices, the key issues are local participation and education; sustainability of costs, supplies, transport systems, and personnel; and the transfer of capacity and responsibility, over time, from the coordinated efforts of international organizations to local communities and governments.

The task of rehabilitation does not end with the successful fitting of a prosthesis and the restoration of mobility. In fact, intensive physiotherapy is necessary before, during, and after the fitting of limbs, and training programs to create local physiotherapists—preferably from among amputee victims of land mines themselves—is urgently needed.

Optimally, rehabilitation includes the psychological and social support needed to restore patients to a productive life and to resume their social roles as workers, parents, or students. The restoration of feelings of individual self-worth and the healing of families and communities are legitimate goals of intervention. In most developing nations, the necessary professional resources to achieve them are sadly lacking.

Conclusion

None of these approaches is a "solution." Some have already been implemented, to various degrees, in land mine–afflicted areas. All of them represent potential contributions to mitigation of land mine effects on human populations. The key is the recognition of land mine injuries as a major public health problem, similar in many respects to disease entities that are more familiar, and the mobilization of public health approaches and techniques in response. This strategy is not limited to developing nations; one may see a striking parallel to the belated recognition of gun-related violence in the United States as a public health problem, requiring intervention on all three levels of prevention, rather than being merely an issue of medical care and of law, order, and criminal justice.

Finally, human rights groups have a role to play, supplementing the work of humanitarian, national, and international organizations. In the vanguard of humanitarian and human rights groups calling for an outright ban on mines are the ICRC, UNICEF, Handicap International, Physicians for Human Rights, Human Rights Watch, and Medico International. Apart from taking this political stance, health professionals in these groups have made, and must continue to make, contributions at every level: documenting the medical and social effects of mines on individuals, families, and communities; attending to the immediate physical injuries of mine victims, providing rehabilitative and therapeutic care after these patients leave the hospital; and educating communities in mine awareness and basic first aid skills.

Recognizing and responding to the global toll of land mine injuries as an epidemic is more than a semantic device. Epidemics are never merely biological phenomena. In their causes and in their consequences, they are always also social, economic, and political events—a truth recognized by the Greek physician Hippocrates more than two millennia ago and by the German pathologist Virchow in the last century. The land mine epidemic is, in that respect, a classic example. Epidemics are never controlled by the strategies of a single discipline, but the collective and coordinated actions of the many disciplines that are relevant can, over time, end them.

11

Developing Indigenous Amputee Programs: Lessons from Nicaragua and Somalia

KEVIN M. CAHILL, M.D.,
AND ABDULRAHIM ABBY FARAH

I n recent years, many civil wars have occurred in developing countries where, under the best of circumstances, the population's daily
struggle is for social and economic survival, and for life itself. The
countries share high infant mortality, low life expectancy, and grossly
inadequate health services. Unfortunately, the introduction of mine warfare has added a new and ominous dimension to their internal conflicts.
Even when the war has ended, the menacing presence of land mines
continues to cause death, mutilation, and suffering among countless
innocent people.

Most of the affected countries have neither the financial nor the technical resources to clear mines, and they can seldom provide mine victims
with the medical treatment and rehabilitation programs needed. Typical
of the countries that fall in this category are Afghanistan, Nicaragua,
Cambodia, Ethiopia, Somalia, Mozambique, and Angola. They are listed
among the least developed nations of the world. They all suffer acute
shortages of medicines and equipment, have too few hospitals to cope
with even routine illnesses, and have an inadequate number of trained
medical and surgical personnel.

With so much competition for limited health services, amputees
requiring prostheses are accorded a low priority. In conflict and disaster

situations, the medical triage principle demands that resources go to the critically ill and wounded, while the rehabilitation of those with chronic disabilities is seen as an unaffordable luxury.

To address such situations, we report on two attempts—separated in place and time—to devise and apply an approach to rehabilitating amputee victims that would be suitable for underdeveloped countries. These efforts were built around a prosthesis technology—the Jaipur foot—that was inexpensive and effective, simple to teach and learn, and easily standardized, and that had an assured supply source. The prosthesis itself could be fitted in an outpatient setting, thereby not burdening an already overworked and fragile hospital system. The Jaipur foot is a preformed, rubberized, durable, and flexible unit that requires little repair or replacement over a reasonable period of time. The sophisticated prosthetic devices used in the West, by contrast, usually require major surgical intervention, elaborate rehabilitation, and expensive time in hospital.

The experience gained in two war-torn countries—Nicaragua and Somalia—indicates some of the public health lessons that can be learned only in the field, where the most carefully prepared plans, caught in the conflict between aspirations and reality, are liable to go awry, but where careful analysis of failure can point the way to success.

Nicaragua

In 1987—the seventh year of the Contra-Sandinista war in Nicaragua—this country of 3 million people had over 6,000 amputees. The country was under a strict U.S.-imposed economic embargo, which did not exempt medical supplies, despite rhetoric to the contrary. In a situation where patients died as respirators failed for lack of parts, and critical surgery had to be done without anesthesia, the needs of amputees could be deferred almost indefinitely. Through the late 1980s, one could see the same amputees awaiting treatment in the same beds for years on end.[1]

As the Nicaraguan amputee project began, it offered exceptional prospects for success. Support was promised by the United Nations Development Programme (UNDP), the governments of India and Nicaragua, and by the U.K.-based Hamlyn Foundation. Valuable contributions were also promised by the Jaipur Medical Center. Over many months, multiple planning conferences took place in the relevant Nicaraguan ministries, within the United Nations, at the central ministries in Delhi, at the regional government headquarters in Jaipur, and between all the various sponsors.

The Nicaraguan government provided a well-appointed building to accommodate the Jaipur foot program; it also assigned highly trained medical personnel from its armed forces to serve as staff for the center. It promised to pay their salaries and give them the necessary leave from other duties for training in Jaipur and for establishing the new center in Managua. The Nicaraguan government also provided housing in Managua for a team from India during its three-month stay to establish the workshop. The UNDP, for its part, bore the cost of air passages to and from India for the Nicaraguan team to receive training in Jaipur, and then for the Indian experts' travels to Nicaragua. The Indian government contributed in-country costs for maintenance and travel of the Nicaraguans.

The UNDP was particularly attracted to the project because it would give a practical demonstration of technical cooperation among developing countries—a development objective strongly promoted by the United Nations. The Hamlyn Foundation provided a $100,000 grant to construct a workshop and other facilities on the site of the assigned building. These funds were also intended to cover the purchase of aluminum for leg molds and other materials and equipment.

The directorate of the amputee center had the enthusiastic support of the Nicaraguan foreign minister, who became chairman of the Nicaraguan Jaipur foot program. Certainly, from the planning perspective, the project appeared to have everything working in its favor. The bright promise of the project led the UNDP to feature it on the cover of the June 1989 issue of its magazine, and the *New York Times* ran a lengthy article in its international section on September 1, 1990.

Unfortunately, what was achieved fell far short of expectations. The slow movement of almost any government bureaucracy was accentuated by the war conditions in Nicaragua, jurisdictional conflicts between regional and central ministries in India, and the need for formal signed documents at every stage, between both governments and the United Nations. The absence of an ambassador on vacation once delayed the entire project for four months. Time-consuming procedures, unforeseen political developments, the lack of firmly based community support, and other factors presented obstacles that could not be overcome. The U.S. embargo caused considerable delays and heavy expenses in the procurement of supplies. It was difficult, for example, to purchase the aluminum except at exorbitant prices in neighboring countries. In giving the project public visibility, the Nicaraguan government had selected senior staff, many of whom were overqualified for the work expected of them, and in any case were not committed exclusively to the amputee project. Perhaps of greatest import, the amputee center was widely viewed as a Sandinista facility and not as a purely humanitarian service. When the Sandinista government lost the 1990 elections, just as the amputee center was to open, the incoming authorities withdrew all support. A demobilization program affected the army personnel who had staffed the center, and their salaries were stopped. The foreign minister—a keen supporter of the project—was replaced, and funds that had been donated for the maintenance and operation of the center were frittered away on unessential activities. As a sad footnote to the history of the project, the ownership of the site of the amputee center is now the subject of litigation in the Nicaraguan courts.

After four years of intense planning and preparation, and the expenditure of a considerable amount of effort and resources, the project had fitted only 150 amputees with the Jaipur foot. Regrettably, at the time the project ceased to operate, the remaining amputees—and there were many thousands—were still waiting in the same overcrowded hospitals for locally improvised limbs, and they were being fitted at the same slow, almost imperceptible pace. The project had come full circle.

If it were not for the bitter but important lessons it taught, the Nicaraguan project could be considered an utter failure. However, from this disappointing experience, new fruit would flourish in Somalia, where a successful amputee project has been established in spite of far more formidable obstacles presented by interclan conflict and near anarchic conditions that prevailed throughout the territory in 1993.

Somalia

In 1993, northwestern Somalia (Somaliland), with nearly a quarter of its 2 million people either in refugee camps in neighboring countries or internally displaced, had been the scene of a drawn-out civil war, complicated by a prolonged armed confrontation on the borders between Somalia and Ethiopia. In the course of these conflicts, land mines were extensively planted, causing a high proportion of amputees among war veterans, as well as among civilians. Antipersonnel mines were laid at watering points, along trade and stock routes, in pasture and agricultural lands, and within townships; even civilian homes were deliberately mined.

Over 1 million land mines have been laid in Somaliland.[2] No countrywide study has yet been made to determine the number of persons who have become amputee victims or rendered physically incapacitated as a result of mine blast. The chaotic security conditions and ongoing clan conflicts made it difficult to gather reliable information on the number of amputees. The majority were thought to live in villages in rural areas, while a substantial number were reported in refugee camps in neighboring countries.

Having known the people, illnesses, and health system—such as it is—of Somalia for many years,[3] the authors decided to implement the philosophy of the Center for International Health and Cooperation (CIHC)[4] by establishing an amputee project in Hargeisa, the capital of Somaliland. The African Development Bank provided a grant for a basic rehabilitation center and a mobile unit.

Establishing an entirely new health facility in such a war-torn and unstable area was extremely challenging. A fledgling local government, which existed more in form than in substance, was barely functioning, and its authority hardly extended beyond the walls of its headquarters; only the rudiments of a police force existed within the capital, and almost all of the region's social and economic infrastructure was in ruins. Towns and villages had been leveled; more than 80 percent of the buildings in Hargeisa were uninhabitable. All electric power stations and telecommunications systems were destroyed. Health, education, and sanitation services were nonexistent, and roads were extremely insecure.

It was obvious that it would take years for Somalia to recover sufficiently for its government to provide basic services, and given the extreme shortage of medicines and the intense pressure for the few available hospital beds, public health programs such as the rehabilitation of land mine victims would have to take their place far back in the long queue of competing priorities. We believed that if we could establish a successful amputee program in such a chaotic setting, it would offer immediate help to a neglected group, the disabled, as well as provide a highly visible sign of a recovery in a basic public health problem. Few examples of a functioning health service are more dramatic than having hundreds of legless persons suddenly walking around the town. The program might also be replicable in other war settings where simple, inexpensive, and rapid public health programs are needed.

As daunting as the situation in Somaliland was at the time when the CIHC project was envisaged, we were convinced that with proper planning, experienced leadership, and a good field team, a rehabilitation center for amputees could be constructed and equipped within three to four months of a suitable site's being secured. In fact, Somaliland provided the setting for an excellent experiment. If we could get a project working there in the midst of anarchy, and document an approach that could be duplicated elsewhere, we would have achieved a unique accomplishment.

One advantage we had was that the Nicaraguan experience had given us a good idea of what to avoid and what guidelines to follow. We would ensure the humanitarian and nonpolitical nature of the project and its managerial independence. We would avoid formal governmental involvement whenever possible. We would not spend our limited resources on housing and production facilities, expensive foreign training programs, overqualified staff, and the creation of a program that could not be supported locally when our phase of the project was over. We would also maintain the independence of the rehabilitation center from the hospital so that our work would not be affected by other public health priorities.

Three major objectives have guided our project; all are encompassed by our local motto, "Help the Somalis to help themselves." They are as follows:

- Establish the rehabilitation center as an operation run entirely by local Somalis. To that end, Somali personnel are to be involved from the very start in the planning, execution, and operation of the project.
- Create a center that would be effective and relatively inexpensive to operate, and within the resource capability of the government to sustain when conditions return to normal.
- Ensure that the services offered by the center are available to all leg amputees free of charge and without discrimination of any kind.

Two retired, highly respected Somali civil servants joined the project's local board and served as our bridge to the local community. From the outset, we involved local leaders, veterans, and disabled and women's groups to the maximum extent possible so that the future of the project would be as much their responsibility as ours. We attended the time-honored Somali traditional meetings—the *shir*—where we explained our objectives and plans to assembled religious, political, and civic leaders. The humanitarian motive—in Somali *sama fal* (doer of good deeds)—was frequently emphasized to underscore the common obligation toward the needy and the helpless.

Until CIHC initiated its project, the region had virtually no services for the disabled. A military facility some fifty miles east of Hargeisa had had a project that was abandoned in 1990, while a recently established workshop for leg amputees provided very few and very basic wooden legs and crutches. When beds and supplies permitted, the Hargeisa hospital offered acute care to amputee victims, but this often resulted in tying up critically needed beds for long periods. The hospital had no resources to provide rehabilitative services, and we felt an amputee project would thrive best outside the hospital's understandable routine priorities.

IMPLEMENTATION OF THE PLAN

Both of the authors visited Hargeisa in August 1993, and one remained for the full four-month construction period. By this personal overseeing, we could attend to problems immediately, without encountering the long delays and bureaucratic obstacles that had destroyed the Nicaraguan experiment. In any case, conditions prevailing at the time left no other realistic alternative. There were no public or commercial telecommunication links with CIHC headquarters, and the majority of problems required complete understanding of local conditions and of the people themselves. Modifications would need to be made on the scene if the planned starting date was to be achieved. The project manager was granted full discretionary powers in the construction of the facility, and in developing close relations with the authorities, community leaders, local nongovernmental organizations, and the disabled community. The goodwill generated by these contacts provided immeasurable support for the project.

Contrary to the approach in Nicaragua, we did not develop elaborate facilities or expensive preparatory arrangements that divert resources from the basic needs of patients. We secured a site adjacent to but separate from the hospital, one that gave us relative freedom in the design and operation of the center. We could manage and operate the property as we chose, and could rehabilitate, modify, and expand the building according to our needs.

From the start, we established a close relationship with the community we were to serve through the local Handicapped Veterans Association. We hired all skilled and nonskilled labor required for the construction of the center from the disabled ranks. Their employment not only provided the handicapped workers with much needed wages, but gave a considerable boost to their morale and self-esteem, and secured our acceptance as full partners in their plight.

In the absence of a local police force, security constituted a major problem. We built a high perimeter wall and hired even our security guards from among the handicapped community. At the same time as the construction phase began, we hired four Somali technicians and a surgeon to work with expert Indian counterparts who came from Jaipur for an intensive training period. We minimized theoretical and classroom training by selecting Somalis with some knowledge of rehabilitative work. Attention was concentrated on the practical aspects of the manufacture and application of the Jaipur foot. The Somali team were expected to be adequately trained to take over the greater part of the work from their Indian counterparts within a matter of weeks.

PUTTING THE PIECES TOGETHER

By the end of three months, the plan that we had carefully put together began to materialize as construction progressed, materials and equipment were delivered, and staff began to take up their positions. Our experience with the Jaipur foot technology and the contacts that we had cultivated in India allowed the project to have the necessary professional guidance and technical backup, and a reliable source for the materials needed for the manufacture of the prostheses.

Inevitably, we encountered some logistical problems. We had underestimated the difficulties in getting supplies air-freighted from neighboring countries, particularly since the port city, Berbera, was still out of bounds to most ships. An airline charter company used the Berbera airport, but this involved a rather dangerous and insecure road haulage to Hargeisa—110 miles to the west—where vehicles had to pass through numerous road blocks manned by groups of armed tribal militia.

One may ask why it was necessary to bring in supplies from India, Kenya, and elsewhere, and why it was not possible to manufacture some essential components of the prosthesis—the rubber foot, for example. In the first place, the civil war had resulted in the looting of all removable properties. Not a single workshop or factory had escaped plunder. Second, neither the resources nor the technical know-how were available locally to construct the necessary facilities for production. Third, in emergency situations, the cost-benefit factor must be taken into consideration. Since we could meet our needs relatively cheaply, easily, and without delay from abroad, there was no justification for holding up the project indefinitely while a local production capacity was being developed.

One of our major problems was communications—not only with the outside world, but internally. The national radio broadcast station and the telecommunications system had been destroyed, so contacts with the population had to be made primarily by word of mouth. In order to launch an awareness and registration campaign in Hargeisa for the amputee center, we hired a van with a loudspeaker and toured the township on three consecutive days, urging leg amputees to register themselves for treatment before a fixed date.

We deliberately restricted registration in the initial period to below-the-knee amputees, since they could be easily fitted and they seemed to constitute the major proportion of amputees. Moreover, we felt that the most practical inducement for registration would be the visible presence in public of known amputees walking. During the first three days of registration, 160 men, women, and children registered for artificial limbs. Within a month, that figure had more than doubled. As we had expected, news of the center and of the service it offered traveled quickly. More women and children began to register, and amputees from outlying districts did not wait for the mobile clinic to visit their areas, but traveled to Hargeisa for treatment.

The center's first patient was a six-year-old girl whose parents had been killed during the civil war. Just six months before the center opened, she had lost both legs while playing near her aunt's home. When she was brought to the center, she could move around only on her buttocks. Two days after she received her new legs, she was walking with the help of training bars. One month later, she was walking without help and able to play once again with her friends. A sixty-five-year-old nomad was also among our first patients. He had lost one of his legs by stepping on a mine while tending his camels. He was able to walk firmly without any support within an hour of being fitted with his prosthesis. In sharp contrast to the numbers achieved in Nicaragua, the Hargeisa center averaged *100 patients a month* during the first four months of its operation.

The operation of a mobile clinic is an integral part of the Somaliland project. Many amputees living in outlying population centers find it extremely difficult to undertake the long journey to Hargeisa for treatment, and the mobile clinic has obviated the need for such travel. This service consists of a surgeon, a technician, and a nurse. They spend ten to fourteen days in each district registering patients, taking measurements and ascertaining the condition of the stump, and determining which patients might require surgery. The data collected are taken back to the center's workshop, where individual artificial limbs are produced to the measurements given. Patients are given a date when the mobile clinic will return to the district to fit them and make corrective adjustments to their prostheses on the spot. A period of three to ten days is allowed for the patients to receive physiotherapy and instruction in the use and care of their artificial limbs.

Many land mine victims receive their injuries when they are far from medical assistance. Consequently, many die from their wounds, while others often have to undergo crude emergency operations under the most primitive conditions and without the services of a skilled surgeon. Those who are brought to hospitals often arrive when their wounds have already developed extensive gangrene or sepsis and, in consequence, suffer with sensitive and painful stumps. Those patients often require minor corrective surgery before receiving a prosthesis, and we have been able to accomplish this at a relatively modest cost.

Organizational egocentricity should have no role in humanitarian crises. From the outset, we tried to forge close links with kindred agencies, and to interest them in the rehabilitation center. The response has been most encouraging, and a number of organizations have made important contributions to the Hargeisa amputee project. The United Nations High Commission for Refugees provided funds for the patients transit ward; the World Food Programme supplies both the food component for the transit ward and a ration allowance for the lower paid medical workers; the United Nations Organization for Somalia provided a grant for the installation of a water distribution system, and has helped in the airlift of our supplies from Nairobi; African International Airlines has generously transported, free of charge, the bulk of our supplies from Nairobi to Berbera; Catholic Relief Services provided administrative and logistical support, as well as assistance during the construction phase.

UNFILLED NEEDS

At this time, the Hargeisa rehabilitation center has resources for dealing only with leg amputees, but we were regularly confronted with land mine victims who had lost arms, hands, or sight; who had become quadriplegic; who had suffered internal injuries from shrapnel; or who manifested serious psychological and emotional problems arising directly from mine-related injuries and shock. They have as legitimate a claim to assistance as the leg amputees, and it was our difficult task to explain that we could not help them because of financial and other constraints.

There are also no facilities in Hargeisa, or anywhere in Somaliland, where emotionally disturbed persons can receive treatment. A fifty-bed mental hospital was closed during the civil war, and the building has since been stripped of all its equipment and left in a ruinous condition. Merely fitting prostheses on amputees does not constitute a comprehensive land mine rehabilitation program. The development of occupational training programs, so that the disabled can become gainfully employed, is an important aspect we have not yet been able to address. Public health education and mine awareness programs are other important needs that should, ideally, be communicated to a largely illiterate nomad population via radio. Unfortunately, there is no national radio station functioning, and public health is a major loser.

Public Health Lessons

Obviously, there are specific local and national conditions and characteristics peculiar to each of the countries plagued by large-scale land mine infestations. Nonetheless, the experience gained from public health projects for the rehabilitation of land mine victims in Nicaragua and Somalia teach valuable lessons that have significant relevance for postwar situations elsewhere.

1) Given the political instability that inevitably prevails in civil war settings, a rehabilitation center should be seen as an independent institution, not tied to any particular political entity.

2) A rehabilitation center, such as that established in Hargeisa, should maintain a discreet but not total distance from the hospital. In uncomplicated cases, the center is quite capable of working alone. However, reconstructive surgery requires consultation between the center's surgeon and the hospital. In general, the rehabilitation program needs to be free from triage pressures and other valid but constraining hospital priorities.

3) Strong links with the local community are necessary to provide a foundation for support and continuity. When governmental and hospital involvement weakened in Nicaragua, the project shriveled for lack of an alternative base. In Hargeisa community relationships were strengthened by the hiring of local staff at all levels of the project—managerial, professional, technical, and secretarial. In addition to building bridges to the community, we strengthened our operation by having the benefit of the local staff's intimate knowledge of the cultural, social, and political environment, and of their commitment to a national cause. Our almost exclusive reliance on the disabled for construction, security, and semi-

skilled jobs generated goodwill and gave us ties both to the special community we were serving and to the community at large.

4) Public health issues transcend purely medical concerns. Practical and organizational considerations were as important as those of policy, particularly in the midst of the harsh, anarchic conditions of Somaliland. Here we found that humanitarian goodwill is no substitute for careful planning. The success of a public health project is as much a question of leadership and organization in every aspect—technology, supply, building, finance, training, and public education—as it is a question of medical and surgical technique. In Hargeisa, tasks as varied as modifying and equipping the water supply, scheduling trainers and trainees, developing a patients list, and measuring stumps all had to be precisely managed.

5) Public health projects in wartorn areas should be based on the simplest and least expensive technology available. The choice of the Jaipur foot repeatedly confirmed the importance, in developing countries, of using a technology without complex requirements in terms of production, treatment of patients, housing, equipment, training, and staff.

6) In public health, there are no national barriers: epidemics do not respect borders. So, too, the world must be viewed as a global market. Time and energy should not be wasted on production that can be done more economically and better elsewhere than the local scene. The best markets for acquiring materials should be sought farther afield if national and regional sources have limitations. In the case of Nicaragua, the search for production materials in neighboring countries was time-consuming and economically draining. In Somalia, supplies were brought from India, where they were inexpensive and readily available.

7) Appropriate selection, training, and supervision of staff are essential elements in all public health projects in developing lands. An unnecessary, time-consuming, and expensive foreign training program, and the assignment to the project of overqualified medical professionals, proved to be negative factors in the Nicaraguan program. The use in Somalia of on-the-job, in-country training of technicians was both effective and economical. Much depends on the careful selection of the surgeon/supervisor and the small team of technicians, whose ability to relate to the disabled, as well as their medical and teaching skills, spreads public confidence in the project. The necessity of integrity and commitment on the part of the staff cannot be overemphasized, especially in the midst of social chaos, when theft and neglect of duties are

almost understandable. Lax standards in a health project will prove rapidly contagious and ultimately fatal.

8) In initially confining the Somalia project to leg amputees, we followed a basic public health lesson: address the needs of the most easily treatable majority of the affected group. This approach had several results. The need for professional surgical services was kept to a minimum, and the relatively large number of amputees who could be fitted immediately showed the effectiveness of the prosthesis and induced others to come forward. In a traumatized and relatively closed society, this practical demonstration was an effective way of giving publicity to the work of the center and, in fact, to the very possibility of reestablishing a basic public health service.

9) Cooperation is the key to successful public health. The speedy establishment and popularity of the Somalia project increased the prospect of gaining additional support to extend the service to arm amputees. When an amputee project proves its viability, other international or local agencies with relevant mandates are more likely to avoid the waste of duplicating existing skills and facilities by contributing to an already successful program.

10) Every public health project needs an education campaign. Despite the widely available press, radio, and television coverage available in Nicaragua, the media were not used properly to win local understanding and support. In Somaliland, where no national media existed, the lesson of adaptation to local conditions was driven home. The same techniques of public health education used in more sophisticated places to build interest, morale, and pride, and to engender patient lists, were employed through meetings with community leaders anu veterans groups. A car driven through the town with a loudspeaker had to substitute for newspapers or electronic media, but that was no reason not to reach out and build support.

Conclusion

Taken together, the public health lessons learned in Nicaragua and Somalia point to two wider considerations: much can be accomplished with relatively modest resources if the right approaches are used, but much remains to be done by the international community. In particular, we would urge agencies with special mandates for the welfare of the disabled and of children, as well as those states that bear some culpability in the matter of land mine production, export, and use, to apply their resources to help rehabilitate innocent civilian victims. We have developed a public health model that can be replicated in other wartorn areas. Successful amputee rehabilitation projects not only return individuals to a better life, but serve as a highly visible example of man's humanity—and obligation—to his fellow man.

III

New Directions

12

An International Approach Toward Humanitarian Assistance and Economic Development of Countries Affected by Land Mines

JAN ELIASSON

Recently, there has been a surge of interest in—and outrage at—
the land mine plague around the world. Televised reports have
shown graphic illustrations of its effects, and the enormity of
the problem has been made abundantly clear in newspaper articles and
academic studies. The United Nations, the International Committee of
the Red Cross (ICRC), and others have identified the issues and have
indicated the direction we have to go.

Still, both globally and nationally, we are far away from programs of
action and timetables for concrete measures. These are necessary next
steps if we are to avoid succumbing to the size and complexity of the
task. Facing a problem of this nature, we easily fall prey to helplessness
and frustration. In such a situation it is important to recognize and
understand the problem and divide it into manageable parts so that we
only have to deal with "one hell at a time," and formulate the solutions
as correctly as possible.

Perhaps the most striking feature of the mine problem is its many

The author acknowledges the assistance of George D'Angelo in the preparation of this
chapter.

layers, its manifold ramifications. It affects not only the individual and the family, but the village, the region, and the nation. Mines can physically disable their victims, and can also leave deep psychological scars. They are a medical problem as well as a moral, political, social, and economic challenge. To deal with the mine problem we need to develop not only a legal strategy but also a plan of action for training, development of appropriate technology, resettlement of the afflicted population, rehabilitation, and normalization of economic life.

We need at this juncture to focus on the problem and let institutional consequences flow from actual needs and the priorities we set. For the next century we will walk over innumerable killing fields if we do not respond to the mine plague with passion and compassion, with respect for human life and dignity, and with determination to formulate and implement a concrete program of action.

The Multifaceted Land Mine Problem

The international community can no longer ignore the tremendous human suffering and loss of resources inflicted by land mines throughout the world. The horror of land mines indiscriminately killing or maiming innocent civilians long after conflicts have ended has been well documented. The destruction tears the social fabric and cripples economies, leaving the victimized country in a condition of reduced independence and increased vulnerability—and mined countries usually have the most fragile economies and greatest need of development. The international donor community eventually will have to bear a great part of the increased cost of relief for such ravaged countries, and provide additional substantial resources to deal with mine-induced problems.

The land mine problem is truly a globally interwoven one. An estimated 5 to 10 million mines are manufactured every year by thirty supplier countries, mainly in the industrialized world. Over sixty countries are directly affected by mines. International organizations and the donor community are also involved as they attempt to respond to the humanitarian and developmental needs of the affected countries. Ironically, many of the largest donors supporting humanitarian activity to overcome the consequences of land mines are also among the states producing and exporting them.

When more mines are being laid per year than can possibly be cleared, when the costs to the international community for dealing with mines take a significant portion of the resources available for international relief and development, when land mines impede national development, and when untold suffering is being perpetuated indiscriminately on civilian populations, it is time for this staggering problem to be addressed with a coherent strategy.

Thanks to several UN member states and nongovernmental organizations (NGOs), important aspects of the problem are now being examined more closely. The UN, during its debate in October 1993, recognized the presence of mines as a critical factor impeding the return to normalcy of a number of countries. Yet, while we have been learning more about the devastating effects of land mines on the social fabric of affected countries, we are only just beginning to address the problem. An attempt is made here to present a blueprint for urgent international action to deal with the multifaceted land mines question.

A Call to Action

UN General Assembly resolution 48/7 of October 19, 1993, attests to the increasing international concern about land mines. It stresses the need for coordinating mine clearance activities and strengthening the UN's capacity for solving the problems created by mines, and requests a comprehensive report of the problems that they cause. Additionally, the forty-eighth General Assembly referred to the land mine issue in three other resolutions, further highlighting the growing concern of the world community.

It is essential to view the land mine problem as central to peacebuilding programs rather than merely as a factor on the margin of a country's development. Land mines are truly a global problem. Nothing less than an internationally coordinated strategy will be adequate to deal with it. Three distinct areas for action should be considered.

First, mine proliferation must be stopped. In the last several years, approximately 3 million mines were laid annually, while probably fewer than 150,000 were extracted. Mathematically and practically speaking, the problem can only get worse unless effective curbs are placed on land mine production, trade, and usage.

Second, a coordinated strategy involving the UN, international lending institutions, the ICRC, and NGOs involved in mine clearance must be developed to address the immediate problem of mine removal. The strategy should include mine clearance, research and development (R&D) in detection and clearance technology, and mine awareness and education programs.

Third, the international community needs to clearly understand and appreciate the long-term social and economic effects of land mines on a country's relief needs and development plans, and must address these issues.

The heightened awareness within the international community of the land mine problem and its long-term effects on a country's development must be translated into action. The international community can address the multifaceted land mine problem in several ways, but if the problem is to be dealt with effectively, solutions must be globally conceived, properly coordinated, and adequately funded.

The international community must assume a large degree of responsibility in assisting affected countries on their road to normalcy, and the foundation of lasting development can be found in the guiding principles of humanitarian assistance which are:

- international assistance must be provided at the request of the affected state;
- the affected state must accept primary responsibility for relief and protection of its own citizens when able, although the international community may be required to assist; and
- the affected state must be willing to render whatever assistance it can to support organizations actively engaged in resolving mine-related problems.

The following are specific suggestions for dealing with the land mine problem from global and national perspectives.

FUNDING

Any realistic attempt to deal with the mine problem must be prefaced with a discussion of funding options. Without the political will to generate sufficient funds, all talk of solutions becomes mere rhetoric.

General Assembly resolution 48/7 of 1993 provides a novel concept for funding: it requests the secretary-general to report on "the advisability of establishing a voluntary trust fund to finance, in particular, information and training programs relating to mine clearance and to facilitate the launching of mine clearance operations." This trust fund is a prerequisite for a meaningful strategy to deal with the mine problem.

Such a voluntary trust fund should be operational in two areas. First, funding is needed to deal with the general nature of the problem. Funding to provide information, coordination, and research of the overall land mine issue requires a separate source, a general trust fund. This funding should be used to establish a staff to define and address the multifaceted nature of the issue more precisely. It should be used to obtain and maintain visibility over the diverse components of the problem, and to coordinate the resources where necessary.

Second, country-specific funds should address mine-related development programs such as mine clearance, mine education, and responses to medical and social dimensions of land mine injuries.

The secretary-general has delegated responsibility to the UN Department of Humanitarian Affairs (UNDHA) for a "comprehensive report of the problems caused by the increasing presence of mines, and on the manner in which the United Nations contribution to the solution of problems relating to mine clearance could be strengthened," which was required by resolution 48/7. UNDHA should take the initiative in exploring all aspects of the funding issue, possibly convening a conference that would consider contribution possibilities from member governments, the World Bank, the International Monetary Fund, charitable institutions, and other segments of the financial community. All UN agencies and other governmental and nongovernmental entities involved with the mine problem should be encouraged to provide input and to actively participate.

COORDINATION

General Assembly Resolution 48/7 was explicit in stressing "the importance of coordination by the United Nations of activities . . . relating to mine clearance, in particular those activities relating to information and training with a view to improving the effectiveness of operations in the field." This reference to coordination must be broadly interpreted. UNDHA, as the designated coordinating entity, and as chair of the UN Interagency Standing Committee, is clearly in the position to assume leadership in defining the global nature of the problem, and assuring that all aspects of it are dealt with as an integrated whole. UNDHA should promote a functional division of labor among the UN agencies affected by the land mine problem.

Coordination can best be accomplished by establishing an integrated coordination and management working unit. This unit must be operationally oriented, with the full support of member states, to assure that the land mine problem is kept on a firm track. Close coordination with

UN peacekeeping mine experts should be maintained. Especially at the critical first stage, it is important that adequate resources, including personnel, be made available to define and address the diverse dimensions of the problem.

COUNTER–LAND MINE PROGRAMS

To be effective, counter–land mine programs must address two issues: mine detection and clearance technology, and mine awareness.

The technology in mine detection and clearance is largely outdated. Member states must develop a system to share existing antimine technology and must launch a coordinated campaign to advance the state-of-the-art in mine detection and clearance. This will entail assessing technologies and promoting an accelerated R&D program. Consideration should be given to devising reliable, cost-effective technologies that can be easily applied in developing societies. The challenge is to find technologies that are effective, yet simple to use.

The UN must be given resources and authority to coordinate and disseminate information. It should set a goal of establishing a global mine clearance database of information on all facets of land mine clearance, including R&D. Using resolution 48/7 as the basis for action, member states should be required to provide information, and personnel if necessary, to assure the operational success of this important function.

In repatriation schemes, mine awareness education programs are critical. The UN High Commissioner for Refugees (UNHCR) provides such programs that include surveying and demarcation of minefields for returning refugees. UNICEF has developed mine awareness programs in Central America and Africa. The effectiveness of these programs needs to be evaluated. They also must be coordinated with the work of other international agencies and NGOs, and be available to all affected populations, including displaced persons returning to their homes. Cultural sensitivities must be borne in mind in any effective program. UNDHA can provide an important service by assuring that available information on the subject of mine awareness is shared and properly disseminated.

SOCIAL AND ECONOMIC PROGRAMS

It is clear that land mines severely affect the postconflict development of countries. Addressing this issue entails finding effective countermeasures as well as securing adequate funding.

Infrastructure

The capability to rebuild a strong infrastructure is a major element in a country's return to normalcy. Severely mined countries often have a totally disrupted infrastructure. Either for defensive or for offensive reasons, land mines are concentrated around power plants, power lines, airports, bridges, roads, riverbeds, and water supplies. The result is disruption of services and a marked decrease in a country's ability to repair and use affected facilities. For example, after eighteen years of civil war, and 2 million land mines later, most major roads in Mozambique are unusable.

Viable infrastructures are necessary to lessen human suffering and to support peace-building efforts. The costs in resources and time of repairing a country's transportation system and other basic facilities can be enormous. The inability to do so often becomes the greatest impediment to a nation's development.

Priority must go to mine clearance as an integral part of restoring a functioning infrastructure. As demining can be a long and laborious process, the international community should not be expected to continue to support these activities only through the United Nations. Rather, as national capacities are developed, financial support must be shifted to bilateral donors or the Bretton Wood institutions.

The UN needs to assure that the land mine problem is considered in each World Bank development program for mine-affected countries, and that funding is requested specifically for mine clearance activities. Efforts to assure financial support of land mine programs are essential. UNDHA must at least for the foreseeable future, take the lead in assuring that these avenues are known to international institutions and groups concerned with land mine issues.

Agriculture Programs

The availability of arable land greatly determines a nation's ability to support its population. The presence of land mines reduces the amount of arable land available for food production, thus increasing the need for international food aid. The proportion of land taken out of production is difficult to assess, especially in countries still in conflict, but it is considerable.

A Cambodian vice governor of the fertile western province of Battanbang has estimated that one-third of the province's arable land is unusable because of mines. In some parts of the province, 68 percent is unusable. The resultant decrease in production capacity will mean

172 · JAN ELIASSON

either a corresponding increase in food aid or perpetuation of the lethal cycle of malnutrition for the province's 500,000 residents. The associated costs of land mines on a country's food aid needs can be significant. In Angola alone, a World Food Programme (WFP) officer estimated that 20 percent of the 1994 WFP food aid budget of $160 million will be used to meet nutritional needs that result from the land mine problem. Additionally, farmers and others dependent upon agriculture disrupted by land mines need to find other employment, or may have to move to another part of the country to find suitable farmland. They may then expose themselves to further risks of land mine accidents by entering unfamiliar areas. The costs of these "hidden" effects of mines are difficult to calculate accurately but may point toward the true economic costs of land mines.

Rapid demining of arable land is essential. Most countries affected by land mines derive a large part of their gross national product from agriculture. For many nations, inability to produce their most vital product severely impedes their return to normalcy. This must be remedied quickly, especially when the return to farming will significantly reduce the country's dependency on food aid. A cost analysis of mine clearance activities versus food aid dependency should be a part of every development assessment.

Medical Programs

An estimated 800 people die each month around the world as a result of land mine injuries. Many of these, together with another estimated 800 victims who survive land mine accidents, require immediate emergency treatment. Only a fraction of those disabled receive care from medical NGOs. The rest are cared for by medical personnel who have little training in mine-related injuries and must work with inadequate facilities, supplies, and medicines. Countries severely affected by land mines have a critical need for specially trained medical personnel to deal with these uniquely traumatic wounds. Since many of the injuries occur in inaccessible areas, it may take considerable time to get adequate emergency care. Measures are needed not only to increase the quantity and quality of emergency medical facilities, but to instruct people in heavily mined areas on elementary first aid to mine victims.

In Cambodia, where over 36,000 people suffer from mine injuries, the ICRC and other medical NGOs have begun programs to increase the medical capacity and training of emergency physicians to deal with mine-related injuries. Total costs to the affected countries, international medical groups, and donors are significant and must be taken from scarce medical resources.

More programs and funding of emergency training for doctors and other medical personnel are required, especially in the area of mine-related injuries. There should be recognition of the uniqueness of mine injuries and of the need for more medical research in the treatment of such injuries in the medical institutions of the developing countries. This is an area that lends itself to funding by a large and, as yet, untapped pool of charitable foundations. The United Nations should formally advise such foundations that medical, rehabilitative, and social programs for countries plagued by mines play an essential part in their development and deserve special support.

Rehabilitation and Welfare Programs

Rehabilitation for mine victims is almost nonexistent in the most se-verely affected countries. Permanent disability, while being personally devastating, also places a heavy burden on government resources. Greatly affected by cultural mores, amputees often are socially ostra-cized, and in cultures where the handicapped are devalued or unable to find employment, large segments of society may be reduced to begging. Programs are needed that can integrate amputees into productive society.

The social dependency created by debilitating injury is a significant cost factor for struggling governments as well as for donor countries. The Vietnam Veterans Foundation of America is conducting research in Afghanistan, Cambodia, and Mozambique to better understand the social and economic effects of land mines and their associated costs. Preliminary information indicates a pressing need to establish rehabilita-tion facilities, follow-up medical support, prostheses refitting, and other long-term welfare services. In 1991, in Cambodia alone, the ICRC spent $9.6 million to build and operate orthopedic centers and to train local personnel to produce prosthetic devices; yet, these activities cover only a small portion of the overall needs of mine-wound victims. In very limited area of prostheses manufacture and fitting alone, the global cost is tremendous.

Mine-wound victims have special needs, and it is essential to gener-ate physical and psychological rehabilitation for amputees. Certain gen-eral considerations apply to most cases, while others are country- or culture-specific. Along with the urgency of developing adequate local prostheses manufacturing, there is the need for a serious and adequately funded prostheses R&D program. Such programs should be submitted to charitable foundations for funding.

A country's social welfare system should also provide job retraining and consider provisions to protect the disabled. Greater efforts must be made to enable handicapped persons to become productive members of society, thus restoring their sense of dignity and overcoming social and cultural stigma. A sad fact is that after twenty-one years of conflict in Cambodia, the country still has no rehabilitation centers and no laws that protect disabled persons against discrimination or exploitation.

Refugee and Displaced Persons Programs

After the peace is won in a country or region, repatriation becomes a primary humanitarian consideration. Land mines are a serious obstacle to the safe repatriation and reintegration of many of the world's refugees and displaced persons. According to the U.S. State Department, land mines were responsible for slowing the rate of return of refugees to Cambodia in 1992 from an expected 10,000 to approximately 1,000 per week.

Repatriation is often restricted by mining of the routes of return. The areas around villages and communities are often so extensively mined that normal habitation patterns are impossible to follow; ordinary movement and gainful employment are no longer feasible. There is a fear of returning to mined areas when stories of death and maiming by land mines filter back to the displaced populations. It is little wonder that victims are reluctant to leave the relative safety of temporary shelter in foreign locations to return to areas strewn with land mines.

The UN humanitarian coordinator in Angola has stated that the mine issue is at the center of problems affecting the return and repatriation of refugees and displaced persons. UNHCR is increasingly addressing these repatriation problems through mine awareness education and other related activities. These types of programs also need to be applied to internally displaced persons and local populations. The return of residents over mined roads and into mined areas greatly increases the risks, complexity, and expense of repatriation.

Approximately 1.5 million refugees in Pakistan are awaiting repatriation to Afghanistan. The most common reason given for the slowness of return is the danger of land mines. Financial assistance from the government of Pakistan and international organizations needed to maintain the minimal living conditions in refugee camps is significant. While the hardships the refugees continue to endure cannot be quantitatively assessed, UNHCR expenditure in Pakistan for refugee programs was $48.4 million in 1993. The great human and financial costs of slow repatriation require that innovative approaches to the issues of displaced populations should be considered in light of the specific problems presented by land mines.

Dislocated Populations

Another consideration, which is seldom quantified, is the destabilization caused by the influx of asylum seekers, especially in poor countries already suffering under the burden of overpopulation. The mining of rural areas often makes people move into urban areas, whose resources are already overstressed as a result of the conflict. Competition in the marketplace and unemployment increase sharply. As tension rises, so do dangers of instability. Temporary, squatter settlements often proliferate. Illicit market practices are fostered, creating further destabilization.

Psychological Impact

Perhaps the least quantifiable problem in mined areas is the fear of mines and the ensuing fear of movement. Land mines are basically weapons of terror. Their random destruction produces a degree of uncertainty and risk whose effect is hard to determine. In Afghanistan and Somalia, mothers have been known to tie their children to trees to prevent them from wandering into mined areas. In one respect, the fears generated by mines can be paralyzing; in another respect, their omnipresence may produce a sense of complacency, especially for children, that can actually increase the danger of mines. In northern Iraq, mines are so much a part of daily life that children often trade them and use them as toys. In Cambodia, farmers use them to demarcate their paddy fields.

There is also the long-term effect on the individuals coping with disfigurement, and the effect on society of dealing with a large amputee population. These effects can only be expected to grow. As a proportion of the entire population, Cambodia's estimated 36,000 amputees would be roughly equivalent to 1.3 million amputees in the United States. One can imagine the effect such numbers would have on the national psyche of a country seeking normalcy.

The international community needs to understand the effect that fear of mines has on the development of a country in a postconflict environment and must assist such countries in dealing with these problems. The Vietnam Veterans Foundation of America is studying the long-term psychological effects of mines on adults and children. UNDHA should work closely with this organization to assure that the results of the study are made available to groups that can address the findings.

Environmental Impact

Land mines are recognized as having a devastating environmental impact. Their severe and long-term effect on land usage, water supply, and infrastructure make them among the most toxic of all man-made pollutants. Protocol I to the 1949 Geneva Conventions, article 35(3), prohibits means of warfare "which are intended, or may be expected, to cause widespread, long term and severe damage to the natural environment." Article 55(1) provides for a "prohibition of the use of methods or means of warfare which are intended, or may be expected, to cause such damage to the natural environment and thereby to prejudice the health or survival of the population." Land mines clearly fall into this category; they degrade very slowly and render land and other natural resources unusable for years, even generations.

HUMANITARIAN ASSISTANCE

International humanitarian resources are strained by the presence of land mines in a country. The cost of the consequences of mine pollution must be met either from the national budget of the affected country or from the development and humanitarian assistance budgets of donor governments and NGOs.

Another major problem—which is becoming ever more acute as global relief efforts increase—is the impediment mines present to the effective delivery of relief. Whether it is a doctor caring for the sick in rural areas or a food convoy delivering to the needy, the ever-present danger of mines impedes the effort. The welfare of relief workers is a major concern, and the danger for them becomes more acute as their humanitarian activities take them into mine-infested areas.

In an eleven-day period in 1993, three land mine accidents occurring in Mozambique, Senegal, and Somalia killed fourteen and injured ten relief workers. These incidents are examples of the indiscriminate nature and tremendous potential for large-scale, continuous destruction of land mines. Additionally, even with excellent training and supervision, eighty deminers were killed or maimed in 1993 while carrying out mine clearing duties in Afghanistan and Cambodia alone.

Mine awareness programs should be an integral part of relief personnel training. Again, UNDHA is well situated to provide leadership to the international governmental and nongovernmental organizations that are assisting in mine-ravaged countries.

The interrelationship of all the issues raised by the presence of land mines requires a single entity to coordinate information and serve as an intermediary between official and unofficial groups. Although UNDHA need not be that operational entity, it is best positioned to work closely with NGOs to assure that the work is being accomplished.

MINE PROLIFERATION

A total ban on the manufacture and use of antipersonnel land mines should be the goal of the international community. Regardless of the likelihood of this solution being chosen now, it should still be recognized and remain the aim of international and national groups concerned with land mines. When all the facts are in, it will be obvious that any short-term advantage gained by use of antipersonnel land mines will be more than offset by the short-, medium-, and long-term damage caused by their indiscriminate deployment and their costs in terms of permanent warfare.

In anticipation of a total ban, worthwhile measures can be taken to limit the use of land mines. For example:

1) Land mines should be placed immediately on the United Nations registry of Conventional Weapons to provide an increased degree of knowledge regarding their use.

2) The General Assembly resolution of December 16, 1993, calling for an immediate international ban on the export of land mines should be vigorously pursued as a step toward a total ban.

3) Stronger provisions should be adopted to expand the restrictions in Protocol II to the 1980 Conventional Weapons Convention, and to close its existing loopholes. General Assembly resolution 48/79 calls for a review conference, which will provide an opportunity to strengthen the Convention and its Protocols. Additionally, competent NGOs should be admitted as observers to the experts meetings leading to the conference.

4) States should be encouraged to sign the Convention on Inhuman Weapons. General Assembly resolution 48/79 calls for all states to become parties to the Convention.

5) The United Nations should officially encourage increased interna-

tional public awareness of the land mine problem and its consequences.

By dealing effectively with the land mine problem, the United Nations
best serves its mandate laid down in the Charter, "to achieve international
co-operation in solving international problems of an economic, social,
cultural or humanitarian character, and in promoting and encouraging
respect for human rights and for fundamental freedoms for all without
distinction as to race, sex, language or religion."

The land mine, with its inability to tell friend from foe or soldier
from innocent child, affronts the principles the United Nations was created to protect. Its debilitating effects on the basic social, economic, and
humanitarian fabric of society can no longer be tolerated. The time to
act is now.

13

Turning Principles into Practice: The Challenge for International Conventions and Institutions

YVES SANDOZ

T he use of antipersonnel mines has reached proportions that take the issue beyond purely humanitarian concerns. The problem's economic and social implications, as well as its impact on the environment and its effects on population movements in particular, give it a universal dimension.

Different actors must address the problem at different levels, pursuing a variety of aims, with local or worldwide objectives, in the short or the long term. But the key word for all these efforts is *complementarity:* they should not compete with each other, but be designed to be mutually supportive.

To overcome the current crisis, the emphasis must be placed on preventive action. This will involve compliance with clear, effective, and universally accepted rules, which must be drawn up without delay. Two main levels of preventive action may be identified: the prevention of wars (*jus ad bellum*) and the prevention of abuses during wars (*jus in bello*). The reasoning applied to each is different, but the two must not be regarded as contradictory. A third level comes between these two and has a bearing on both of them: disarmament and arms control.

Prevention of Wars

One cannot disregard the fact that, whatever the circumstances, wars cause immeasurable suffering, and that the need for an international mechanism capable of imposing a ban on the use of force between states and of preventing, as far as possible, recourse to force within states is becoming ever more pressing.

The proliferation of mines is certainly a further argument in favor of such a mechanism. This type of solution is, however, a long-term prospect with little bearing on the current massive use of land mines.

Arms Control and Disarmament

Even in the short term, the problem of mines cannot be seriously addressed without being viewed as part of arms control and disarmament, fields that extend beyond the scope of international humanitarian law.

Given the reality of the proliferation and transfer of weapons, it is evident that a ban on the use of a certain weapon will not be completely effective as long as the weapon continues to be manufactured and stockpiled. Arms control and disarmament measures are therefore indispensable.

Such measures might include the prohibition or the restriction of exports, destruction of existing stocks that do not comply with possible new manufacturing standards, prohibition of the manufacture of certain types of mines, and establishment of verification mechanisms to accompany all these measures.

States should therefore seriously examine the possibility of a multilateral agreement to ban the development, manufacture, transfer, and use of at least certain types of land mines and the destruction of all existing stocks of those types. To this end, they should introduce the subject of mines in the Conference on Disarmament and could look to the process that led to the adoption of the Chemical Weapons Convention as a source of inspiration.

As an immediate and unilateral measure, an export moratorium on mines, as instituted by the United States and some other countries, should be encouraged.

Preventing the Use of Mines During Armed Conflicts: The General Framework of International Humanitarian Law

International humanitarian law originally limited the damage caused by weapons by altogether prohibiting the use of weapons that were perceived as excessively cruel or "barbaric." The customary prohibition of the use of poison was based on the perception of its treacherous nature and the fact that poisoned weapons inevitably caused death.[1] The prohibition of the use of explosive bullets by the St. Petersburg Declaration of 1868[2] was similarly based on the wish to outlaw weapons that inflicted excessively cruel injuries or that usually killed the victim. Subsequently, humanitarian law prohibited the use of expanding (dum-dum) bullets.[3] For the same reason, but also because of their indiscriminate nature, the use of chemical weapons, mentioned in the Treaty of Versailles in 1919 as contrary to international law,[4] was specifically prohibited, together with the use of bacteriological weapons, by the Geneva Protocol of 1925.[5]

Between 1925 and the adoption of the 1980 Conventional Weapons Convention, however, international humanitarian law did not make any significant progress in prohibiting the use of specific weapons, despite the numerous discussions on incendiary weapons[6] that took place between the two world wars and the reaction to the use of nuclear weapons on Hiroshima and Nagasaki.[7]

As for the general rules of international humanitarian law governing the conduct of hostilities, it is primarily in the 1977 Additional Protocol I to the Geneva Conventions of 1949 that they were reaffirmed and developed. It is evident that rules limiting the use of weapons and methods of warfare "of a nature to cause superfluous injury or unnecessary suffering"[8] have little chance of being effective unless they are supplemented by rules specifying which weapons or methods of warfare are prohibited.

The importance of the reaffirmation in 1977 Protocol I of the ban on the use of "a method or means of combat which cannot be directed at a specific military objective"[9] and of the other rules that protect civilians cannot be denied. They reflect the very essence of international humanitarian law—that is, the distinction between combatants and noncombatants.

But the key question is the relationship between the specific rules introduced in the 1980 Convention, in particular those governing the use of land mines, and the general rules of international humanitarian law. There is no doubt that the rules governing the use of land mines are based on the principles and rules laid down in 1977 Protocol I. Furthermore, Protocol I reaffirmed and developed international humanitarian law. Whereas certain provisions, such as those specifically concerning the environment, are obviously developments, others are a reaffirmation of preexisting rules, often considered as preemptory norms of general international law (*jus cogens*).[10]

Thus it can be claimed that the indiscriminate use of antipersonnel mines is a violation not only of the 1980 Convention, but also of Additional Protocol I, and even of a rule of *jus cogens*.

Review of the 1980 Convention

The military view on mines is expounded elsewhere in this volume, and we shall not dwell on it here. It should just be recalled that a meeting of experts on the subject convened by the International Committee of the Red Cross (ICRC) came to the conclusion that "no alternative fulfils the military requirement in the way that anti-personnel mines do" and that "the anti-personnel mine is the most cost-effective system available to the military."[11]

This is a very important point because, as experience has shown, international humanitarian law has no chance of imposing exigencies that would have a decisive effect on the outcome of a conflict. If the law is to be applied, it must be seen as useful, or at least not detrimental, to all concerned. Military commanders will not take the risk of giving up an effective weapon unless it is guaranteed that their potential adversaries have also done so.

Consequently, among the numerous conditions that have to be met to ensure that the review of the 1980 Convention brings real progress, the first, apart from parallel action in the field of disarmament, is universal acceptance of the Convention's rules.

UNIVERSAL ACCEPTANCE OF THE CONVENTION'S RULES

Everything possible must be done to ensure that the 1980 Convention is universally accepted. The fact that only forty-one states are party to the Convention makes its revision almost futile. The review process should, therefore, prompt a large-scale mobilization of the international community to incite states to ratify or accede to the Convention, especially in regions, notably in Asia and Africa, where mines have taken and are still taking such a heavy toll.

Furthermore, since the 1980 Convention and its three Protocols reflect the rules reaffirmed or developed in Additional Protocol I of 1977, they also concern the states party to 1977 Protocol I, or even all states in some respects. It is therefore important that all states ratify or accede to the Additional Protocols of 1977, so as to give their provisions as broad a base as possible. In view of the U.S. role in the international scene, it seems evident that ratification by the United States of the 1977 Additional Protocols could give new impetus to the indispensable progress of international humanitarian law toward universal acceptance. This objective can be achieved in the medium term, and its achievement would certainly have a favorable effect on the global land mine problem. Meanwhile, we need to consider interim measures.

REDEFINING THE SITUATION OF THE
CONVENTION AND THE REVIEW PROCEDURE

This review system provided for in the 1980 Convention is flexible,[12] allowing for rapid adaptation to developments in the weapons field. Indeed, the procedure can be seen as an intelligent manner of implementing article 36 of 1977 Protocol I, which stipulates: "In the study, acquisition or adoption of a new weapon, means or method of warfare, a High Contracting Party is under an obligation to determine whether its employment would, in some or all circumstances, be prohibited by this Protocol or by any other rule of international law applicable to the High Contracting Party."

Antipersonnel laser devices that could be used to blind combatants are a prime example of a newly developed weapon that could, and indeed should, be the subject of a further protocol.[13]

A major difficulty, however, is that the high contracting parties are bound by the Convention, six months after ratification, only in relation to other party states. This is also the case for the annexed Protocols. This aspect is far from satisfactory for two reasons: First, it gives the impression that the prohibitions or restrictions in question arise entirely from the Convention itself. In fact, for the most part they are only an illustration of the more general rules contained in the 1977 Additional Protocols, or of rules that form part of *jus cogens*. Who, then, is to determine which rules are binding only on states party to the 1980 Convention and the Protocol concerned, which ones are also binding on states party to 1977 Additional Protocol I, and which ones are binding on all states? No one; hence the deplorable situation of uncertainty in a domain in which states, and their armed forces in particular, have to know exactly where they stand. Second, since certain restrictions have obvious military implications, how will a state's armed forces go about imposing rules on their soldiers in certain circumstances (for instance, when they are in conflict with another state party) and not in others? Should the troops nevertheless be trained in the use of weapons prohibited by the Convention?

These considerations raise the question of whether it might be necessary to rethink the entire philosophy of the 1980 Convention and make it an instrument that is linked much more closely with the Additional Protocols of 1977.

In reality, everything would be much easier and clearer if participation in the Additional Protocols of 1977 automatically meant participation in the 1980 Convention, which would become a sort of technical annex that could be adapted to keep pace with technical developments. Additional Protocol I of 1977 already has one such technical annex, in the form of regulations concerning identification, which has the purpose of allowing procedures for the identification of medical personnel, units, and transports to be adapted in accordance with technical advances. Indeed, this annex has its own review procedure.[14]

This review procedure should also have a bearing on the reflection on the 1980 Convention. Under this procedure, any amendment proposed by a conference of states party is communicated to the parties to the Convention by the depositary, and "shall be considered to have been accepted at the end of a period of one year after it has been so communicated, unless within that period a declaration of non-acceptance of the amendment has been communicated to the depositary by not less than one third of the High Contracting Parties." The amendment then "shall enter into force three months after its acceptance for all High Contracting Parties other than those which have made a declaration of non-acceptance."[15]

Such a procedure has enormous advantages. First, it is very speedy. The 132 states party to 1977 Protocol I are today bound by the revised technical annex to the Protocol,[16] only four years after the start of the review process. Second, it obliges states to take a position, since they have to declare their *nonacceptance* of proposed amendments rather than their agreement to be bound by them. This is a vital point when one considers the heavy workload and, occasionally, the apathy of government administrations. Indeed, it is probable that a great majority of the states that have not ratified the 1980 Convention have failed to do so not because they reject its provisions, but simply because they have not found the time to examine them.

This type of procedure has other precedents, as well. One can be found in the Convention on International Civil Aviation, signed in Chicago on December 7, 1944. That Convention provides that international standards and recommended parties, designated as annexes to the Convention, "shall require the vote of two-thirds of the Council at a meeting called for that purpose and shall then be submitted by the Council to each contracting State. Any such Annex or any amendment of an Annex shall become effective within three months after its submission to the contracting States or at the end of such longer period of time as the Council may prescribe, unless in the meantime a majority of the contracting States register their disapproval with the Council."[17] Here, the procedure goes even further than the one provided for in the technical annex to 1977 Protocol I, since the new rules become binding even on minority states that have refused to accept them. This is quite understandable in the case of rules governing international civil aviation, which obviously have to be standard.

This further step, or some similar measure, could perhaps be taken in regard to prohibitions or restrictions on weapons that will be fully complied with only if those bound by them are convinced that their potential adversaries will do likewise. In any event, all these matters should provide us with food for thought. Although such a proposal should prevent neither an immediate mobilization in favor of the 1980 Convention nor efforts to improve its efficiency during the ongoing review procedure, it should be submitted to states without delay for examination as a medium-term objective.

EXTENSION OF APPLICABILITY[18]

The 1980 Convention formally applies only to international armed conflicts. However, in recent times, most conflicts have been internal, and it is these conflicts that are largely responsible for the human suffering caused by land mines. It is therefore of the utmost urgency to formally extend the scope of application of the Convention to noninternational armed conflicts through an amendment specifying this new scope.

Nevertheless, we cannot disregard that some states would undoubtedly object to such an extension of the applicability of the Convention, invoking national sovereignty. This foreseeable reaction probably arises from a misunderstanding. Several states, particularly in the Southern Hemisphere, oppose the tendency toward intervention on humanitarian grounds to bring assistance to people in need. They fear that such operations might have a destabilizing effect on governments or might even serve as a pretext for seeking to overthrow them. They are therefore extremely reluctant to see any development of rules pertaining to noninternational armed conflicts.

Such views can perhaps be understood in regard to large-scale relief operations. They are totally unwarranted, however, when it comes to the weapons issue: the application of rules banning the use of weapons does not imply any outside intervention. From a moral standpoint, moreover, it is inconceivable that a government would consider using against its own population weapons it has agreed not to employ against an enemy state because of their cruel nature.

But there again, the military advantages of a weapon might make a government hesitate if it fears that insurgents might easily be able to lay their hands on it. Hence the importance of universal rules and parallel efforts in the sphere of disarmament. The Chemical Weapons Convention demonstrates that if the manufacture, possession, and transfer of a weapon are prohibited, the question of its use is automatically resolved, and controversies on possible different approaches to international and noninternational armed conflicts become pointless. In the framework of international humanitarian law, the formal link between general rules and specific weapons envisaged above should relate to both Additional Protocols of 1977, and not only to Protocol I.

It should be noted, finally, that progress toward harmonization of the rules governing hostilities in all types of armed conflict might be achieved by establishing cooperation among the military, particularly in terms of drawing up military training manuals. In practice, military training generally makes no distinction between preparations to use weapons and means of warfare in international or in internal conflicts.

INTRODUCTION OF IMPLEMENTATION MECHANISMS

Although the 1980 Convention contains no implementation provision, it reaffirms the rules of international humanitarian law found in other treaties. Implementation measures under those treaties are therefore also relevant to the 1980 Convention. Nevertheless, it may be desirable to include specific measures in the 1980 Convention; these could be drawn mainly from the humanitarian law treaties, or from other instruments of international law. It bears emphasis, however, that this possibility should be considered as secondary to the more radical reform suggested above, whereby the 1980 Convention would become an annex to the 1977 Additional Protocols.

Provision of Legal Advisers

This is now required under article 82 of Additional Protocol I to the Geneva Conventions. A similar provision in the 1980 Convention could provide for legal advisers to give guidance on matters relating to the use of weapons, to be incorporated at all levels down to brigade or equivalent level, and to be included in planning staff.

Requirements for Training in Humanitarian Law

The requirement to instruct the armed forces in the law is embodied in the Hague Convention IV of 1907, the four Geneva Conventions of 1949, and their Additional Protocols of 1977. Such a requirement ought to be contained also in the 1980 Convention, including such provisions as the following:

- Training in the use of weapons in accordance with humanitarian law should be given in cadet academies and during all command and staff training courses;
- Manuals on weapon systems should include the law specifying their correct use, in the languages of the user countries;
- The packaging of weapons should bear a warning as to the legal limitations on their use; and
- All military training of foreign nationals should include training in humanitarian law.

Incorporation in Domestic Law

The 1980 Convention should be translated into local languages, and appropriate national laws and regulations should be adopted. This suggestion is similar to the provision set out in article 84 of 1977 Protocol I.

International Fact-Finding Commission

The international fact-finding commission provided for in article 90 of Additional Protocol I to the Geneva Conventions could also be used to investigate possible violations of the 1980 Convention. In the context of the 1977 Protocol, the commission's competence is based on consent that can be given either in advance, in the form of a declaration, or on an ad hoc basis. It would have to be decided whether the same formula would be appropriate for the 1980 Convention and whether it should also be based on confidentiality, as in the 1977 Protocol.

Creation of a Supervisory Body

A number of international treaties create supervisory bodies designed to help implement the treaty. These bodies typically receive periodic reports submitted by states parties on the measures they have taken to implement the treaty. They also receive complaints about alleged violations, undertake investigations, and discuss their findings with the states concerned. They often undertake promotional activities to improve compliance with the law.

The review conference could consider whether it might be appropriate to create an analogous body for the 1980 Convention, or whether the role of the international fact-finding commission could be extended to cover this Convention.

NECESSARY CLARIFICATIONS OF PROTOCOL II[19]

Article 3, enumerating general restrictions on the use of mines, booby traps, and other devices, is based on the generally accepted distinction between military objectives and civilian objects. Such a distinction, however, is difficult to maintain once a military target has moved away from a mined area, leaving behind antipersonnel mines. Moreover, the duty to protect civilians from the effects of those weapons is couched in very weak terms, as paragraph 4 of this article makes reference to all "feasible" precautions. The term *feasible* allows for considerable flexibility in interpretation. Furthermore, the provision is weak because feasible measures would include installation of fences or signposts, although these tend to be removed by members of the local population, either out of ignorance or for the sake of the profit to be derived from such items. This article might be the right place to introduce a ban on the use of antipersonnel mines without a self-destruct mechanism.

Article 4, restricting other types of mines, has the same shortcomings as article 3.

Article 5 prohibits the placement of remotely delivered mines outside areas that are military objectives unless one of two conditions is fulfilled: that their location can be recorded or that they are fitted with self-neutralizing mechanisms. It is difficult to record accurately the location of mines delivered by fixed-wing aircraft, artillery, and rockets. The recording requirements in the absence of a neutralizing mechanism, set out in paragraph 1(a), are therefore not applicable when these methods of delivery are used. Problems remain with the implementation of paragraph 1(b), regarding self-destruct and self-neutralization devices, because these devices are not reliable enough to guarantee the safety of a mined area; moreover, there is no maximum time limit for the active life of these mines. The wording of paragraph 1(b) also creates confusion between self-destruct and self-neutralizing mechanisms. Furthermore, paragraph 2 of this article requires but does not define "effective advance warning."

In fact, article 5 embodies a striking contradiction between an approach based on the military utility of the weapon and a view of the problem that takes the economic and social cost of its use into account. As pointed out above, mines have an acknowledged "military utility," especially in countries that do not have the technological capacity to develop alternatives. Moreover, from the military standpoint, mines would be slightly less cost-effective if there was a general obligation to fit them with self-destruct or self-neutralizing mechanisms. This requirement, too, would have a greater impact on technologically less-advanced countries, where the production of such devices might be problematic.

It is thus the poorer countries that put up the most vigorous opposition to a total ban on antipersonnel mines or to a general obligation to fit all mines with self-destruct or self-neutralization mechanisms. Yet it is these same states that suffer most from the effects of mines, and in which the concept of the "military utility" of these weapons becomes absurd in view of the economic and social costs to which they give rise.

Article 7, on the recording and publication of the location of minefields, mines, and booby traps, contains a major flaw in that it gives no definition of a "preplanned" minefield, which is the only type that requires recording. With regard to all other minefields, parties are required only to "endeavor" to record them, which is a rather weak provision. In practice, there are still other difficulties. For instance, regular armies have followed strict procedures with respect to mine laying, and there are clear rules for marking and recording minefields. However, such records are properly created and kept by only very few armies. They also are quite frequently lost.

Even with such records, successful minefield clearance rarely can be guaranteed for a number of reasons. Mines tend to move, sometimes long distances, over a period of time, owing to the effects of the weather, soil erosion, and on occasion the action of animals. This is especially true in the case of scatterable mines. Furthermore, even the most conscientiously maintained minefield record can be subject to human error by soldiers who may be tired or under stress.

Article 8, addressing the protection of UN forces and missions from the effects of mines and other such devices, should be expanded to cover organizations other than the UN, such as CSCE missions and private mine clearance agencies. In fact, the UN itself has acknowledged the need to coordinate mine clearance activities, and for that purpose, the Department of Peacekeeping Operations, which includes the Mine Clearance Center, has established a database to which any contributions are welcome. Expert reports from other mine clearance organizations point out that, more often than not, mine clearance is an extremely hazardous exercise, principally because records are not properly kept and there are often no maps or signposts. As of April 1993, in Afghanistan, for instance, mine clearance activities had resulted in twenty-four deaths and twenty-eight amputations, and no fewer than nineteen operatives had been blinded.[20]

Mine clearance is expensive given the high cost of experts' fees, personnel insurance premiums, and such support expenses as medical and casualty evacuation costs. Article 8 should therefore be extended to afford protection to third-party missions and, logically, to humanitarian organizations working in regions affected by mines.

Article 9, on international cooperation in the removal of minefields, mines, and booby traps, does not impose an obligation to remove mines, as the words used therein are "shall endeavour to reach agreement." Moreover, this agreement relates only to "the provision" of such information and assistance as "necessary to" remove or render ineffective mines and minefields, and thus in no way imposes a specific obligation to actually do so. This is a major shortcoming of the law. Further, this article does not deal with other issues of crucial importance in a mine-devastated country after the cessation of active hostilities, such as repatriation and land reclamation requirements.

PROHIBITION OF UNDETECTABLE MINES

A ban on undetectable mines should be viewed as secondary or complementary to other proposals. It must be mentioned, however, because the difficulty in detecting mines makes mine clearance—so vitally needed today—an almost insurmountable task.

If a provision on the subject is introduced, it should stipulate that the detectable element in the mine not be easily removable. Provisions should also be made for verification that mines not conforming to these specifications are not manufactured.

SPECIFICATIONS FOR ANTITANK MINES

The mines considered here are essentially antipersonnel mines. Antitank mines frequently have self-neutralizing devices because they are expensive and often need to be reused. It would therefore be useful to require that all antitank mines be fitted with neutralizing mechanisms, and it would have to be verifiable that only this type is manufactured.

Reparation for Damage

Although the principle of reparation is reaffirmed in international humanitarian law,[21] its application has proved uncertain. Cases in which an arrangement is reached between belligerent parties are generally settled after the armed conflict is over, on terms imposed by the victor. At this stage, considerations associated with *jus ad bellum* apply, and not the humanitarian exigencies of *jus in bello*. Moreover, requests that the responsible state make reparation are submitted through the state of origin of the injured persons (individuals or bodies corporate).

The ambiguous nature of many current conflicts and the frequent lack of a clear passage from war to peace make the problem doubly difficult to resolve. The question of reparation for damage resulting from acts contrary to international humanitarian law is, however, a very topical issue, owing in particular to the work of the International Law Commission and the reports of the special rapporteur of the subcommission on the prevention of discrimination and protection of minorities on questions relating to "the right to restitution, compensation and rehabilitation for victims of gross violations of human rights and fundamental freedoms."[22]

In the framework of this chapter, the key point is that no progress in the field of reparation will be possible unless responsibility for violations of international humanitarian law can be clearly determined. That can be achieved only if the rules are explicit, and this is an additional argument in favor of formulating prohibitions that are precise and cannot be circumvented.

Repression

Responsibility for punishing those who commit grave breaches of international humanitarian law lies first and foremost with governments in regard to their own population, and in particular to members of their armed forces. At the international level, two events have created a new impetus for fulfillment of the obligation incumbent on each state party to the Geneva Conventions to punish or extradite any war criminal on its territory: the establishment of an international tribunal for the prosecution of persons suspected of perpetrating grave violations of international humanitarian law committed on the territory of the former Yugoslavia since 1991,[23] and the examination of a draft code of crimes against the peace and security of mankind and of a draft statute for an international criminal tribunal.[24]

The preventive role that such tribunals can play, insofar as they meet the challenges before them (stringency, consistency, independence, cooperation of states, and so forth) cannot be underestimated. But the rules pertaining to mines must be clear so that acts committed in violation of international humanitarian law, war crimes in particular, can be determined unequivocally and action can be taken to prosecute the perpetrators.

Role of Humanitarian Institutions:
The Example of the ICRC

International and nongovernmental organizations that are directly or indirectly concerned with the problem of mines can certainly play an important role in this collective effort. The ICRC feels that it has a special mission in this respect, in view of the mandate entrusted to it by the international community to work for the application and development of international humanitarian law.[25]

The ICRC's operational work in the field, carried out with the support of National Red Cross and Red Crescent Societies, gives it, first of all, the role of a witness: the surgeons it sends to the theaters of war are only too well placed to see the devastating effects of mines on the civilian population, and on children in particular; the orthopedic technicians it sends to set up and manage orthopedic workshops in many countries can but acknowledge that the needs greatly exceed their capacity. The thousands of ICRC delegates and local employees who work in conflicts worldwide are faced every day with the destruction wrought by mines. The ICRC therefore feels duty-bound to alert the general public and governments to the magnitude of the problem, and to this end has published a number of brochures that have been widely distributed.[26] Through its regional delegations and its cooperation with National Red Cross and Red Crescent Societies and their International Federation, the ICRC seeks to spread awareness in all parts of the world of the mines problem, and indeed of all issues concerning international humanitarian law.

Second, the ICRC has tried to grasp all the aspects of the problem and to make them clear to others. In particular, it organized a multidisciplinary symposium in Montreux, Switzerland, in April 1993. The general objective of the symposium was to collect the facts and ideas necessary to coordinate future action by bodies interested in improving the situation of mine victims and in taking preventive action. Its more specific aims were to gain as accurate a picture as possible of actual mine use and the consequences thereof; to analyze available methods designed to limit such use or alleviate the suffering of the victims, and to identify the inadequacies of such methods; to decide on the best remedial action; to establish strategies for coordinating the work of the different bodies involved in such action; and to draft a report that could be used as a reference for future efforts.[27] The symposium took place in a positive atmosphere. Following intensive work by the different working groups, the participants stressed the necessary complementarity of the various courses of action envisaged. These courses were set out in a highly detailed report.[28]

Third, the ICRC feels that it has a moral duty to make its position public. The organization's president has done this, coming out in favor of a total ban on the use of antipersonnel mines.

With regard to international humanitarian law, the ICRC takes action on two levels. The first involves consolidation of the basic rules of international humanitarian law. To this end, the ICRC has published commentaries on the Geneva Conventions and their Additional Protocols[29] and engages in diplomatic approaches to encourage states to ratify or to accede to these treaties. It also organizes numerous seminars throughout the world, in cooperation with the local National Red Cross or Red Crescent Societies, to make the law more widely known and to invite states to adopt national legislation and other measures necessary for its implementation.

In parallel, the ICRC has always helped prepare for the development of the instruments of international humanitarian law. As regards conventional weapons, it organized two meetings of experts in the mid-1970s, whose results were published and served as a basis for the conference that drafted and adopted the 1980 Convention.[30]

In preparation for the review of the 1980 Convention, the ICRC has organized four experts meetings and has published a detailed report on a recent and terrifying invention, namely, blinding weapons.[31] It has also held a conference of army experts to examine the military utility of mines and the possibility of finding alternatives. Finally, it has drafted a report for the review conference containing many suggestions for improvement of the Convention itself, and more particularly of the Landmines Protocol.[32]

Finally, the entire International Red Cross and Red Crescent Movement is engaged in ongoing efforts to bring help to the victims of mines. Numerous other organizations are also involved in the mobilization against the use of mines, especially in relation to mine clearance and in raising public awareness.[33] All these efforts are important and necessary, but considerable room for development remains.

Conclusion

In view of its social, economic, and ecological implications, the massive use of antipersonnel mines in present-day conflicts is a problem that concerns us all. Greater awareness and large-scale mobilization among the public are necessary if governments are to be spurred to make a genuine commitment to address the issue. But the problem is a complex one and should be tackled simultaneously on different fronts, with the accent on cooperation rather than confrontation. Strengthening the means of preventing war, seeking a total ban on the use of antipersonnel mines, or seeking the prohibition of the use of certain mines in wartime are valid objectives that stem from the conviction that the current situation is unacceptable. They are just different levels of the same endeavor.

The goal of a world organized in such a way as to eliminate war, considered Utopian by some, is at any rate a distant prospect. The military utility of mines leads one to believe that a total prohibition can be contemplated only within the framework of a disarmament agreement comprising strict verification procedures, and this is bound to take time. Immediate efforts to broaden, strengthen, and clarify existing agreements are therefore also necessary.

The following practical proposals, while not constituting a plan of action as such, are useful steps toward alleviating the land mine crisis.

1) Efforts to mobilize public opinion must be increased, especially in countries that suffer the most from mines. Everything possible must be done to alert the public to the scale of the phenomenon, its pernicious nature, and its dramatic consequences in the long term. Land mines cause horrendous damage in human, social, economic, and ecological terms, and there is a critical shortage of resources to cope with that damage, particularly in the countries worst affected. All these considerations call for vigorous and determined action on the part of the entire international community.

2) There is little hope of serious progress unless the issues of the production and transfer of land mines are addressed. Prohibition of *certain uses* of mines is not enough, as effective control of illicit use is practically impossible for this type of weapon, and such a measure would thus have only marginal effects. It is therefore essential to set standards that will make it possible to tackle the matter at the levels of production and trade, in the framework of disarmament negotiations. Such standards will have to be accepted by a wide consensus and be accompanied by verification procedures. As in the case of a contagious disease, measures taken to control the use of mines will be effective only if they are universal. Like microbes, mines do not stop at borders.

3) A total ban on antipersonnel mines would be by far the best solution. If this objective is not immediately attainable, the standards chosen must be capable of containing the problem. The active life of a large proportion of the mines produced today is almost unlimited, and they are extremely difficult to detect. At the very least, every mine should be fitted with a self-destruct mechanism, or a self-neutralization mechanism in the case of the larger models, and include an element making it easier to detect. The cost of self-destruct mechanisms or elements facilitating detection is negligible in comparison with the extra cost of clearing mines that are not fitted with such devices.

4) Rules requiring extra expenditure and technological expertise must

not, however, be seen as favoring rich countries. Such requirements must be accompanied by a dialogue that takes this aspect of the problem into consideration and envisages the transfer of technology and financial assistance.

5) Universal recognition of the rules governing the use of certain weapons during armed conflict must be secured to avoid any ambiguity: members of the armed forces need clear directives and have to know the rights and duties of their adversaries. Whereas the Geneva Conventions have achieved almost universal acceptance, only about two-thirds of states are party to their Additional Protocols of 1977.[34] Three of the permanent members of the UN Security Council, which in that capacity have a special responsibility in regard to the use of force, are not yet party to the Protocols: France (party to Protocol II only), the United Kingdom, and the United States. It is essential that ratification, examination, or reexamination under way in those states be speeded up and completed, so as to give a decisive boost to universal acceptance of the rules of international humanitarian law.

6) Moreover, a clearer, more formal, and more automatic link between the general instruments of international humanitarian law and the rules that prohibit or restrict the use of certain types of weapons would be highly desirable. In addition, the review procedure for those rules must be flexible, allowing for rapid adaptation to new developments and for the universal acceptance, within a very short period, of new or amended rules. The possibility of making them an annex to the 1977 Additional Protocols, along the lines of Annex I to Protocol I, merits consideration.

7) At the same time, a considerable effort of mobilization must be made to persuade states to ratify or accede to the 1980 Convention.

8) It is morally and militarily unjustifiable for weapons banned during international armed conflicts not to be prohibited during internal conflicts. Moreover, disarmament measures aimed at prohibiting the production of such weapons imply a total ban on their use. Any prohibition on the use of antipersonnel mines or of certain types of mines must therefore also apply to noninternational armed conflicts.

9) Preparations for the future cannot be made without regard to the past; the entire international community must make a concerted effort to clear the vast tracts of land rendered unusable by mines and to provide mine victims with the care and assistance they need

and deserve. Those who use mines, but also those who produce them and states that tolerate the mines trade, must assume their responsibilities.

10) These objectives call for an effort on the part of all who are aware of the scale of the problem and who refuse to see this evil that is afflicting our planet spread further.

The measures taken may be directed toward a whole range of short-term or long-term goals. Care must be taken, however, to ensure that the different approaches do not appear contradictory, and that they are seen as a coherent attempt to achieve a common objective. In a wider perspective, the effort to control mines is also an effort for peace.

14

Eliminating the Threat of Land Mines: A New U.S. Policy

CYRUS VANCE AND HERBERT S. OKUN

With international attention focused on negotiations to destroy nuclear weapons and prevent new nuclear arms races on the Korean peninsula and in South Asia, some may think that land mines, those tiny weapons that can fit in the palm of a hand, are hardly a threat to world peace.

In fact, while reducing the threat of nuclear war must remain the first priority of international arms control efforts, it is small weapons that are killing and wounding far more people every day. The U.S. Department of State has noted that land mines "may be the most toxic and widespread pollution facing mankind."[1] This is true, but *pollution* is too benign a word. Land mines have caused and continue to cause human and economic catastrophe of monumental proportions.

People often speak of an idea whose time has come; the use of land mines is an issue whose time has come. The accumulation of land mines across the globe is a crisis that can, without exaggeration, be characterized as epidemic. Further, there is a broad consensus in the United States and in the international community regarding the need to combat the wide array of problems caused by land mines. Although encouraged by the many solutions suggested throughout this volume, we are convinced that nothing less than a total ban on the production, possession, transfer, and use of antipersonnel land mines will move us closer to the goal of completely eliminating this scourge. And, we believe the United States should take the lead to achieve this goal.

With this in mind, we will, in this chapter, describe the magnitude and nature of the crisis, examine the evolution of U.S. policy toward land mines, and outline why U.S. policy should focus on a total ban.

The Crisis

During World War II, the Korean conflict, and a few other large-scale conventional wars, land mines were used as defensive weapons against enemy soldiers—to guard a perimeter or to channel the enemy into a specific area. But that purpose changed in Vietnam, and since then, the overwhelming majority of mines have been used as offensive weapons against civilians.

Cheap to buy, easy to make and transport, mines have become a weapon of choice of Third World armies and insurgent groups. Their purpose is not just to maim and kill, but to destroy the social and economic fabric of a society by isolating whole communities, depopulating vast areas, and preventing the return of refugees. In dozens of countries where people survive by growing their own food, land mines have turned huge areas of scarce arable land into useless death traps.

Land mines can be scattered by aircraft dropping thousands per minute. Each mine then lies in wait for weeks, months, or years, until an unsuspecting person, usually a civilian, steps on it, with disastrous consequences: a mine the size of a shoe polish can is powerful enough to blow the leg off an adult or pulverize a child.

Mines are easy to lay, but extremely difficult to detect and life-threatening to remove. They are often made of plastic and thus are undetectable by metal detectors. They blend in with the soil or ground cover, and are quickly obscured by a layer of dust or vegetation. Tragically, far more land mines are being deployed today than are being cleared. The statistics are appalling: an estimated 80 percent of all land mine casualties are civilians.

As we seek to address the new conflicts that have emerged in the post–Cold War world, we see the legacy of this new kind of mine warfare:

• In Afghanistan, the worst case, land mines have caused some 350,000–500,000 casualties.[2] And the U.S. Department of State estimates as many as 35 million mines may have been deployed.[3] The United Nations has launched an extensive mine clearance program in Afghanistan but estimates that it will take its twenty-seven mine clearance teams at least fifteen years to clear designated priority zones.[4]

- In Angola, there are at least 9 million mines, or the equivalent of twenty for every square mile.[5] The country has over 30 thousand amputees and only a minimal capacity to produce artificial limbs.[6] According to one estimate, 150–200 new mine injuries occur each week.[7]
- In Cambodia, where an estimated 4–7 million mines remain unexploded,[8] one out of every 236 citizens is an amputee.[9]
- Between 1991 and the spring of 1994, over 3 million mines were laid in the former Yugoslavia.[10] And these devices have wrought terrible damage on innocent human beings.
- In Vietnam, more than 7,300 American soldiers were killed by mines or booby traps, and many more were injured.[11]
- In Kuwait, which spent nearly $800 million to get rid of two-thirds of the Iraqi mines laid there, more than eighty deminers have died.[12] That is more than all the American troops killed in the Persian Gulf War. Hundreds of Kuwaiti civilians have been killed by mines since the war ended.

In the absence of action by the international community, the proliferation of mines is unlikely to abate in the near future. Each day, they continue to be laid at a rate far exceeding current demining efforts. Indeed, the number of countries producing and exporting land mines, particularly in the developing world, increases each year. But we cannot blame the Third World for this tragedy. It is primarily the industrialized nations that have created increasingly sophisticated mine technology, making mines ever more lethal, difficult to detect, and easily sown in extremely large numbers.

Moreover, even after the fighting has stopped and troops have gone home, land mines remain a major obstacle to postconflict peace and reconstruction. In addition to impeding the return of refugees and displaced persons, the presence of land mines causes loss of manpower, exhaustion of medical and rehabilitation services, destruction of infrastructure, environmental damage, and loss of agricultural land. Since most land mines are found in the developing world, where resources to respond to these problems are scarce, the international community will continue to bear the costs of demining and rebuilding these countries, if it is to be done at all.

The magnitude of the problem is such that in Cambodia, the UN has estimated that to demine the entire country, not to mention rebuild it, would require every citizen to contribute every dollar of his or her income for the next 5–7 years.

This crisis of land mines may not be the most pressing issue on the American foreign policy agenda, but it is a haunting problem that will not disappear and that deeply affects U.S. efforts to promote international peace, security, and economic development. A successful campaign by the United States, resulting in a total ban on land mines, would be a concrete and substantive measure to make peacekeeping and humanitarian operations, be they American or UN, safer and less costly in both lives and human suffering. And by reducing the financial and human costs of both, the United States would take a giant step forward on the road to a more peaceful and stable world.

Evolution of U.S. Policy

In 1980, the United States and fifty-two other countries signed the Conventional Weapons Convention, including the Landmines Protocol. The signing of this document was initially accompanied by support from the Reagan administration and served to focus international attention on the land mine problem.

The Protocol was designed to regulate the use of land mines and reduce the harm to innocent civilians by adapting generally accepted principles of international humanitarian law to the specifics of mine warfare. Although the Protocol has focused attention on the global threat of land mines and contains important limitations on their use, it has had insufficient practical impact and is generally considered a flawed document.

Part of the reason the Protocol has failed to emerge as a useful instrument was the loss of American leadership. Although the United States encouraged other countries to ratify the Conventional Weapons Convention and its Protocols, including the Landmines Protocol, neither the Reagan nor the Bush administration submitted it to the Senate for ratification. The fact that only forty-one countries have ratified the Convention is due, at least in part, to the U.S. reluctance to ratify.

The United States had lost momentum as a leader in the fight to eliminate the threat of land mines until 1989, when Sen. Patrick Leahy began the War Victims Fund as part of the U.S. foreign aid program to send American doctors and prosthetists to help land mine victims. Since that time, Senator Leahy has emerged as a bold and effective leader in the campaign to focus American and international attention on the issue.

In 1992, Senator Leahy introduced the Landmine Moratorium Act, which imposed a one-year moratorium on all U.S. exports, sales, and transfers of antipersonnel mines. The legislation calls on the president to submit the 1980 Conventional Weapons Convention, along with the Landmines Protocol, to the Senate for advice and consent. It declares that U.S. policy is to actively seek verifiable international agreements or a modification of the existing international Landmines Protocol in order to prohibit the sale, transfer, or export of land mines, and further limit their use, production, and deployment. In September 1993, the Senate voted 100–0 to extend the unilateral American moratorium for an additional three years. Significantly, although the moratorium is not a long-term solution, it has served as a catalyst for further action in both U.S. and international fora.

Since passage of the Landmine Moratorium Act, the U.S. government has become increasingly active in addressing the land mine issue. In August 1993, the Department of State submitted to Congress its landmark report *Hidden Killers: The Global Problem with Uncleared Landmines.* The report, which estimates there are 85–100 million unexploded land mines in more than sixty countries, has proven to be an invaluable resource in creating awareness of the magnitude of the problem.

Hidden Killers also describes the tragic legacy of land mines: "Anyone who has seen the pictures of children with limbs mangled by landmines, or young men with no legs, or women torn and blinded by landmine explosions, will forever be haunted by the images. Mines are indiscriminate killers that can be lethal for decades. . . . An average of twelve people per year are still injured in the Netherlands from World War II landmines. Between 1945 and 1977, roughly fifteen million World War II vintage mines were cleared from Poland. During this period 13,000 civilians were killed or injured by mines."[13] The report acknowledges that "uncleared mines pose a significant challenge to the achievement of key U.S. foreign policy objectives."[14]

Additionally, the United States established the interagency working group to provide direction and policy guidance for American demining efforts. The stated strategy of the group, which is chaired by the Department of State's Bureau of Political-Military Affairs and cochaired by the Secretary of Defense's office of Democracy and Peacekeeping, is based on four goals:

- Reducing global proliferation and illegitimate use of antipersonnel land mines through domestic and international agreements;
- Providing mine awareness programs in nations with significant land mine problems to help affected populations cope with uncleared mines;
- Establishing demining training programs to help countries solve their land mine problem; and
- Developing technologies that can assist in international mine detection and clearing.

Much of American policy has focused on demining. In addition to supporting demining programs in Nicaragua, and assisting ongoing programs in Afghanistan, Cambodia, Mozambique, and Somalia, the United States is funding mine awareness programs and research and development efforts. In fiscal year 1993, the Department of State and the Agency for International Development allocated approximately $9 million for such assistance.

The United States is not alone in its efforts to deal with the global crisis. Belgium has decided to stop all production of antipersonnel mines, and prohibits the transit of such mines within its territory. The Netherlands has enacted a moratorium restricting trade to countries that are parties to the 1980 Convention. France has been respecting a voluntary de facto moratorium since 1985. Greece, Germany, and South Africa have also announced export moratoriums. In Sweden, the famous arms manufacturer Bofors has announced that it is ceasing all production of antipersonnel mines. And the European Parliament has passed a resolution calling for a five-year moratorium on the export of mines and training to place them.

In the fall of 1993, the United States took an important first step to reduce international proliferation of mines, by introducing a resolution in the UN General Assembly calling for a global moratorium on the export of antipersonnel mines. On December 16, 1993, the General Assembly unanimously adopted a resolution based on the American export moratorium. Since that time, the United States has called on other UN members who produce land mines to adopt three- to five-year unilateral moratoriums on export, sale, and transfer of antipersonnel land mines.

The General Assembly has also passed a resolution setting up a UN conference to review the 1980 Conventional Weapons Convention, including the Landmines Protocol. A series of meetings of governmental experts has begun to prepare for that conference. Unfortunately, on the same day that the General Assembly adopted the American resolution calling for an export moratorium, the United States was one of only three countries to abstain on the resolution setting up the review conference. Although the United States formally supports the review conference, it abstained because an amendment to the resolution asked the conference to discuss all aspects of the land mine problem, including a total ban. In explaining the abstention, President Clinton stated, "While we fully supported the overall thrust of the resolution, we could not vote for it because the U.S. Armed Forces continue to require landmines to accomplish certain military missions."[15]

Notwithstanding this action, to its credit the Clinton administration has indicated a desire to submit the Convention to the Senate for ratification. To this end, an administration review of the Conventional Weapons Convention is under way. Although the Protocol, with its complex rules, broad exceptions, and discretionary language, is routinely violated, the Senate should ratify it so the United States can participate fully in the review conference.

At the first UN meeting of governmental experts, held in Geneva in March 1994, the United States argued forcefully in favor of granting observer status to nongovernmental organizations (NGOs). This is appropriate, as NGOs have much to contribute to the deliberations and governmental decisions on land mines. The administration has also made several constructive proposals. For example, it proposed that remotely delivered mines contain self-destruct and self-neutralizing devices, that all mines be detectable, and that a verification regime be established. These proposals, while not going far enough, stand in sharp contrast to the modest proposals offered by other governments.

With further UN experts' meetings scheduled, this is a crucial time for U.S. leadership. The scope of the review conference, and indeed the outcome of those negotiations, will largely be determined in these meetings.

Future U.S. Policy

The next stage of U.S. policy will focus on the Conventional Weapons Convention review conference. This conference represents the best opportunity for legal and political initiatives to eliminate the threat of mines. If the United States is to seize this opportunity, constructive leadership will be needed. As noted, the United States is actively participating in the experts meetings leading up to the conference, and the

United States should move promptly to ratify the Convention and the Landmines Protocol so that it can participate fully in the conference.

Even more important, the United States should reconsider its position on excluding discussion of a total ban. In this regard, the administration should heed the advice of Senator Leahy:

> The goal of the Review Conference should be nothing less than thorough revision of the Protocol or, if necessary, negotiation of another international agreement that imposes restrictions that can stop the killing of civilians by anti-personnel landmines. If we are to have a realistic chance to achieve that goal, . . . we must approach the Conference with a presumption that anti-personnel landmines should be banned, because they have indiscriminate effects and cause unnecessary suffering.[16]

In this connection, it is of interest that the International Committee of the Red Cross (ICRC), UNICEF, and numerous other NGOs have also called for a complete ban on the production, transfer, and use of land mines.

The ICRC, which for years has provided medical aid to land mine victims around the world, has been a leading force against land mines. In report after report, the ICRC has documented the effects of mines, which it describes as "fighters that never miss, strike blindly, do not carry weapons openly, and go on killing long after hostilities are ended."[17] In 1994, the ICRC announced that "from a humanitarian point of view, . . . a worldwide ban on anti-personnel mines is the only truly effective solution."[18] We agree.

According to the UNICEF report titled *Anti-personnel Landmines: A Scourge on Children,* there is already one land mine for every twenty children in the world.[19] It states that "given the destruction and damage anti-personnel landmines can cause to children and to their development and living environment, arguments in favor of such weapons cannot be morally justified."[20] The United States must take the lead here because of the enormous impact American leadership can have. It was, after all, the American export moratorium that transformed the landscape from one of ignorance and apathy to one that presents an unprecedented opportunity to stop the ongoing carnage.

Nobody doubts that land mines have some military use: anything that can wound or kill has a military use. But land mines are killing and maiming over 1,200 innocent people a month. If children walking to school or playing in a field in Manhattan, Maine, or Monterey were having their legs blown off, the U.S. government would certainly be doing everything possible to stop it. This is happening, however, in for-eign places where medical care is often almost nonexistent, and physical labor is necessary for survival.

Therefore, we must ask ourselves whether land mines are so useful militarily that they are worth the immense costs that society is forced to pay to repair the enormous damage and ease the horrendous suffering they cause. It is time to ask whether we really need these weapons, whose victims are overwhelmingly innocent civilians. We believe the clear answer is no.

Let us examine the arguments advanced by those in and out of gov-ernment who favor fine-tuning, or otherwise tinkering with, the Land-mines Protocol. Essentially, they advocate redressing the weaknesses of the Protocol in two main ways: by strengthening or adding to its regula-tion of land mine use; or by prohibiting certain types of land mines.

The defects in the Protocol have been described in detail by others. Briefly, they are as follows:

- The Protocol covers only international conflicts, while most land mines have been placed during internal conflicts.
- It does not regulate the production, stockpiling, transfer, or export of mines.
- It lacks any provision for monitoring compliance and has no system of enforcement.
- It has no system of penalizing the use of mines against civilians.
- It fails to take into account the inherent indiscriminate effects of land mines due to their time-delay character.
- Its complex rules, discretionary language, and broad exceptions limit its utility.

Numerous, detailed proposals address each of these points. However, near universal agreement exists that there is no need to further burden an already dense and faulty document with even more complex and potentially unenforceable rules and regulations. Some proposals for improving the Protocol involve prohibiting certain types of mines—for example, antipersonnel mines not fitted with self-neutralizing or self-destruct mechanisms. In other words, all mines in use would have a mechanism to make them inert over time. While these proposals are well intentioned, they are faulty in concept and, in practice, would actu-ally impede realization of a total ban.

Self-neutralizing mines become inert when their batteries expire or through some other mechanical, chemical, or electronic means. But it is never clear that such mines have, in fact, been neutralized. Their explosive charge remains in the ground and can become more dangerous over time as it chemically degrades. These mines can also be dug up, refitted, and resold. Thus their threat can never be completely eliminated. Permitting mines with self-destruct mechanisms is also unrealistic, since by definition, self-destructing mines eventually explode and during the period they are active cannot distinguish between a civilian and a soldier any better than any other mines. In addition, most self-destructing mines are randomnly strewn—thousands at a time. This is particularly important because the failure rate of self-destructing mines is about 10 percent. In the absence of 100 percent effectiveness, such mines will continue to endanger civilian populations.

In sum, while current U.S. proposals are welcome as far as they go, they do not go nearly far enough. Indeed, they are based on the faulty premise that the limited military utility of land mines justifies their continued use, despite the immense, long-term social, economic, and environmental damage they cause. Such proposals ignore the fact that because of these weapons' inherent delayed-action characteristics, land mines have undiscriminating effects regardless of how they are used or who the intended target may be. And these proposals ignore the fact that land mines are a favorite weapon of terrorists and insurgent groups who use them to implant fear among civilian populations.

A total ban is needed for several reasons. The most practical reason is that, compared with a rule restricting use, a total ban would be easier to monitor, verify, and enforce. The breach of a complete ban would be readily evident, while the violation of a partial restriction would be less obvious and subject to discretion and argument. If some types or uses of mines are legal, there will always be room for argument over whether a particular use or export is legal. Even if the review conference could address every criticism of the Protocol through regulation or restrictions on certain mines, the compliance mechanism for enforcing such a partial agreement would be financially and administratively burdensome. Compliance measures for a total ban, on the other hand, would not be as complicated.

The reality is that nothing short of a total ban on the production, transfer, and use of antipersonnel land mines will stop the killing and maiming of civilians. This is so because no matter how these weapons are used, they are undiscriminating. No matter how sophisticated the technology, they cannot distinguish between an innocent civilian and a combatant. Bombs can be aimed at military targets and bullets fired by soldiers against soldiers, but land mines are radically different, lying in wait—as they do—until triggered by the target.

Because land mines are so cheap and easy to produce and transport, the only way to stop widespread use is by stigmatizing them, as other indiscriminate weapons are stigmatized. While this will not stop the Hitlers of the world, it could drastically reduce the use of land mines, as it has that of chemical and biological weapons. No doubt, there would not be a chemical weapons treaty today had it not been for strong support from the United States. Nor would preparations be under way to review the Landmines Protocol were it not for the American export moratorium. As the world's most powerful nation, the United States has both a responsibility and an opportunity to press for a solution to eliminate the land mine threat.

Therefore, the administration as a matter of policy should seek an international prohibition on the production, possession, transfer, and use of antipersonnel land mines. This should be its unequivocal position at the review conference in Geneva. Governments that wish to continue producing, transferring, or using these weapons should bear the burden of proving that they do not have undiscriminating effects.

With strong American leadership, a complete ban on antipersonnel land mines is possible. Further, in a time of ethnic and regional conflicts in countries where land mines are widely used and UN peacekeeping forces are sent in significant numbers, a global ban would benefit the entire international community. Among those who share our view in this regard is the United Nations secretary-general (see his foreword to this volume).

In fact, the Arms Project of Human Rights Watch contends that the use of land mines is already prohibited by the following provisions of customary international humanitarian and treaty law:

• Indiscriminateness: combatants in conflicts must employ means of warfare that distinguish between civilian and military objectives. This fundamental rule is meant to protect civilians from indiscriminate attacks; and
• Proportionality: parties to a conflict must weigh the expected military utility of a particular weapon against the expected human toll.[21]

A total ban on land mines would also be part of an established and working legal tradition for banning whole categories of weapons that are intolerably harmful. For example, the 1972 Biological Weapons Convention bans the use, production, and transfer of biological and toxic weapons, on the grounds that their use "would be repugnant to the conscience of mankind." Given this criterion for banning a weapon, the use of land mines most definitely warrants it.

Short of a ban, certain interim measures, if coupled with a strong verification regime, could help to protect civilians from mines and lay the foundation for a complete ban. These include the following:

- An in-depth analysis of the military utility of land mines versus their long-term costs and effects on civilian society;
- A requirement that the location of mines be recorded and marked in a manner visible to civilians;
- A requirement that all mines be detectable with widely available electronic metal-detecting devices;
- A requirement that any party that uses mines be responsible for assisting in clearing them;
- Uniform standards and methods for the discovery, removal, and disarming of land mines;
- Application of these limitations to both internal and international conflicts;
- A strong verification and compliance regime, including requirements that each party register with the UN the number and type of land mines produced and held; report to the UN any transfer of land mines; and agree to permit appropriate inspections to determine compliance, and to be subject to appropriate sanctions for noncompliance.

These partial steps will not eliminate the land mine threat any more than laws limiting the sale and use of handguns will stop a determined criminal. But they will be a step in the right direction, and the United States should pursue them as part of a larger strategy to negotiate a complete ban on land mines.

The review conference should also not lose sight of efforts to alleviate the suffering caused by land mines. To be meaningful, the conference must include in-depth consideration of the long-term medical, social, economic, and environmental effects of land mines. And the United States should take the lead and allocate funds for rehabilitation and medical programs for victims, such as those described in earlier chapters.

Although the current American focus on demining is admirable and has undoubtedly saved lives, it has been limited by financial and time constraints. To make a dent in the problem, demining programs must be expanded; greater funds must be made available; and new technology must be developed to make demining safer, faster, and less costly. In all these areas, the United States could have a real impact. But even with new technologies, it seems unlikely that the financial cost of demining, now ranging from $300 to $1,000 per mine, will be brought down anywhere near the current cost of laying a mine—$10–$20.

At present, when the UN begins a peace operation, a trust fund is set up to finance mine clearance programs. Experience has shown that this is a slow and often inadequate process. The United States should support initiatives to create a UN voluntary trust fund for mine clearance, which would provide funds at the earliest possible stage.

In sum, the United States should therefore acknowledge that it has a moral and practical responsibility to contribute to international efforts ensuring that the threat of land mines is completely eliminated. The time is long overdue to recognize that a total ban is very much in the national interest and should be put into effect as soon as possible.

Conclusion

The land mine crisis, having reached epidemic proportions around the world, demands immediate attention. We can no longer afford merely to compile data, documenting the obvious, or simply indulge in predictable condemnations and continue to issue unenforceable regulations. The phase of impotent outrage and self-deceiving rhetoric is over; we must find *solutions* before whole nations become as permanently scarred as the individual victims who, at an ever-escalating rate, lose lives and limbs as they innocently step on the explosive residue of long-forgotten conflicts. There are over 100 million mines laying in wait in over sixty countries.

The scope and complexity of the land mine crisis are so enormous that no single solution is possible. The contributors to this volume, all experts in their fields, agree that there must be an unequivocal acceptance of a goal—to eliminate the danger of these horrific weapons of indiscriminate destruction—as well as a series of practical, intermediate steps that can quickly arrest the current carnage.

Civilian and military approaches to the land mine crisis need not be mutually exclusive; in fact, the primary function of the United States military is to protect the safety of our citizens and to do so, ultimately, under civilian command. For philosophical as well as practical reasons, the military must play an essential role in solving the land mine crisis.

Responsible military leaders share the ethical concerns about land mines, and must balance the transient benefits these weapons offer against their overwhelming impact on noncombatants and the social and economic price they impose on fragile nations. Only the military currently possesses the information, expertise, and organization that could reverse the land mine crisis. If the military were directed to share their knowledge and skills with civilian forces in a global demining program, immediate progress could be anticipated.

Much of the technology needed to mount an effective demining operation already exists, but the necessary political will and financial commitment have been wanting. International humanitarian law and conventions could easily be strengthened, but, once again, such change demands a political determination that has been sadly lacking. Surgical and public health programs for land mine victims could be standardized, thereby making them more economical and accessible in poorer countries where the burden is greatest. If we are not to perpetuate the present haphazard response system, in which flawed programs are repeatedly launched in different parts of the world, international coordination and cooperation are required. The United Nations Department of Humanitarian Affairs should be designated and funded to undertake this task.

There is an almost palpable feeling that solutions to the land mine crisis can be realized, even if political leaders must be forced to follow the will of an aroused populace. Hope rests on a worldwide movement, a slow, stumbling coalescence of determined private groups influencing governments and international organizations, even if each is motivated by different reasons. There is growing revulsion at the waste of innocent life, at the fear and despair that permeate mine-infested lands, and at the skyrocketing costs to donor and recipient nations alike. There is a reluctant acceptance that current military methods can be changed, if necessary, and that the required technological and legal tools for resolving the crisis are already available or could be developed. Finally, the bright light of public scrutiny has exposed the lack of political thought and leadership on this topic. The hour has come at last; solutions to the land mine crisis are at hand.

KEVIN M. CAHILL, M.D.

NOTES

Kevin M. Cahill, M.D.: Introduction

1. Kevin M. Cahill, M.D., ed. *A Framework for Survival: Health, Human Rights, and Humanitarian Assistance in Conflicts and Disasters* (New York: Basic Books and Council on Foreign Relations, 1993).

Chapter 1. Kenneth Anderson: An Overview of the Global Land Mines Crisis

1. As used in this chapter, "land mines" refers strictly to antipersonnel mines designed to be triggered by pressure or proximity of a person, rather than antivehicle or antitank mines, or command-detonated mines.
2. *Landmines: A Deadly Legacy* (New York: Human Rights Watch, Physicians for Human Rights, 1993), 3.
3. *Hidden Killers: The Global Problem with Uncleared Landmines* (Washington, DC: Department of State Publication, July 1993), 3.

4. Besides Afghanistan and Cambodia, the most severely mined countries and regions are Angola, Burma, Chad, Eritrea, Ethiopia, the Falklands, Georgia, Iran, Iraq (especially Iraqi Kurdistan), Kuwait, Mozambique, Nagorno-Karabakh, Nicaragua, Rwanda, Somalia, Sudan, Thailand, Vietnam, Western Sahara, and the former Yugoslavia (Bosnia, Croatia, and Serbia).
5. *Hidden Killers,* 3.
6. *Landmines,* 143–44.
7. Patrick Blagden, speech before the International Conference of the Red Cross, Montreux Conference, May 1993.
8. See *Acts of Indiscipline and Indiscriminate Fire in the Abkhaz Separatist War in Georgia* (New York: Human Rights Watch, 1994).
9. See *Arming Rwanda* (New York: Human Rights Watch, 1994).
10. Lt. Col. P. R. Courtney-Green, *Ammunition for the Land Battle* (London: Brassey's, 1991).
11. See *Landmines,* chs. 1 and 2.
12. Ibid., ch. 1.
13. Ibid., ch. 3.
14. Ibid.
15. Ibid.
16. Ibid.
17. Ibid.

Chapter 2. Richard H. Johnson: Why Mines?

1. William Seymore, *Yours to Reason Why: Decision in Battle* (New York: St. Martin's Press, 1982), 32.
2. John Keegan, *The Face of Battle* (New York: Military Heritage Press, 1986), 91–92.
3. Jack Coggins, *Arms and Equipment of the Civil War* (New York: The Fairfax Press, 1983), 146–50.
4. Donovan Webster, "Out There Is a Bomb with Your Name," *Smithsonian* (February 1994): 26.
5. Ibid., 28.
6. Both the U.S. M-14 antipersonnel and the U.S. M-19 antitank mines have low-metal-content fuzes, in use since the late 1950s.
7. *United States Army Field Manual 20-32; Mine/Countermine Operations* (Washington, DC: Headquarters, Department of the Army, September 30, 1992), p. 1-8.
8. Ibid., p. 1-5.

9. *United States Army Field Manual 20-32*, p. 2-1.
10. Booby traps may be items disguised to resemble nonhazardous debris found on the battlefield, such as souvenirs, or they may simply be explosive charges in unlikely places.
11. *United States Army Field Manual 100-5; Operations* (Washington, DC: Headquarters, Department of the Army, September 30, 1992), p. 6-16.
12. Geoffrey Regan, *Great Military Disasters* (New York: M. Evans & Co., 1987), 109–220.
13. Charles Whiting, *Kasserine* (New York: Military Heritage Press, 1984), 209.
14. See *Report of the International Committee of the Red Cross for the Review Conference of the 1980 United Nations Convention on Prohibitions or Restrictions on the Use of Certain Conventional Weapons Which May Be Deemed to Be Excessively Injurious or to Have Indiscriminate Effects* (Geneva: International Committee of the Red Cross, 1994). Annex II contains the results of the military meeting.
15. Ibid., 57. The alternatives they examined were wire barricades, ditches, improvised devices, flooding/mud, land force fire, air power, and novel devices. The attributes included delay; canalization; disruption; infliction of casualties; diversion of enemy resources; protection of one's own troops; reinforcement of other obstacles; surprise; force multipliers; low cost of materials; minimal manpower to employ; minimal time to employ; flexibility in battle; reliability in serving desired effects when required; and adverse psychological effects of casualties.
16. This paragraph is a summary of remarks by Gen. Alfred M. Gray, Jr., USMC (Ret.), on April 29, 1994, in New York City at the symposium "Clearing the Fields: Solutions to the Landmine Crisis," cosponsored by the Center for International Health and Cooperation and the Council on Foreign Relations.

Chapter 3. W. Hays Parks: The Humanitarian Law Outlook

Statements contained in this chapter are the views of the author and may not reflect official policy of the Department of the Army, Department of Defense, or any other agency of the United States.

1. See, for example, Senator Patrick Leahy, "Landmine Moratorium: A Strategy for Stronger International Limits," *Arms Control Today*

23, 1 (January/February 1993): 11; Mark Sommer, "Tighter Controls Needed on Spread of Land Mines," *Christian Science Monitor,* May 24, 1993, 19; John Ryle, "The Invisible Enemy," *New Yorker,* November 29, 1993, 120; Donovan Webster, "It's the Little Bombs That Kill You," *New York Times Magazine,* January 23, 1994, 28; *Mines: A Perverse Use of Technology* (Geneva: International Committee of the Red Cross, 1992); and *Hidden Killers: The Global Problem of Uncleared Landmines* (Washington, DC: Department of State Publication, July 1993).

2. Some voices call for a total ban on antipersonnel land mines. (See, for example, the chapter by Cyrus Vance and Herbert S. Okun in this volume.) Supporters of this view may face a dilemma in considering the perspective expressed in this chapter. The dilemma is not new. Representatives of pacifist groups attending the First Hague Peace Conference (1899) were opposed to codification of the law of war inasmuch as it appeared to constitute acceptance of war. Neither that conference, succeeding conferences, nor the practice of nations was able to eliminate war, but the conference did take the first steps toward international codification of the rules related to warfighting. See, generally, Barbara Tuchman, *The Proud Tower* (New York, 1966), 251–67.

3. U.S. Department of Defense, Joint Publication 1-02, *Department of Defense Dictionary of Military and Associated Terms* (Washington, DC: December 1, 1989), 206. The Department of Defense in its implementing directive utilizes the term law of war. Department of Defense Directive 5100.77, DoD Law of War Program (July 10, 1979).

4. See, for example Richard Falk's chapter in this volume.

5. In 1974, the U.S. Department of Defense promulgated Instruction 5500.15, requiring a legal review by the judge advocate general of the appropriate military department to conduct a legal review of any new weapon, weapon system, or munition to ensure its intended use is consistent with the law of war obligations of the United States. Subsequently, the United States was successful in incorporating that requirement into article 36 of the 1977 Additional Protocol I to the Geneva Conventions of August 12, 1949. Although the United States is not yet a party to this treaty, the weapons review program continues.

6. *United States v. Wilhelm List, et al.,* XI *Trials of War Criminals before the Nuremberg Military Tribunals* (1948), 1253.

7. 36 Stat. 2277, TS 539, 1 Bevans 631.

8. The precise title of which is the Protocol Additional to the Geneva Conventions of August 12, 1949, and Relating to the Protection of Victims of International Armed Conflicts of June 8, 1977.

9. See, for example, *Landmines in El Salvador and Nicaragua: The Civilian Deaths* (December 1986); *Landmines in Cambodia: The Coward's War* (September 1991); *Hidden Death: Landmines and Civilian Casualties in Iraqi Kurdistan* (October 1992); *Land Mines in Angola* (January 1993); *Landmines in Mozambique* (March 1994); and *Hidden Enemies: Landmines in Northern Somalia* (Boston, MA: Physicians for Human Rights, 1992).

10. *Landmines: A Deadly Legacy* (New York: Human Rights Watch, Physicians for Human Rights, 1993), 141, 148.

11. Geneva Convention for the Amelioration of the Condition of the Wounded and Sick in Armed Forces in the Field of August 12, 1949 (6 UST 3114, TIAS 3362, 75 UNTS 11); Geneva Convention for the Amelioration of the Condition of the Wounded, Sick, and Shipwrecked Members of Armed Forces at Sea of August 12, 1949 (6 UST 3217; TIAS 3363; 75 UNTS 85); Geneva Convention Relative to the Treatment of Prisoners of War of August 12, 1949 (6 UST 3216; TIAS 3364; 75 UNTS 135); and Geneva Convention Relative to the Protection of Civilian Persons in Time of War of August 12, 1949 (6 UST 3516; TIAS 3365; 75 UNTS 287).

12. Article 3, common to the four 1949 Geneva Conventions, states in part:

> Persons taking no part in the hostilities, including members of armed forces who have laid down their arms and those placed *hors de combat* by sickness, wounds, detention, or any other cause, shall in all circumstances be treated humanely, without any adverse distinction founded on race, color, religion or faith, sex, birth or wealth, or any other similar criteria.

> To this end, the following acts are and shall remain prohibited at any time and in any place whatsoever. . . :

> (1) violence to life and person, in particular murder. . . .

13. The precise title of which is Protocol Additional to the Geneva Conventions of August 12, 1949, and Relating to the Protection of Victims of Non-International Armed Conflicts of June 8, 1977.

14. Article 1, paragraph 1, of Additional Protocol II provides that the Protocol's provisions will apply to a conflict taking place "in the

territory of a High Contracting Party between its armed forces and dissident armed forces or other organized armed groups which, under responsible command, exercise such control over a part of its territory as to enable them to carry out sustained and concerted military operations and to implement this Protocol."

15. *Conference of Government Experts in the Use of Certain Conventional Weapons*, Lucerne, September 24–October 18, 1974 (Geneva: International Committee of the Red Cross, 1975); and *Conference of Government Experts on the Use of Certain Conventional Weapons*, Lugano, January 28–February 26, 1976 (Geneva: International Committee of the Red Cross, 1976).

16. The complete resolution is contained in *Commentary on the Additional Protocols of 8 June 1977 to the Geneva Conventions of 12 August 1949* (Geneva: International Committee of the Red Cross, 1987), 1527–28.

17. The official title is the Convention on Prohibitions or Restrictions on the Use of Certain Conventional Weapons Which May Be Deemed to Be Excessively Injurious or to Have Indiscrminate Effects of October 10, 1980 (249 UNTS 240). The title reflects language in diplomatic conference Resolution 22. As some delegates pointed out, however, the title was inaccurate inasmuch as the UN conference concluded that none of the weapons met these characteristics, and if they had, they would have been illegal per se. The Convention is discussed in William J. Fenrick, "The Conventional Weapons Convention: A Modest But Useful Treaty," *International Review of the Red Cross* 279 (November–December 1990): 498–509; and Frits Kalshoven, "The Conventional Weapons Convention: Underlying Legal Principles," *International Review of the Red Cross* 279 (November–December 1990): 510–20.

18. The umbrella portion of the Convention and Protocol I are addressed in J. Ashley Roach, "Certain Conventional Weapons Convention: Arms Control or Humanitarian Law," *Military Law Review* 105 (Summer 1984): 3–72; Protocol III is discussed in this author's "The Protocol on Incendiary Weapons," *International Review of the Red Cross* 279 (November–December 1990): 535–50.

19. See, for example, Stockholm International Peace Research Institute, *Anti-personnel Weapons* (New York, 1978), in which land mines and booby traps are discussed in an uncritical tone, and on only 12 of the book's 299 pages; and Richard Falk's four volumes on *The Vietnam War and International Law*, which do not identify a problem with their use.

20. Personal observation of the author, who attended as a member of the U.S. delegation.
21. See, for example, Burrus M. Carnahan, "The Law of Land Mine Warfare: Protocol II to the United Nations Convention on Certain Conventional Weapons," *Military Law Review* 105 (Summer 1984): 73–95; and A. P. V. Rogers, "Mines, Booby-traps and Other Devices," *International Review of the Red Cross* 279 (November–December 1990): 521–34.
22. Article 25.
23. The term *neutralize* in article 5 (1)(b) is explained in the article ("render harmless or destroy a mine"), but nonetheless has caused confusion. A mine may self-destruct, at which time it detonates, or it may render itself harmless (that is, inert) when its power supply is exhausted. The latter also occurs if a mine intended to self-detonate fails to do so.
24. States parties to the Convention are Australia, Austria, Belarus, Benin, Bosnia-Herzegovina, Bulgaria, China, Croatia, Cuba, Cyprus, Czech Republic, Denmark, Ecuador, Finland, France, Germany, Greece, Guatemala, Hungary, India, Japan, Lao People's Democratic Republic, Latvia, Liechtenstein, Mexico, Mongolia, the Netherlands, New Zealand, Niger, Norway, Pakistan, Poland, Russian Federation, Slovak Republic, Slovenia, Spain, Sweden, Switzerland, Tunisia, Ukraine, and Yugoslavia. The number of parties was inflated slightly by the dissolution of Czechoslovakia and Yugoslavia. The United States, the United Kingdom, and Canada are in the concluding phases of ratification. The United States signed the Convention on April 8, 1982, and on May 12, 1994, President Bill Clinton forwarded the Convention and its Protocols I and II to the U.S. Senate for its advice and consent as to ratification. Even though the United States is not yet a party, U.S. military doctrine for land mine employment is consistent with the Landmines Protocol, and the United States has actively participated in the development of standardization agreements (STANAG) for the North Atlantic Treaty Organization in implementation of the Convention within that alliance. See, for example, NATO STANAG 2963 (January 23, 1992), Coordination of Field Artillery Delivered Scatterable Mines; NATO STANAG 2990 (March 16, 1992), Principles and Procedures for the Employment in Land Warfare of Scatterable Mines with a Limited Laid Life; and NATO STANAG 2036 (September 16, 1993), Land Mine Laying, Marking, Recording and Reporting Procedures.

25. Article 8, paragraph 3. The Convention entered into force on December 2, 1983.

26. General Assembly Resolution 48/79 (December 16, 1993).

27. Dated December 22, 1993. It was submitted identifying as sponsors the governments of Australia, Austria, Belarus, Benin, Bulgaria, China, Cuba, Cyprus, Czech Republic, Denmark, Ecuador, Finland, France, Germany, Greece, Guatemala, Hungary, India, Japan, Lao People's Democratic Republic, Latvia, Liechtenstein, Mexico, Mongolia, the Netherlands, Niger, Norway, Pakistan, Poland, Russian Federation, Slovakia, Slovenia, Sweden, Switzerland, Tunisia, Ukraine, and Yugoslavia. However, neither China, Cuba, Guatemala, India, Lao People's Democratic Republic, Niger, nor the Russian Federation signed it.

28. UN CDA/1-94/CCW I-1 dated January 4, 1994.

29. Its efforts are reported in *Report of the International Committee of the Red Cross for the Review Conference of the 1980 United Nations Convention on Prohibitions or Restrictions on the Use of Certain Conventional Weapons Which May Be Deemed to Be Excessively Injurious or to Have Indiscriminate Effects* (Geneva: International Committee of the Red Cross, February 1994), Annex I.

30. Invitees (attending in their personal capacity) represented Argentina, Cambodia, China, El Salvador (one from the government, another from the Farabundo Marti National Liberation Front), Eritrea, Ethiopia, France, Germany, India, Israel, Italy, Mozambique, Russia, South Africa, United Kingdom, and the United States, Human Rights Watch, Vietnam Veterans of America, and the United Nations office for demining operations. Several were combat engineers with experience in land mine warfare.

31. Reported in *Report of the International Committee of the Red Cross for the Review Conference of the 1980 United Nations Convention on Prohibitions or Restrictions on the Use of Certain Conventional Weapons Which May Be Deemed to Be Excessively Injurious or to Have Indiscriminate Effects* (Geneva: International Committee of the Red Cross, February 1994), Annex II, 50.

32. Ibid. As a United States Marine, the author served in Vietnam in 1968–69, in an area where land mines were the major casualty producer among U.S. forces. Most were field expedients developed from unexploded ordnance recovered by the Viet Cong on the battlefield.

33. John Barham, "Falklands Mine Accord Claimed," *Financial Times* (London), April 22, 1994, 6.

34. This raises a question: Do demining initiatives, which play such an important humanitarian role, encourage nations to use low-technology antipersonnel land mines that increase civilian risk? The answer at this time appears to be no, as the parties to the conflicts where the more indiscriminate uses of antipersonnel land mines have occurred have not had access to high-technology land mines.

35. This was the thinking at the International Committee of the Red Cross meeting of military experts in January 1994. The rationale is simple. When a land mine self-destructs, it ceases to be a threat. If it self-neutralizes, it is impossible to discern whether the self-neutralizing mechanism actually worked, and the mine must be treated as active.

36. The global positioning system, using twenty-four satellites and a ground control center, permits commercial users to determine their position on earth to within 128 feet. It would enhance the accuracy of the location of remotely delivered land mines by confirming the position from which they were employed. See Ralph Vartabedian, "Eye in the Sky," *Los Angeles Times* (Wash. Ed.), May 2, 1994, B5.

37. For example, in language appropriate for consideration for incorporation into the Conventional Weapons Convention, article 147 of the 1949 Geneva Convention Relative to the Protection of Civilian Persons in Time of War defines as a grave breach "wilful killing . . . wilfully causing great suffering or serious injury to body or health, . . . and extensive destruction and appropriation of property, not justified by military necessity and carried out unlawfully and wantonly."

38. In this regard, see Umesh Palwankar, "Measures Available to States for Fulfilling Their Obligation to Ensure Respect for International Humanitarian Law," *International Review of the Red Cross* 298 (January–February 1994): 9; and Nikolay Khlestov, "International Conference for the Protection of War Victims—What Is to Follow Up the 'Follow Up'?" *International Review of the Red Cross* 298 (January–February 1994): 6. The International Conference for the Protection of War Victims was hosted by the government of Switzerland in Geneva from August 30 to September 1, 1993, to develop and adopt a resolution reaffirming the existing law of war.

39. Department of Defense Directive 5100.77 requires that all military personnel receive law of war training "commensurate with their duties and responsibilities." A separate program, Department of Defense Instruction 5500.15, provides for a review of each new weapon, weapon system, or munition to ensure its consistency with

the law of war obligations of the United States. The success of these programs in Operation Desert Storm was obvious, and is described in U.S. Department of Defense, *Final Report to the Congress: Conduct of the Persian Gulf War* (Washington, DC: April 1992), 605–32.

40. A program to institutionalize human rights and law of war training requires funding and leadership support within the host nation and the United States. A U.S. Army program in Peru required funding from the U.S. Southern Command CINC Initiative Funds (10 U.S. Code, section 166a). Other funding sources (depending on the state in question and availability) include military-to-military contact funds under 22 U.S. Code, section 5901, and LATAM-COOP funds under 10 U.S. Code, section 1050.

Chapter 4. Thomas E. McNamara: The U.S. Approach Toward Land Mines

1. *Hidden Killers: The Global Problem with Uncleared Landmines* (Washington, DC: Department of State Publication, July 1993).
2. In 1987, seven concerned countries created the MTCR to restrict the proliferation of nuclear-capable missiles and related technology. Since 1987, eighteen more countries have joined the regime. The MTCR is not a treaty but rather a common export policy applied to a common list of controlled items, including virtually all equipment and technology needed for missile development, production, and operation.

Chapter 5. Richard Falk: Walking the Tightrope of International Humanitarian Law

1. The argument here is that international humanitarian law can effectively challenge combat practice only when the professional military is convinced, or at least divided, on questions of propriety and battlefield utility; this precondition for effective regulation has not been satisfied with respect to land mines.
2. The halfhearted legal attempts to prohibit strategic air bombardments of heavily inhabited cities or to banish unrestricted submarine warfare are illustrative.
3. In some circumstances, the gap can be politically beneficial. Human

rights activists often rely upon legal standards hypocritically accepted by governments to exert pressure on violative behavior. The success of the Helsinki Process in Eastern Europe during the 1980s was partly a result of activists and dissident elements exploiting the gap between law and practice, thereby undermining the legitimacy of the governing process itself in these countries.

Would the gap be helpful in relation to the struggle to banish land mines from the battlefield? It is unclear, as much would depend on whether the campaign to banish can be sustained and intensified, and its reach extended to Third World settings.

4. If breaking the will of the opponent is regarded as crucial to winning the war, then commanders and planners treat cruelty beyond the battlefield as an aspect of military necessity, although it is rarely acknowledged as such, and is criticized as "barbaric" or "terroristic" if done by the adversary.

5. Nuclear weaponry exists at the interface between a strong taboo and powerful military imperatives, perhaps explaining, in part, the compromise by way of legitimate "use" only in passive modes— deterrence, deployment, and development.

6. A variant on this position underlies Neil Sheehan's important book on the Vietnam War, *A Bright Shining Lie: John Paul Vann and America in Vietnam* (New York: Random House, 1988); such an analysis also bears on the failure of U.S. and UN efforts in Somalia during 1993, and on the problem posed by the challenge of land mine use.

7. The "de Martens clause" is named after its drafter and proponent, Feodor de Martens, the principal Russian delegate to the First and Second Hague Peace Conferences in 1899 and 1907, where the modern law of war was codified in a series of treaties.

8. Article 1(1). Article 1(2) exempts from coverage "internal disturbances and tensions," such as "riots" and "sporadic acts of violence."

9. Article 51(5) further specifies the character of an indiscriminate tactic by reference to attacks directed at inhabited areas that contain distinct military objectives or that are likely to produce "an incidental loss of civilian life, injury to civilians . . . which would be excessive in relation to the concrete and direct military advantage anticipated."

10. Article 14 prohibits reliance on tactics that interfere with access to food and water needed to ensure the physical survival of the civilian population.

11. For some analysis along these lines, see Richard Falk, *Revolutionaries and Functionaries: The Dual Face of International Terrorism* (New York: Dutton, 1988).

12. These "success stories" of international humanitarian law are ongoing processes with no assurance of happy endings; their interpretation is subject to controversy. For example, Iraq used chemical weaponry extensively against heavily populated Kurdish villages in the late 1980s, receiving only a mild slap on the wrist from the international community. And some Third World countries regard chemical warfare, and even biological warfare, as the poor man's atomic bomb, and seem to be covertly challenging these regimes of prohibition by engaging in development and production activities. The effectiveness of the prohibitions of specific classes of weaponry useful for secondary states seems also eroded by the unwillingness of nuclear powers to renounce their discretion to use nuclear weapons, much less to eliminate nuclear weaponry. For a useful discussion, see Susan Wright, ed., *Preventing a Biological Weapons Arms Race* (Cambridge, MA: MIT Press, 1991).

13. Revealingly, prior to the emergence of significant capabilities to inflict damage from the air, halfhearted efforts were made to restrict aerial bombardment in relation to the broad customary law principles of international humanitarian law. See text of 1923 Hague Rules of Aerial Warfare, especially Articles 22–26, in Adam Roberts and Richard Guelff, eds., *Documents on the Law of War*, 2nd rev. ed. (Oxford, 1989), 123–35. These provisions seeking to draw a clear dividing line between civilian society and military operations resemble in many respects the 1980 Landmines Protocol, with a similar behavioral irrelevance. The difference between the two contexts is that from a high-technology perspective, air war is an indispensable instrument, both strategically and bureaucratically (that is, by its influence within military establishments), while land mines are essentially a convenience for high-technology belligerents. Given this asymmetry, one would expect an effort to restrict the use of land mines to be more serious than one concerning bombing, but not nearly so serious as to be effective.

14. As soon as restrictions on use, rather than a prohibition, is agreed upon, especially in the absence of a verification capability, battlefield perceptions of military utility inevitably will dominate. Compare the international experience with "the definition of aggression," a normative enterprise that peace groups pushed hard and geopolitical forces resisted; the result was a formulation full of

loopholes, which has been totally ignored despite the fanfare surrounding the drafting and the agreed wording.

15. *Landmines: A Deadly Legacy* (New York: Human Rights Watch,
    Physicians for Human Rights, 1993), 289. I also share the impor-
    tant observation contained in that volume (p. 262) that "customary
    rules forbidding means of warfare that cause indiscriminate or
    excessive harm, particularly as codified in articles 51(4) and (5)
    and 35(1) and (2) of 1977 Additional Protocol I of the 1949
    Geneva Conventions provide *stronger protection* to civilians than the
    Landmines Protocol itself" (emphasis supplied). I do not, however,
    share the assessment attributing the failure to a "fatally incom-
    plete" analysis by the drafters, who allegedly "placed undue heavy
    emphasis on military need" (p. 273). This emphasis on perceived
    military utility is exactly what should have been expected from a
    diplomatic initiative in the land mines context, and it will again, I
    would assume, prevent significant reform if a review conference is
    held in the next year or so in accordance with article 8 of the 1980
    Conventional Weapons Convention. This retention of professional
    support for the military utility and legitimacy of certain uses of
    land mines has already been expressed in the report of the Interna-
    tional Committee of the Red Cross January 1994 experts meeting.
16. Some specialists in international humanitarian law favor an overall
    ban on weaponry with cruel features. See, for example, *Blinding
    Weapons: Reports of the Meetings Convened by the International Com-
    mittee of the Red Cross on Battlefield Laser Weapons, 1989–1991*
    (Geneva: International Committee of the Red Cross, 1993).
17. International Committee of the Red Cross Military Experts Report,
    January 1994.
18. Ibid., 3.
19. Ibid., 3–5.
20. Whether this effort is sufficient is beyond the scope of this chapter.
    The claim that any use would be contrary to international law is
    now being tested by a request from the World Health Organization
    to the World Court for an advisory opinion; a determination of
    "illegality" might strengthen the disposition to pursue nuclear disar-
    mament and achieve a nuclear-free world.
21. A combat dimension remains in relation to the quantity and charac-
    ter of land mines available for arms purchase by likely adversaries.
22. Presumably, so-called backlash states would remain outside a sup-
    pliers regime, as might China and several other important suppliers.
23. Of course, this may sound far-fetched, but it would represent a

cost-effective way of reducing land mine harm outside belligerency without altering the play of forces on the battlefield itself.

Chapter 6. Janne E. Nolan: The Arms Control Dimension

1. See, for instance, *Landmines: A Deadly Legacy* (New York: Human Rights Watch, Physicians for Human Rights, 1993).
2. The major suppliers of land mines in the past were the Warsaw Pact nations, especially the Soviet Union, Yugoslavia, Czechoslovakia, Bulgaria, and Hungary, and the NATO members, particularly Italy, Belgium, the United Kingdom, the United States, and France.
3. For further discussion of various kinds of mines, see, for example, Gerald C. Cauderay, "Anti-personnel Mines," *International Review of the Red Cross* (July–August 1993).
4. For a more detailed discussion of this measure, see the chapter by Cyrus Vance and Herbert S. Okun in this volume.
5. United Nations General Assembly Document A/C/1/48/ L. 42, November 1993, p. 2.
6. For further discussion of these negotiations, see Janne E. Nolan, "The US-Soviet Conventional Arms Transfer Negotiations," in Alexander George et al., *U.S.-Soviet Security Cooperation: Achievements, Failures, Lessons* (Oxford: Oxford University Press, 1988), 510–23.

Chapter 7. J. Bryan Hehir: A Political-Moral Assessment

1. *Landmines: A Deadly Legacy* (New York: Human Rights Watch, Physicians for Human Rights, 1993), Appendix 8.
2. Stanley Hoffmann, *Duties Beyond Borders: On the Limits and Possibilities of Ethical International Politics* (Syracuse, NY: Syracuse University Press, 1981), 16–27.
3. Michael Walzer, *Just and Unjust Wars: A Moral Argument with Historical Illustrations* (New York: Basic Books, 1977), 3–13.
4. For historical and philosophical perspectives on the Just War ethic, see J. F. Childress, *Moral Responsibility in Conflicts: Essays on Nonviolence, War and Conscience* (Baton Rouge: Louisiana State University Press, 1982), 63–94; J. T. Johnson, *Just War Tradition and Restraint of War: A Moral and Historical Inquiry* (Princeton, NJ: Princeton University Press, 1981); J. C. Murray, *We Hold These*

Truths: Catholic Reflections in the American Proposition (New York: Sheed and Ward, 1960), 249–73; R. B. Potter, *The Moral Logic of War* (Philadelphia, PA: Board of Christian Education, The United Presbyterian Church, n.d.).

5. Childress, *Moral Responsibility*, 69. Childress draws the phrase from Robert Nozick, professor of philosophy at Harvard University.

6. Potter, *Moral Logic*, 10. This summary of the Just War ethic draws principally from Potter's account of its logic.

7. For a fuller explanation of each of the criteria, see Childress, *Moral Responsibility*, and Potter, *Moral Logic*.

8. The classical defense of the principle is found in J. Ford, "The Morality of Obliteration Bombing," *Theological Studies* 5 (1944): 261–309. The preeminent contemporary commentary can be found in Walzer, *Just and Unjust Wars;* and P. Ramsey, *The Just War: Force and Political Responsibility* (New York: Charles Scribner's Sons, 1968).

9. Murray, *We Hold These Truths*, 269.

10. *Landmines*, 3.

11. Ibid., 9.

12. Ibid.

13. Ford, "Morality of Obliteration Bombing."

14. McGeorge Bundy, *Danger and Survival: Choices About the Bomb in the First Fifty Years* (New York: Random House, 1988), 95.

15. Ibid.

16. *Landmines*, 9.

17. Ibid., 317.

18. Patrick Leahy, "Landmine Moratorium: A Strategy for Stronger International Limits," *Arms Control Today* 23 (January–February 1993), 11.

19. Ibid.

20. Ibid., 13.

21. *Landmines*, Appendix 8.

22. Leahy, "Landmine Moratorium," 11.

Chapter 8. Patrick Blagden: The Use of Mines and the Impact of Technology

The views expressed here are those of the author, and do not necessarily represent the official policy of any of the organizations for and with whom the author has worked. The figures quoted are the best estimates available to the author, but like most estimates in the secretive world of mines, may be in error.

1. See, for example, Dan Raschen, *Send Port and Pajamas!* (Buckland Publications Ltd., 1987), and Norman Schwarzkopf, *It Doesn't Take a Hero* (New York: Bantam, 1992).

Chapter 9. Thomas R. Evans: Technology Beyond the Probe

1. All figures cited in this chapter are from *Landmines: A Deadly Legacy* (New York: Human Rights Watch, Physicians for Human Rights, 1993).

Chapter 10. Chris Giannou, M.D., and H. Jack Geiger, M.D.: The Medical Lessons of Land Mine Injuries

1. *Hidden Killers: The Global Problem with Uncleared Landmines* (Washington DC: Department of State Publication, July 1993).
2. *Report of the Symposium on Anti-personnel Mines: Montreux 1993* (Geneva: International Committee of the Red Cross, 1993), 271.
3. *Landmines: A Deadly Legacy* (New York: Human Rights Watch, Physicians for Human Rights, 1993), 117–40.
4. In Mongkol Barei Hospital, Cambodia, during the four months prior to the May 1, 1991, cease-fire, 51 percent of 428 war-wounded were landmine victims. During the first four months *after* the cease-fire, 61 percent of 168 wounded had been injured by land mines. In the Jalalabad Public Health Hospital in Afghanistan, land mine victims rose from 35 percent to 60 percent of war-wounded during the first few months of 1993, when hundreds of thousands of Afghan refugees began returning to their homes from the Peshawar refugee camps in Pakistan. (Unpublished statistics, internal medical reports from the International Committee of the Red Cross.)
5. D. Morris, W. Sugrue, and E. McKenzie, "At War: On the Border of Afghanistan with the International Committee of the Red Cross," *New Zealand Medical Journal* 98 (1985): 750–52; J. Rautio, Paavolainen, "Afghan War Wounded: Experience with 200 Cases," *Journal of Trauma* (1988): 523–25; M. K. Bhatnagar and G. S.

Smith, "Trauma in the Afghan Guerilla War: Effects of Lack of Access to Care," *Surgery* 105 (1989): 699–705; and R. Fasol, S. Irvine, and P. Zilla, "Vascular Injuries Caused by Anti-personnel Mines," *Journal of Cardiovascular Surgery* 30 (1989): 467–72.

6. R. Russbach, "Les units chirurgicales du Comittee Internationale de la Croix Rouge: Le personnel, la materiel, les costs," *Medecine et Hygiene* 49 (1991): 27–29.

7. G. W. Odling-Smee, "Ibo Civilian Casualties in the Nigerian Civil War," *British Medical Journal* 2 (1970): 592–96; C. M. De Wind, "War Injuries Treated Under Primitive Circumstances: Experiences in an Ugandan Mission Hospital," *Annals of the Royal College of Surgeons* 69 (1987): 193–95; D. A. Ityavyar and L. O. Ogba, "Violence, Conflict and Health in Africa," *Social Science and Medicine* 28 (1989): 649–57; and B. Eshaya-Chauvin and R. M. Coupland, "Transfusion Requirements for the Management of War Injured: The Experience of the International Committee of the Red Cross," *British Journal of Anesthesia* 68 (1992): 221–23.

8. *Mines: A Perverse Use of Technology* (Geneva: International Committee of the Red Cross, 1992).

9. Eshaya-Chauvin and Coupland, "Transfusion Requirements."

10. *Landmines in Cambodia: The Coward's War* (New York: Physicians for Human Rights and Asia Watch, 1991); *Hidden Enemies: Landmines in Northern Somalia* (Boston, MA: Physicians for Human Rights, 1992); *Landmines in Mozambique* (New York: Physicians for Human Rights, 1994).

11. M. L. Fackler, R. F. Bellamy, and J. A. Malinowski, "A Reconsideration of the Wounding Mechanism of Very High Velocity Projectiles—Importance of Projectile Shape," *Journal of Trauma* 28, Suppl. (1988): S53–57; and Y. Liu, X. Chen, S. L. X. Chen, R. Guo, D. W. X. Fu, S. Jiang, and S. Xu, "Wounding Effects of Small Fragments of Different Shapes at Different Velocities on Soft Tissues of Dogs," *Journal of Trauma* 28, Suppl. (1988): S95–98.

12. D. Dufour, S. Korman Jensen, M. Owen-Smith, J. Salmela, G. F. Stenning, and B. Zetterstrom, *Surgery for Victims of War* (Geneva: International Committee of the Red Cross, 1988); R. M. Coupland, "Technical Aspects of War Wound Excision," *British Journal of Surgery* 76 (1989): 663–67; R. M. Coupland, "Amputation for Antipersonnel Mine Injuries of the Leg: Preservation of the Tibial Stump Using a Medical Gastrocnemius Myoplasty," *Annals of the Royal College of Surgeons* 71 (1989): 405–8; and R. M. Coupland,

Amputation for War Wounds (Geneva: International Committee of the Red Cross, 1992).

13. Rautio, "Afghan War Wounded."

14. D. Johnson, J. Crum, and S. Lumjiak, "Medical Consequences of the Various Weapons Systems Used in Combat in Thailand," *Military Medicine* 146 (1981): 632–34.

15. F. King, *Landmine Injury in Cambodia: A Case Study* (London: London School of Tropical Medicine, unpublished thesis, 1992).

16. *Landmines*, 165–83.

17. Ibid.

18. A. Garachon, "ICRC Rehabilitation Programmes on Behalf of War Disabled," in *Report of the Symposium on Anti-Personnel Mines: Montreux 1993* (Geneva: International Committee of the Red Cross, 1993), 83.

19. J. P. Grant, ed., *The State of the World's Children, 1993* (New York: Oxford University Press, 1993), 6.

20. J. M. Last, ed., *Maxcy-Rosenau Public Health and Preventive Medicine*, 11th ed. (New York: Appleton-Century-Crofts, 1980), 4–5.

21. The Arms Project of Human Rights Watch, "Landmines in International Law: Why Is a Complete Ban Required?" Memorandum, March 4, 1994.

22. At the village level, Halo Trust also seeks to first clear mines from areas that will affect the livelihood of the greatest number of people. For example, Halo Trust will demine a village footpath to a water well, or the area around a school, before clearing a farmer's house or field.

Chapter 11. Kevin M. Cahill, M.D., and Abdulrahim Abby Farah: Developing Indigenous Amputee Programs

1. Kevin M. Cahill, "Holidays in Nicaragua," *America* (1988), 1, 9; and Kevin M. Cahill, "Bridges to Peace," *J. Publ. Health Policy* 229 (1987).

2. *Hidden Killers: The Global Problem with Uncleared Landmines* (Washington, DC: Department of State Publication, July 1993), *Landmines: A Deadly Legacy* (New York: Human Rights Watch, Physicians for Human Rights, 1993), 510; and Physicians for Human Rights, *Hidden Enemies: Landmines in Northern Somalia* (Boston, MA: Physicians for Human Rights, 1992).

3. Kevin M. Cahill, *Health on the Horn of Africa* (London: Spottis-

woode Ballantyne, 1970), 102; Kevin M. Cahill, *Somalia: A Perspective* (Albany: State University of New York Press, 1980) 21; Kevin M. Cahill, "Studies in Somalia," *Trans. Roy. Soc. Trop. Med. and Hyg.* 65, (1971): 28; and Kevin M. Cahill, "Somalia: A Hunger the World Has Never Seen," *New York Daily News,* April 23, 1981.

4. Annual Report of the Center for International Health and Cooperation (New York, 1994).

Chapter 12. Yves Sandoz: Turning Principles into Practice

1. See, in particular, Yves Sandoz, *Des armes interdites en droit de la guerre* (Geneva: Grounauer, 1975), 84.

2. "Declaration Renouncing the Use, in Time of War, of Explosive Projectiles under 400 Grammes Weight, St. Petersburg, 29 November/11 December 1868," in D. Schindler and J. Toman, eds., *The Laws of Armed Conflicts: A Collection of Conventions, Resolutions and Other Documents* (Dordrecht: Martinus Nijhoff Publishers/Geneva: Henry Dunant Institute, 1988), 101.

3. "Declaration (IV, 3) Concerning Expanding Bullets, The Hague, 29 July 1899," in *Laws of Armed Conflicts,* 109.

4. Article 171 of the Treaty of Versailles of June 29, 1919, states: "L'emploi des gaz asphyxiants, toxiques ou similaires, ainsi que de tous liquides, matières ou procédés analogues, étant prohibé ... " For more details about this article, see Sandoz, *Des armes interdites,* 31–32.

5. "Protocol for the Prohibition of the Use in War of Asphyxiating, Poisonous or Other Gases, and of Bacteriological Methods of Warfare, Geneva, 17 June 1925," in *Laws of Armed Conflicts,* 115.

6. See Sandoz, *Des armes interdites,* 106.

7. Ibid.

8. See Article 35, para. 2, of June 9, 1977, Additional Protocol I to the Geneva Conventions of August 12, 1949.

9. See Article 51, para. 4(b), of Protocol I.

10. See Article 53 of the Vienna Convention on the Law of Treaties. On this question, see also, in particular, the "Declaration on the Rules of International Humanitarian Law Governing the Conduct of Hostilities in Non-international Armed Conflicts," *International Review of the Red Cross* 278 (September–October 1990): 404.

11. See *Report of the International Committee of the Red Cross for the*

Review Conference of the 1980 United Nations Convention on Prohibitions or Restrictions on the Use of Certain Conventional Weapons Which May Be Deemed to Be Excessively Injurious or to Have Indiscriminate Effects (Geneva: International Committee of the Red Cross, February 1994), 57.

12. See Article 8, para. 1(a) of the United Nations Convention on Prohibitions or Restrictions on the Use of Certain Conventional Weapons Which May Be Deemed to Be Excessively Injurious or to Have Indiscriminate Effects, October 10, 1980.

13. On this subject, see L. Doswald-Beck, ed., *Blinding Weapons: Reports of the Meetings of Experts Convened by the International Committee of the Red Cross on Battlefield Laser Weapons 1989–1991,* (Geneva: International Committee of the Red Cross, 1993), 371.

14. See Article 98 (Revision of Annex I) of 1977 Additional Protocol I.

15. See Article 98, paras. 4 and 5, of 1977 Additional Protocol I.

16. Of the 132 states, only 2 expressed minor reservations on the amended Annex 1.

17. Article 90 of the Convention on International Civil Aviation, Chicago, December 7, 1944.

18. On this subject, see *Report of the International Committee of the Red Cross* (1994), 21–24.

19. Ibid., 43–44.

20. *Symposium on Anti-personnel Mines, Montreux, 21–23 April 1993, Report* (Geneva: International Committee of the Red Cross, 1993), 154.

21. See Article 91 of 1977 Additional Protocol I.

22. *Study Concerning the Right to Restitution, Compensation and Rehabilitation for Victims of Gross Violations of Human Rights and Fundamental Freedoms.* Final report submitted by Mr. Theo van Boven, Special Rapporteur, doc. E/CN.4/Sub.2/1993/8, July 2, 1993.

23. See UN Security Council resolution 808 of February 22, 1993.

24. See UN General Assembly resolution 48/31 of December 9, 1993.

25. See Statutes of the International Red Cross and Red Crescent Movement, adopted by the 25th International Conference of the Red Cross, 1986, Article 5, para. 2.

26. See, in particular, *Mines: A Perverse Use of Technology* (Geneva: International Committee of the Red Cross, 1992), 19.

27. To ensure a multidisciplinary approach, the symposium brought together eminent experts in different fields related to the issue of antipersonnel mines use and its effects. They included military strategists; mine specialists and manufacturers; experts in interna-

tional humanitarian law and disarmament; surgeons and orthope-
dists; and representatives of mine clearance agencies, nongovernmental organizations and the media.

28. *Symposium on Anti-personnel Mines*, 321.
29. Jean S. Pictet, ed., *Commentary on the Geneva Conventions of 12 August 1949*, 4 vols. (Geneva: International Committee of the Red Cross, 1952–59); Y. Sandoz, C. Swinarski, and B. Zimmermann, eds., *Commentary on the Additional Protocols of 8 June 1977 to the Geneva Conventions of 12 August 1949* (Geneva: International Committee of the Red Cross, 1987).
30. See *Conference of Government Experts on the Use of Certain Conventional Weapons (Lucerne, 24 September–18 October 1974), Report* (Geneva: International Committee of the Red Cross, 1975), and *Conference of Government Experts on the Use of Certain Conventional Weapons (Second Session: Lugano, 28 January–26 February 1976), Report* (Geneva: International Committee of the Red Cross, 1976).
31. See Doswald-Beck, *Blinding Weapons*.
32. See *Report of the International Committee of the Red Cross* (1994).
33. One product of these efforts that deserves particular mention is the volume *Landmines: A Deadly Legacy* (New York: Human Rights Watch, Physicians for Human Rights, 1993), 510.
34. As of December 31, 1993, 185 states were party to the 1949 Geneva Conventions; 130 states were party to Additional Protocol I of 1977; and 120 states were party to Additional Protocol II.

Chapter 14. Cyrus Vance and Herbert S. Okun: Eliminating the Threat of Land Mines

1. *Hidden Killers: The Global Problem with Uncleared Landmines* (Washington, DC: Department of State Publication, July 1993), 2.
2. Scott MacLeod, "And Still They Kill," *Time*, December 13, 1993.
3. *Hidden Killers*, 42.
4. *Mines: A Perverse Use of Technology* (Geneva: International Committee of the Red Cross, 1992), 14.
5. *Hidden Killers*, 45.
6. U.S. Agency for International Development, "Trip Report, March 1–12, 1994" (Washington, DC: Office of Transition Initiatives, Bureau of Humanitarian Response, USAID).
7. Ibid.

8. *Hidden Killers*, 64.

9. *Landmines: A Deadly Legacy* (New York: Human Rights Watch, Physicians for Human Rights, 1993), 173.

10. Statement of Senator Leahy to the U.S. Senate, February 28, 1994, Congressional Record, S2016–S2017.

11. Ibid.

12. *Mines*, 14.

13. *Hidden Killers*, 5–6.

14. Ibid., i.

15. Letter from President Bill Clinton to Senator Patrick Leahy dated February 22, 1994.

16. Statement by Senator Patrick Leahy, "Anti-personnel Landmines: An International Ban?" November 5, 1993.

17. *Mines*, 4.

18. Statement of the Cornelio Sommaruga, President of the International Committee of the Red Cross, Geneva, February 24, 1994.

19. *Anti-personnel Landmines: A Scourge on Children* (New York: United Nations Children's Fund, May 1994), 5.

20. Ibid., 8.

21. *Landmines*, 261–75.

ABOUT THE AUTHORS

KENNETH ANDERSON is director of the Arms Project of Human Rights Watch, and is the principal editor of *Landmines: A Deadly Legacy*. He lectures on international human rights at both Harvard and Fordham Law Schools.

PATRICK BLAGDEN is the demining expert at the United Nations. Before joining the UN in 1992, he served in the British Army as brigadier general in charge of weapons research. He has been an executive in the defense industry, including a period as mine clearance manager in Kuwait.

KEVIN M. CAHILL, M.D., is president of the Center for International Health and Cooperation. He also serves as director of the Tropical Disease Center in New York, professor and chairman of the Department of International Health at the Royal College of Surgeons in Ireland, and senior medical consultant to the United Nations Health Service and to numerous foreign governments.

JAN ELIASSON is the Conference on Security and Cooperation in Europe's ambassador-mediator for the Nagorno-Karabakh conflict. He served as the first United Nations under-secretary-general for humanitarian affairs, and had previously served as Sweden's permanent representative to the

United Nations, vice president of the Economic and Social Council (ECOSOC), and under-secretary for political affairs in the Foreign Ministry of Sweden.

THOMAS R. EVANS is a member of the Principal Professional Staff of the Johns Hopkins University Applied Physics Laboratory. He has worked extensively with the U.S. Department of Defense in the areas of system analysis and technology policy.

RICHARD FALK is Albert G. Milbank Professor of International Law and Practice at Princeton University. He is author of *Human Rights and State Sovereignty* and, most recently, *Explorations at the Edge of Time: Prospects for World Order.* He also edited a four-volume series on the Vietnam War and international law.

ABDULRAHIM ABBY FARAH is consultant director to the Center for International Health and Cooperation; he previously served as under-secretary-general of the United Nations and senior political advisor on African affairs for twenty years. He has also been Somalia's ambassador to Ethiopia and permanent representative to the United Nations.

H. JACK GEIGER, M.D., is president of Physicians for Human Rights and professor of community medicine at the City University of New York Medical School. He is a founding member and past president of Physicians for Social Responsibility. He has published numerous articles and book chapters on the medical and biological effects of nuclear weapons.

CHRIS GIANNOU, M.D., is a consultant surgeon to the International Committee of the Red Cross. He has worked as a war surgeon in Cambodia, Somalia, and Burundi. His recollections of the war-torn refugee camps of Lebanon are captured in his autobiographical book, *Besieged.*

J. BRYAN HEHIR is professor of the practice of religion and society at Harvard Divinity School and the Harvard Center for International Affairs. Previously he served on the staff of the U.S. Catholic Bishops Conference. Father Hehir has written on the ethics of war, human rights, and Catholic social thought.

COL. RICHARD H. JOHNSON spent thirty years in the U.S. Army, almost all of it in ammunition units and weapons research and development organizations. His assignments included tours as an explosive ordnance disposal officer in the United States, Vietnam, and Egypt, and a variety of other command and staff positions. For the three years preceding his retirement, he was project manager for mines, countermines, and demolitions at Picatinny Arsenal, New Jersey.

THOMAS E. MCNAMARA is the acting assistant secretary of state for the Bureau of Political-Military Affairs. Previously he headed the State Department's Office for Counterterrorism and was the U.S. ambassador to

Colombia from 1989 to 1991. He has served twice on the staff of the National Security Council.

JANNE E. NOLAN is a senior fellow in foreign policy at the Brookings Institution. She has held numerous governmental and foundation positions as an adviser on arms control and defense analysis.

HERBERT S. OKUN capped a thirty-six-year career in the U.S. Foreign Service as ambassador to the United Nations and to the former German Democratic Republic. He is special advisor and deputy to Cyrus Vance on Yugoslav matters and Greek-Macedonian issues.

W. HAYS PARKS has been the special assistant to the judge advocate general for law of war matters since 1979. He served as a combat Marine officer in Vietnam and has taught international law in both civilian and military colleges. He has been the U.S. representative for law of war in Geneva, in the Hague, and at the United Nations.

YVES SANDOZ is director of principles and law at the International Committee of the Red Cross. He has written numerous books and articles on international humanitarian law. He served as the ICRC's delegate in war situations, in particular in Nigeria (Biafra), Israel, Yemen, and Bangladesh.

CYRUS VANCE, former U.S. secretary of state, is personal representative of the secretary-general of the United Nations. A naval officer in World War II, he has also served as secretary of the army and as deputy secretary of defense. He is a partner in the New York law firm of Simpson, Thacher & Bartlett.